Honoré de Balzac

LA COMÉDIE HUMAINE

The Human Comedy

PROVINCIAL LIFE

VOLUME III

BEHIND THE CAPUCHIN CHURCH

At an ill-judged parry on Max's part, Philippe sent his sabre spinning out of his hand.

"Pick it up," he said, suspending operations; "I am not the man to kill a disarmed enemy."

It was the sublimity of atrocity.

THE NOVELS

OF

HONORÉ DE BALZAC

NOW FOR THE FIRST TIME
COMPLETELY TRANSLATED INTO ENGLISH

THE CELIBATES:
PIERRETTE
THE CURÉ DE TOURS
LA RABOUILLEUSE

BY GEORGE B. IVES

WITH TEN ETCHINGS BY EUGÈNE DECISY AND ALFRED
BOILOT, AFTER PAINTINGS BY ORESTE CORTAZZO
AND PIERRE VIDAL

VOLUME II

PRINTED ONLY FOR SUBSCRIBERS BY
GEORGE D. SPROUL, NEW YORK

THE CELIBATES

THIRD STORY

LA RABOUILLEUSE

The following pages, my dear Nodier, deal largely
with deeds of the sort that are protected from the
action of the laws behind the closed doors of private life; but in which the finger of God, so often
called Chance, supplements human justice, and
whose moral, although pronounced by mocking
lips, is none the less instructive and impressive.
The result, in my view, is a fund of useful information both for the family and for the mother. We
shall realize, too late perhaps, the effects produced
by the diminution of paternal authority. This
authority, which in former times ceased only at
the death of the father, constituted the only human
tribunal that had jurisdiction of domestic crimes,
and, on important occasions, the royal power lent
its hand to carry the paternal decrees into effect.
However loving and kind the mother may be, she
no more fills the place of that patriarchal royalty,
than woman fills a king's place on the throne; and,
in the exceptional cases when the place is success-
fully filled, the result is a monster. Perhaps I have
never drawn a picture that shows more clearly than

(3)

this one, how indispensable to European societies is the indissolubility of the marriage tie, how disastrous is female weakness, and what perils are engendered by individual selfishness, when it is unchecked. May a social system based entirely upon the power of wealth shudder to see the impotence of the law in dealing with the schemes of a system which deifies success by pardoning all means that may be resorted to to obtain it! May it speedily have recourse to Catholicism to purify the masses by the sentiment of religion, and by an education other than that afforded by a secular University! The *Scenes of Military Life* contain so many noble characters, so many grand and sublime instances of self-sacrificing devotion, that I may be permitted here to remark how debasing an influence the necessities of war exert upon certain people, who dare to behave in private life as if they were on the battle-field. You have cast upon the times in which we live, an intelligent glance whose philosophy betrays itself in more than one bitter reflection which makes itself felt in your graceful pages, and you have appreciated more fully than any other writer, the havoc that four different political systems have caused in the public spirit of our nation. I could not therefore place this narrative under the protection of a more competent authority. Your name will defend it perhaps against charges that will not fail to be made; where is the sick man who does not lift his voice when the surgeon removes the bandages from his tenderest wounds?

In addition to the pleasure of dedicating this Scene to you is the gratification afforded to my pride by betraying the secret of your kindness to him who subscribes himself

One of your sincere admirers,

DE BALZAC.

LA RABOUILLEUSE

*

In 1792, the bourgeoisie of Issoudun were favored with the services of a physician named Rouget, who was popularly considered to be a profoundly wicked man. According to the statements of some bold persons, he made his wife very unhappy, although she was the most beautiful woman in the town. Perhaps she was a little foolish. Despite the inquisitiveness of friends, the gossip of the indifferent, and the evil-speaking of the jealous, but little was known of the domestic affairs of the family in question. Doctor Rouget was one of those men of whom people say, familiarly: *He's a disagreeable fellow.* And so, during his lifetime, they kept silent about him and treated him courteously. His wife, a Mademoiselle Descoings, who was not in the best of health before her marriage,—that was one reason for the physician's marrying her, so it was said,— bore a son, and later a daughter, who, as it happened, came ten years after the son, and whose coming, it was always said, was not expected by the husband, although he was a doctor. This late arrival was christened Agathe.

These trivial facts are so simple, so commonplace, that there seems to be nothing to justify a historian in placing them at the beginning of the narrative; but, if they were not known, a man of Doctor Rouget's stamp would be deemed a monster, an unnatural father, whereas he simply acted in obedience to evil instincts that many people cloak beneath that shocking axiom: *A man should have a will of his own!* That high-sounding sentence has brought woe to many wives.

The Descoings, Rouget's father-in-law and mother-in-law, were commission merchants in wool, and undertook to sell for the sheep-raisers and to buy for the dealers the golden fleeces of Berri, thus earning a commission from both sides. They became rich in that business, and were misers: the end of many such careers. Descoings junior, Madame Rouget's younger brother, was not contented at Issoudun. He went to Paris in search of fortune, and set up as a grocer on Rue Saint-Honoré. That was his ruin. But what do you expect! the grocer is drawn toward his particular line of business by a force of attraction equal to the force of repulsion that drives artists away from it. Sufficient study has not been expended upon the social forces that constitute the different callings. It would be an interesting thing to ascertain what influences a man to become a stationer rather than a baker, when sons are not forced to adopt their father's trade, as is the case among the Egyptians. In Descoings' case, love had assisted in determining his calling.

He had said to himself: "And I too will be a
grocer!" saying something very different at the
sight of his employer's wife, a beautiful creature,
with whom he fell madly in love. Without other
aids than patience and a little money which his
father sent him, he married the widow of Bixiou,
his predecessor.

In 1792, Descoings was supposed to be doing an
excellent business. The elder Descoings were still
living. They had gone out of the woolen business
and employed their funds in the purchase of national
property: another golden fleece! Their son-in-law,
who was almost certain that he would soon have to
mourn for his wife, sent his daughter to his brother-
in-law in Paris, partly in order that she might see
the capital and partly in pursuance of an artful design. Descoings had no children. Madame Descoings, who was twelve years older than her
husband, was in excellent health, but fat as a
thrush after harvest, and the sly Rouget knew
enough of medicine to foresee that Monsieur and
Madame Descoings, unlike the hero and heroine of
all fairy tales, would live happily and have no children. The husband and wife might take a liking
to Agathe. Now, Doctor Rouget desired to disinherit his daughter and flattered himself that he
could attain his ends by sending her away from the
province. This young woman, who was at this time
the prettiest girl in Issoudun, resembled neither her
father nor her mother. Her birth had been the
cause of a quarrel between Doctor Rouget and his

intimate friend, Monsieur Lousteau, the former sub-delegate,who had just left Issoudun. When a family expatriates itself, the natives of a province so charming as Issoudun are entitled to seek the reasons for such an extraordinary step. According to some sharp tongues, Monsieur Rouget, a most vindictive man, had exclaimed that Lousteau should die by no hand but his. Coming from a medical man, that remark had the effect of a cannon ball.

When the National Assembly suppressed the sub-delegates, Lousteau departed and never returned to Issoudun. After the departure of the family, Madame Rouget passed all her time with the ex-sub-delegate's sister, Madame Hochon, who was her daughter's godmother and the only person to whom she confided her woes. So it happened that the little that the town of Issoudun knew concerning the fair Madame Rouget was told by that good woman, after the doctor's death.

Madame Rouget's first words, when her husband spoke of sending Agathe to Paris, were:

"I shall never see my daughter again!"

"And, unhappily, she was right!" the worthy Madame Hochon would say.

The poor mother thereupon became as yellow as a quince, and her condition did not belie the state-ments of those who claimed that Rouget was killing her by inches. The behavior of her great idiot of a son was calculated to contribute to the unhappiness of this unjustly accused mother. Hardly restrained, perhaps encouraged, by his father, that youth, who

was stupid in every direction, was entirely lacking
in the conduct and the respect that a son owes his
mother. Jean-Jacques Rouget resembled his father
in his evil qualities, and the doctor had but few
good qualities, either moral or physical.

The arrival of the charming Agathe Rouget did
not bring luck to her uncle Descoings. During the
week, or rather during the decade,—the Republic
had been proclaimed,—he was imprisoned at a word
from Robespierre to Fouquier-Tinville. Descoings,
who was imprudent enough to believe the famine to
be artificial, had the folly to communicate his opinion
—he thought that opinions were free—to several of
his customers, male and female, as he attended to
their wants. Citizeness Duplay, wife of the car-
penter with whom Robespierre lived, and who acted
as housekeeper for that eminent citizen, honored
with her custom, unluckily for Descoings, the shop
kept by that native of Berri. The citizeness deemed
the grocer's opinion an insult to Maximilien I. Having previously had reason to complain of the customs of the Descoings' establishment, this illustrious *tricoteuse** of the Jacobin Club regarded the
beauty of Citizeness Descoings as a brand of aris-
tocracy. She exaggerated Descoings' remarks
when she repeated them to her gentle and kindly
master. The grocer was arrested on the commonplace charge of *forestalling*.

Descoings being in prison, his wife bestirred

* Tricoteuse—Knitter. During the Revolution this title was applied to
women who knitted while attending the sessions of the Convention.

herself to procure his release; but the steps she made
to that end were so awkwardly taken, that an observer who had overheard her appeals to the arbiters
of her husband's destiny might have thought that
her real object was to get rid of him.   Madame
Descoings was acquainted with Bridau, one of the
secretaries of Roland, Minister of the Interior, and
the right arm of all the successive occupants of that
post.   She induced Bridau to take the field in the
grocer's behalf.   The incorruptible official, one of
those virtuous dupes who are always so admirable
in their disinterestedness, was careful not to cor-
rupt those persons upon whom Descoings' fate depended; he tried to enlighten them!   He might as
well have asked the men of those days to restore the
Bourbons as to have sought to enlighten them.   The
Girondist minister, who was then struggling against
Robespierre, said to Bridau:

"Why do you meddle with such matters?"

Every man whom the honest official approached
repeated that same atrocious question: "Why do
you meddle with such matters?"   Bridau sagely
advised Madame Descoings to keep quiet; but, instead of assuring the friendship of Robespierre's
housekeeper, she hurled fire and flame at that spy;
she called upon a member of the Convention, who
was trembling for his own safety.

"I will speak to Robespierre," he said.

The fair grocer rested on the strength of that
promise, and her new protector, of course, maintained the most profound silence.   A few loaves of

sugar, a bottle or two of good liquor, bestowed upon Citizeness Duplay would have saved Descoings. This little incident proves that in times of revolution it is as dangerous to employ honest men for one's protection as rascals: one can safely rely only upon one's self.

If Descoings perished, he had at all events the glory of going to the scaffold in company with André de Chénier. On that occasion, doubtless, Grocery and Poetry embraced for the first time, in person, for they had then and always will have secret relations. Descoings' death produced much more sensation than André de Chénier's. Not for thirty years did France realize that she lost more by Chénier's death than by Descoings'. Robespierre's action did this much good, that even in 1830, the terrified grocers did not meddle with politics.

Descoings' shop was within a hundred yards of Robespierre's lodgings. The grocer's successor made a wretched failure there. César Birotteau, the famous perfumer, established himself in that location. But, as if the scaffold had left there the inexplicable contagion of misfortune, the inventor of the *Sultana Double Paste* and the *Carminative Water* ruined himself. The solution of this problem is a matter for the occult sciences.

During the few visits that the secretary paid to the ill-fated Descoings' wife, he was impressed by the calm, cold, guileless beauty of Agathe Rouget. Although he came to console the widow, who was so inconsolable that she did not continue the business

of her second dear departed, he ended by marrying
the charming girl within the decade, and after
the arrival of her father, who was not slow to
make his appearance. The doctor, overjoyed to
find his plans succeeding better than he had hoped,
as his wife had become sole heiress of the Descoings, hastened to Paris, less for the pleasure of
being present at Agathe's marriage, than to see that
the contract was prepared in accordance with his
views. The disinterestedness and excessive passion
of Citizen Bridau left the perfidious physician *carte
blanche*, and he made the most of his son-in-law's
blindness, as the sequel will show you. Thus Madame Rouget, or, to speak more accurately, the
doctor, inherited all the property, real and personal,
of Monsieur and Madame Descoings the elder, who
died within two years of each other. Then Rouget
at last got rid of his wife, who died early in 1799.
He possessed vineyards, he purchased farms and
smithies, and he had wool to sell! His beloved son
knew absolutely nothing; but he destined him for
a landed proprietor, he allowed him to grow up in
wealth and folly, sure that the boy would know as
much as the most learned men, who do no more
than live and die.

In 1799, the calculating minds of Issoudun placed
the elder Rouget's income at thirty thousand francs.
After his wife's death, the doctor continued to live a
dissolute life; but he kept a rein upon it, so to speak,
and confined its ebullitions behind the closed doors
of his own house. This physician, a very strong

character in his way, died in 1805. God alone
knows how the bourgeoisie of Issoudun talked about
him then, and how many anecdotes were circulated
concerning his shocking private life!

Jean-Jacques Rouget, whom his father had at the
last held in strict restraint, realizing his folly,
remained a bachelor for divers weighty reasons,
whose elucidation forms an important part of this
narrative. His celibacy was in part caused by the
doctor's fault, as we shall see later.

At this point it becomes necessary to call attention to the effects of the father's vengeance upon a
daughter whom he did not look upon as his own,
although you may be sure that she did lawfully belong to him. No one at Issoudun had noticed one
of those curious accidents that contribute to make
the mysteries of generation an abyss in which
science loses its way. Agathe resembled Doctor
Rouget's mother. Just as the gout, according to a
familiar saying, often skips a generation, from
grandfather to grandson, so it is by no means rare
to find moral and physical resemblances acting like
the gout.

In like manner, the elder of Agathe's children,
who resembled his mother, had the moral qualities
of his grandfather, Doctor Rouget. Let us bequeath
the solution of this other problem to the twentieth
century, with a fine nomenclature of microscopic
animalculæ, and posterity will write as much nonsense perhaps as our learned societies have already
written upon this obscure question.

Agathe Rouget commended herself to public admiration by one of those faces, which are destined, like that of Mary, mother of Our Lord, to remain virgin forever, even after marriage. Her portrait, which is still in existence in Bridau's studio, displays a face that is a perfect oval in outline with a complexion absolutely fair, without the slightest tinge of redness, despite her golden hair. Many an artist, as he looks to-day upon that pure brow, that innocent mouth, that slender nose, those pretty ears, those long eyelashes veiling deep-blue eyes infinitely tender in expression, in a word, upon that face with its imprint of placidity, asks our great painter : "Is that a copy of one of Raphael's heads ?" Never was man more happily inspired than the departmental second clerk when he married Agathe. She was the ideal housekeeper, brought up in the provinces, who had never left her mother. Pious without being a devotee, she had no other education than that bestowed upon women by the church. Thus she was an accomplished wife only in the ordinary sense, for her ignorance of worldly matters led to more than one disaster. The epitaph of a celebrated Roman matron : *She made tapestry and kept the house,* epitomizes admirably this pure, simple, placid existence.

From the beginning of the Consulate, Bridau became a fanatical partisan of Napoléon, who appointed him chief of division in 1804, a year before Rouget's death. With a salary of twelve thousand francs, and handsome perquisites, Bridau was supremely indifferent to the shameful results of the settlement of his father-in-law's estate at Issoudun, from which Agathe received nothing. Six months before his death, the elder Rouget sold his son a portion of his property, the rest of which eventually came into his hands, either by way of gift or by inheritance. An advance of a hundred thousand francs to Agathe, in her marriage contract, represented her share in the inheritance of her father and mother. Idolizing the Emperor as he did, Bridau seconded, with the blind zeal of a fanatic, the mighty project of this modern demigod, who, finding everything in France overturned, attempted to reorganize everything. The chief of division never cried: *Enough!* Projects, memorials, reports, monographs, he welcomed the heaviest burdens, so happy was he to assist the Emperor; he loved him as a man, he adored him as a sovereign, and would not brook the slightest criticism of his acts or his schemes.

From 1804 to 1808, Bridau was quartered in a large and handsome apartment on Quai Voltaire, two steps from his department and from the Tuileries. A cook and a valet de chambre were their only servants in the days of Madame Bridau's splendor. Agathe, who was always the first to rise, went to market with her cook. While the manservant was putting the apartment in order, she overlooked the preparation of the breakfast. Bridau never went to his office before eleven o'clock. So long as their union lasted, his wife took

2

the same pleasure in preparing an exquisite
breakfast for him, that being the only meal
which Bridau really enjoyed. At all seasons,
and whatever the weather might be when he went
away, Agathe always stood at the window looking
after her husband on his way to the department,
and never turned her face away until he turned
into Rue du Bac. Then she cleared the table herself and glanced over the apartment; after which
she dressed, played with her children, took them
out to walk or received callers until Bridau's return.
When he brought some important work to do at
home, she would station herself beside his table in
his study, silent as a statue, and knit as she
watched him at work, sitting up as long as he sat
up, and going to bed only a few seconds before him.
Sometimes the husband and wife went to the play
and sat in the box belonging to the department.
On those occasions, they always dined at a restaurant, and the panorama there presented always
afforded Madame Bridau the keen pleasure that it
affords those people who have never seen Paris.
Being compelled frequently to accept invitations to
the large formal dinner-parties which were given
to the chief of division who controlled one section
of the Department of the Interior, and which Bridau
conscientiously returned, Agathe complied with the
prevailing fashion of gorgeous toilets; but she gladly
laid aside her splendid state garments when she
returned home, and resumed her provincial simplicity of dress and manner. Once a week, on

Thursdays, Bridau received his friends. On Shrove Tuesday he gave a grand ball. In these few words is comprised the whole story of this conjugal existence, in which there were but three great events: the birth of two children at a distance of three years, and the death of Bridau, from overwork, which took place in 1808, just as the Emperor was about to appoint him director-general, and to make him a count and councillor of state.

In those days Napoléon was devoting particular attention to interior affairs; he overwhelmed Bridau with work and utterly wrecked the health of that intrepid bureaucrat. Bridau had never asked for anything, so that the Emperor took pains to inquire concerning his circumstances and his mode of life. When he learned that that devoted servant had nothing but his office, he recognized in him one of those incorruptible souls who gave moral strength and prestige to his administration, and he determined to surprise Bridau with some signal recompense. Anxiety to finish a tremendous piece of work before the Emperor's departure for Spain, killed the chief of division, who died of an inflammatory fever. Upon his return from Spain, the Emperor, who passed a few days at Paris preparing for the campaign of 1809, exclaimed when he heard of his loss: "There are men who can never be replaced!"

Deeply impressed by a devotion which could be rewarded by none of the brilliant testimonials reserved for his soldiers, the Emperor determined to

create for his civil servants an order with handsome
emoluments, as he had created the Legion of Honor
for his military officers.   The effect produced upon
him by Bridau's death inspired the idea of the
Order of the Reunion: but he had not time to complete that aristocratic creation, all memory of which
has so thoroughly vanished that most of our readers,
upon hearing the name of that ephemeral order, will
ask what its insignia were: it was worn with a blue
ribbon.   The Emperor called the order the Reunion
with the idea of combining the Spanish order of the
Golden Fleece with the Austrian order of the same
name.   "Providence," said a Prussian diplomatist,
"would not permit that profanation."   The Emperor
sought information as to Madame Bridau's position.
The two children each had a free scholarship at the
Imperial Lyceum, and the Emperor charged all the
expenses of their education upon his privy purse.
He also assigned to Madame Bridau a pension of four
thousand francs, reserving to himself, doubtless, the
duty of providing for the future of the two sons.

From her marriage to her husband's death, Madame Bridau had had no connection with Issoudun.
She was on the point of giving birth to her second
son when she lost her mother.   When her father
died, who, she knew, cared nothing for her, the
Emperor's coronation was about to take place and
entailed so much work upon Bridau that she was
unwilling to leave him.   Jean-Jacques Rouget, her
brother, had never written her a word since her departure from Issoudun.   Although she was distressed

by this tacit repudiation by her family, Agathe finally reached a point where she thought but rarely of those who did not think of her. She received a letter every year from her godmother, Madame Hochon, to whom she wrote the merest common-places in reply, without studying the advice which that excellent and pious woman gave her in guarded words. Some time before Doctor Rouget's death, Madame Hochon wrote to her goddaughter that she would get nothing from her father's estate unless she sent her power of attorney to Monsieur Hochon. Agathe was disinclined to annoy her brother. Whether because Bridau supposed that the spolia-tion was in conformity to the laws and customs of Berri, or because that pure and upright man shared his wife's grandeur of soul and indifference in mat-ters affecting their private interests, he would not listen to the advice of Roguin, his notary, that he should take advantage of his position to contest the validity of the documents by which the father had succeeded in depriving the daughter of her *legitimate* share. The husband and wife assented to what was done at Issoudun. However, in these circum-stances, Roguin did force the chief of division to reflect upon his wife's endangered interests. That superior man realized that, if he should die, Agathe would be left without means. He instituted an ex-amination, therefore, into the condition of her affairs; he found that between 1793 and 1805 he and his wife had been compelled to use about thirty thou-sand of the fifty thousand francs in cash which old

Rouget had given his daughter, and he invested the remaining twenty thousand francs in the public funds, which were then at forty. Thus Agathe had about two thousand francs a year from that source.

When she became a widow, Madame Bridau was able to live comfortably on six thousand a year. Still a true provincial, she determined to dismiss Bridau's manservant, to keep only her cook, and to take a different apartment; but her intimate friend, who persisted in calling herself her aunt,—Madame Descoings,—sold her furniture, left her apartment and came to live with Agathe, turning the late Bridau's study into a bedroom. The two widows combined their revenues and found themselves possessed of twelve thousand a year. This step seems a simple and natural one. But nothing in life demands more careful attention than the things that seem natural, for we always distrust the extraordinary; thus you see that men of experience—solicitors, judges, physicians, priests —attach enormous importance to trivial matters; they deem them the most troublesome. The serpent under the flowers is one of the most valuable myths that antiquity has bequeathed to us for the conduct of our affairs. How often do fools, to excuse themselves in their own eyes and others', exclaim:

"It was so simple that anyone would have been taken in by it!"

In 1809, Madame Descoings, who did not divulge her age, was sixty-five years old. She had been

called in her day "the fair grocer," and was one of
the few women whom time respects, being indebted
to an excellent constitution for the privilege of re-
taining her beauty, which nevertheless would not
endure a searching scrutiny.   Of medium height,
plump and fresh-looking, she had lovely shoulders
and a slightly ruddy complexion.   Her light hair,
which bordered on chestnut, had not begun to turn
gray, notwithstanding the shocking fate of Descoings.   Being excessively dainty, she loved to
make nice little dishes for herself; but, although
she seemed to think a great deal of the table, she
also adored the play, and cultivated a vice which
she enveloped in the most profound mystery: she
invested in the lottery!   May not that be the pitfall
that mythology warns us against in the fable of the
sieve of the Danaides?

La Descoings—that is the way a woman should
be spoken of who invests in the lottery—spent a
little too much on dress, perhaps, like all women
who have the joy of remaining young for many
years; but, saving these slight drawbacks, she was
the most agreeable of women to live with.   Always
of the opinion of everybody else, offending nobody,
she attracted people by a mild and contagious cheer-
fulness.   She possessed one essentially Parisian
quality that fascinates retired clerks and elderly
tradesmen; she knew how to take a joke!—If she
did not marry a third time, it was undoubtedly the
fault of the epoch.   During the wars of the Empire,
marriageable men secured young, lovely and wealthy

wives too easily to take up with women of sixty.
Madame Descoings sought to enliven Madame
Bridau's life, she often took her to the play and to
drive, she arranged excellent little dinners for her,
she even tried to bring about a match between her
and her son Bixiou. Alas! she confessed to her the
terrible secret, carefully guarded by herself, the deceased Descoings and her notary. The young, the
giddy Descoings, who said that she was thirty-six,
had a son of thirty-five, named Bixiou, already a
widower and a major in the Twenty-first Regiment
of the line. He was killed, a colonel, at Dresden,
leaving an only son. La Descoings, who never saw
her grandson Bixiou except in secret, passed him off
as her husband's son by a first wife. It was an act
of prudence on her part to confide in her friend; the
colonel's son, who was educated at the Imperial
Lyceum with Bridau's two sons, had a half scholarship there. He was a cunning, mischievous boy at
the Lyceum and later made a great reputation for
himself as an artist and a wit.

Agathe cared for nothing in the world but her
children and desired to live only for them; so she
refused to marry again for cause as well as through
fidelity. But it is easier for a woman to be a good
wife than a good mother. A widow has two tasks,
whose obligations run counter to each other: she is
a mother and she is called upon to exercise the
authority of a father. Few women are strong
enough to understand and play this double rôle.
And so poor Agathe, despite her virtues, was the

innocent cause of much unhappiness. As a result
of her lack of wit and of the trustfulness to which
noble hearts are addicted, Agathe fell a victim to
Madame Descoings, who brought a terrible calamity
upon her head.

La Descoings cherished a favorite combination of
numbers, and the lottery did not give credit to those
who invested in it. As she kept the house, she
was able to use in her lottery investments, the
money intended for the household expenses, and she
allowed the bills to run on and on, in the hope of
enriching her grandson Bixiou, her dear Agathe and
the little Bridaus. When the debts amounted to
ten thousand francs, she invested more heavily than
ever, hoping that her favorite combination, which
had not won for nine years, would fill the yawning
abyss of the deficit. From that time, the debts increased rapidly. When they reached the figure of
twenty thousand francs, La Descoings lost her head,
and still the combination did not win. Then she
wished to pledge her own fortune to reimburse her
niece; but Roguin, her notary, showed her that that
honorable design was impossible of execution. The
late Rouget, at the death of his brother-in-law Descoings, had taken over his property, buying off Madame Descoings with a life estate chargeable upon
the property of Jean-Jacques Rouget. No usurer
would care to lend twenty thousand francs to a
woman of sixty-seven on a life-estate of four thousand francs a year, at a time when safe investments
at ten per cent abounded.

One morning La Descoings threw herself at her niece's feet, sobbing bitterly, and confessed the condition of things; Madame Bridau did not utter a word of reproach; she dismissed the manservant and the cook, sold all her superfluous articles of furniture, sold three-fourths of her stock in the Funds, paid everything and gave her landlord warning of her purpose to leave her apartment.

*

One of the most horrible corners of Paris is, beyond question, the portion of Rue Mazarine that lies between Rue Guénégaud and its junction with Rue de Seine, behind the palace of the Institute. The high gray walls of the college and library presented by Cardinal Mazarin to the city of Paris, where the Académie Française was one day to have its abiding-place, cast chilly shadows upon this corner of the street; the sun rarely shows itself there, the north wind reigns supreme.

The poor ruined widow went into lodgings on the third floor of one of the houses situated in this damp, cold, dark corner. In front of the house arose the buildings of the Institute, where the cages of the wild beasts known to the bourgeois by the name of artists, and by that of *rapins* in the studios, were to be found. A young man entered there a *rapin,* and might come out a pupil of the government at Rome. This operation did not take place without extraordinary turmoil, at those times of the year when the rival candidates were confined in the aforesaid cages. To win the prize they must have executed within a given time—if a sculptor, the clay model of a statue; if a painter, one of the pictures you can see at the École des Beaux-Arts; if a musician, a cantata; if an architect, a design for a monument.

At the moment of writing these lines, this menagerie had been transferred from those cold, dark buildings to the beautiful home of the École des Beaux-Arts, a few steps away.

From Madame Bridau's windows one looked out upon those barred cages, a profoundly melancholy sight. Toward the north, the prospect is limited by the dome of the Institute. As you go up the street, the only recreation for the eye is afforded by the line of cabs at the upper end of Rue Mazarine. So the widow finally placed in her windows three boxes filled with earth, and cultivated one of those aërial gardens that are prohibited by the police ordinances and which exclude light and air. The house stands back to back with another house on Rue de Seine and is necessarily very shallow—so shallow that the staircase turns upon itself. The third floor is the last. There are three windows and three rooms: a dining-room, a small salon and a bedroom, and across the landing, a tiny kitchen; above are two single attic rooms and a vast garret, not used for any purpose. Madame Bridau selected this apartment for three reasons: the moderate rent of four hundred francs, at which price she took a lease for nine years; the proximity to the Imperial Lyceum, which was only a short distance away; and lastly, she remained in the quarter in which she was accustomed to live.

The interior of the apartment was in harmony with the house. The dining-room, the walls of which were hung with yellow paper with green flowers, and the red tiled floor unpolished, contained only what was absolutely necessary: a table, two sideboards, six chairs, all from the apartment she had left. The salon was embellished with an Aubusson carpet, given to Bridau when the department offices were refurnished. The widow placed in the room one of the common mahogany cabinets, with Egyptian heads, which Jacob Desmalter made by the gross in 1806, upholstered in green silk with white roses. Above the couch Bridau's portrait, done in crayons by a friendly hand, also caught the eye. Although true art might detect some shortcomings therein, the firm will of that great obscure citizen could be read upon the brow. The serene expression of his eyes, at once mild and proud, was well depicted. The sagacity to which his prudent lips bore witness, the frank smile and the whole air of the man, to whom the Emperor applied the phrase: *Justum et tenacem*, were reproduced with truth at least, if not with talent. As you looked at the portrait, you felt that there was a man who had always done his duty. His countenance expressed the incorruptibility which is universally accorded to several men employed under the Republic. Opposite, above a card-table, the portrait of the Emperor, done in colors by Vernet, shone resplendent; it represents Napoléon galloping by, followed by his escort.

Agathe indulged in two large bird-cages, one filled with canaries, the other with parrots. She had taken up that childish taste after the loss she had met with, a loss irreparable to her as to many people.

As to the widow's bedroom, it became within three months what it was destined to remain until the ill-fated day when she was obliged to leave it: an abode of disorder to which no description could do justice. The cats made their homes on the couches; the canaries, which were sometimes allowed to fly about the room, left their marks on all the furniture. The poor dear widow placed canary seed and chickweed for them in various places. The cats found delicate morsels in chipped saucers. The clothing was thrown about. The whole room was redolent of the province and of fidelity to the dead. Everything that had belonged to the late Bridau was preserved with pious care. His clerical utensils received the attention that a paladin's widow would have bestowed upon his armor in the old days. A single instance will enable everyone to understand her touching devotion. She had placed a pen in an envelope, sealed it up and written on the outside: "The last pen my dear husband used." The cup from which he had drunk his last draught was kept under glass on the mantelpiece. Caps and false hair were perched, later, on the glass globes that covered those precious relics.

After Bridau's death there was not the slightest trace of coquetry or womanly care of her person in this woman of thirty-five. Parted from the only man she had ever known, esteemed and loved, and

who had never given her a moment's sorrow, she
no longer felt that she was a wife, everything was
indifferent to her; she paid no heed to her dress.
Never was anything more simple or more complete
than this abandonment of conjugal happiness and
coquetry. Certain mortals receive from love the
power to transport their *I* into another person; and
when he is taken from them, life becomes impossible to them. Agathe, who had no desire to live
except for her children, felt infinitely sad when she
saw how great privations her ruin was destined to
impose upon them. From the time that she moved
to Rue Mazarine, there was a tinge of melancholy
in her expression that made her face extremely
touching. She relied somewhat upon the Emperor,
but the Emperor could do no more than he was doing for the moment; each child had six hundred
francs a year from his privy purse, in addition to
the scholarship.

As for the brilliant Descoings, she occupied an
apartment similar to her niece's, but on the second
floor. She had assigned to Madame Bridau a thousand crowns a year from the income of her life interest. Roguin the notary had arranged matters
in proper form for Madame Bridau in that regard,
but it would require seven years for the damage to
be repaired by this gradual method. Roguin, who
was entrusted with the task of restoring the lost
fifteen hundred francs a year, laid aside the sums
thus held back. La Descoings, reduced to twelve
hundred francs a year, lived with her niece, in a

very small way.   The two honest but feeble creatures hired a woman for the morning only.   La
Descoings, who loved to cook, prepared the dinner.
In the evening, a few friends, clerks in the department, who owed their appointments to Bridau, came
in to play cards with the two widows.   La Descoings still cherished her lottery combination, which
refused to come out, from sheer obstinacy, she said.
She hoped to return, at a single stroke, all that she
had forcibly borrowed from her niece.   She loved
the two little Bridaus more dearly than her own
grandson Bixiou, she felt so strongly her own guilt
toward them, and admired so warmly her niece's
kindness in never saying a reproachful word to her
even in her greatest misery.   So you may believe
that Joseph and Philippe were made much of by La
Descoings.   After the manner of all persons who
have a vice for which they seek forgiveness, the
old investor in the imperial lottery of France
arranged little dinners for them and loaded them
with sweetmeats.   Later, Joseph and Philippe found
it extremely easy to obtain money from her pocket,
the younger for crayons, pencils, paper and prints,
the elder for apple-tarts, marbles, twine and knives.
Her passion had led her to restrict her expenses to
fifty francs per month, so that she might gamble
with the balance.

For her part, Madame Bridau, by reason of her
mother-love, did not allow her expenses to exceed
that sum.   To punish herself for her confidence, she
heroically sacrificed her little pleasures.   As in the

case of many timid souls of limited intelligence, a single sentiment wounded and her distrust aroused, led her to display one defect so extensively that it assumed the consistency of a virtue. The Emperor might forget, she said to herself, he might be killed in battle, and her pension would die with her. She shuddered when she saw how many chances there were that her children would be left penniless. Incapable of understanding Roguin's figures, when he tried to show her that in seven years, a yearly payment of three thousand francs out of Madame Descoings' income would enable her to repurchase the consols she had sold, she refused to trust the notary, her aunt or the State; she relied upon herself alone and upon her privations. By putting aside a thousand crowns out of her pension each year, she would have thirty thousand francs at the end of ten years, which would yield her fifteen hundred francs a year for one of her sons. At thirty-six she was justified in believing that she might live twenty years longer; and, by adhering to that system, she would be able to give each of them what was absolutely necessary. Thus these two widows had passed from false opulence to voluntary poverty, one under the guidance of a vice, and the other under the impulse of the purest virtue.

There is not one of all these trivial details that does not contribute to the wealth of useful information that will result from this narrative, which deals with the most ordinary interests of life, but whose scope will be perhaps the more extended on that account.   The sight of the cages, the frisking of the *rapins* in the street, the necessity of looking up at the sky to seek relief from the ghastly sights by which that damp corner is surrounded, the aspect of the portrait, full of soul and grandeur as it was, despite the amateurish work of the artist, the spectacle of the rich, but softened and harmonious colors of that pleasant and tranquil interior, the flowers in the aërial gardens, the poverty of the household, the preference of the mother for her elder son, her opposition to the tastes of the younger, in a word, the *ensemble* of the facts and circumstances which serve as a preamble to this narrative, contains, it may be, in germ, the causes to which we owe Joseph Bridau, one of the greatest painters of the present French school.

Philippe, the elder of Bridau's two children, bore a striking resemblance to his mother.   Although he was a fair-haired boy, with blue eyes, he had a swaggering air which was easily mistaken for animation and courage.   Old Claparon, who entered the department with Bridau, and was one of the faithful friends who came in the evening to play cards with the two widows, said to Philippe two or three times a month, tapping him on the cheek:

"Here's a young rascal who will not fail for want of dash!"

Thus stimulated, the child acquired, through mere bravado, a sort of resolution.   This bent once imparted to his character, he became skilful in all bodily exercises.   By dint of fighting with his fellows at the Lyceum, he acquired that personal courage and contempt for pain which lead to military valor, but he naturally contracted the greatest aversion to study, for public education will never solve the difficult problem of the simultaneous development of the body and the intellect.   Agathe reasoned from her purely physical resemblance to Philippe that there also existed a moral likeness to her, and firmly believed that she would some day find in him her delicacy of feeling enhanced by his manly strength.

Philippe was fifteen years old at the time that his mother took up her abode in the gloomy apartment on Rue Mazarine, and the winning manners of children of that age tended to confirm the mother's belief.   Joseph, who was three years younger, resembled his father, but only in his undesirable qualities.   In the first place, his abundant black hair was always unkempt, whatever one might do; while his brother, notwithstanding his activity, was always sleek and pretty.   In the second place, by some unknown fatality—but a too constant fatality becomes a habit—Joseph could never keep any of his clothes clean: if he were dressed in new clothes throughout, they soon became old. The elder, through self-love, took care of his belongings.   The mother insensibly fell into the habit of scolding Joseph and holding his brother up to him as an example to be followed.   She did not always show the same face to the two children; and when she went to fetch them, she would say of Joseph:

"What condition shall I find his clothes in?"

These trivial things forced her heart into the bottomless pit of maternal favoritism. Not one among the extremely ordinary beings who composed the social circle of the two widows, neither Père du Bruel, nor old Claparon, nor Desroches the elder, nor even Abbé Loraux, Agathe's confessor, noticed Joseph's tendency to close observation. Completely dominated by his one taste, the future colorist paid no attention to any of the things that really concerned him; and, during his childhood, this disposition bore so close a resemblance to torpidity, that his father had some anxiety about him. The extraordinary size of the head, the expansive brow, had caused some fear at first that the child was hydrocephalic. His restless face, whose originality may be considered ugliness in the eyes of those who do not know the moral value of a face, was extremely ungenial during his boyhood. The features, which developed in due time, seemed then to be contracted, and the profound attention the child paid to everything contracted them still more.

Thus Philippe flattered his mother's vanity at every point, while she never had a pleasant word for Joseph. Philippe constantly let fall one of those bright remarks, those quick retorts, which lead parents to believe that their children will be remarkable men, while Joseph was always taciturn and musing. The mother hoped for marvels from Philippe, but she did not count upon Joseph at all.

Joseph's predisposition to art was developed by a

most commonplace circumstance: in 1812, during the Easter holidays, as he was returning from a walk in the Tuileries garden, with his brother and Madame Descoings, he spied a pupil drawing on the wall a caricature of some professor, and he stood speechless with admiration, in front of that sketch in chalk, which sparkled with malice. The next day the child stationed himself at the window, watched the pupils going in through the gate on Rue Mazarine, went stealthily down and glided into the long courtyard of the Institute, where he saw statues, busts, unfinished works in marble, clay and plaster of Paris, at which he gazed feverishly, for his instinct was revealing itself, his calling was stirring him. He entered a lower room, the door of which was ajar, and saw ten or twelve young men designing a statue; he at once became the target of innumerable jests.

"Here, boy! here, boy!" said the first one who saw him, taking up some bread crumbs and tossing them to him.

"Whose child is that?"

"God! how ugly he is!"

For fully quarter of an hour, Joseph sustained the assaults of the great sculptor Chaudet's studio; but after they had made sport of him to their heart's content, the pupils were impressed by his face and by his persistence, and asked him what he wanted. Joseph replied that he was very anxious to learn how to draw; and, thereupon, one and all did their utmost to encourage him. The child, won over by their friendly manner, told them that he was Madame Bridau's son.

"Oho! if you're Madame Bridau's son, you may become a great man," was the cry from every corner of the studio. "Vive Madame Bridau's son! Is your mother pretty? If we're to judge by your mug as a specimen, she must be a beauty!"

"Ah! you want to be an artist," said the oldest, leaving his place and coming to Joseph to join in the attack upon him; "but do you know that you must be a swaggering blade and put up with great hardships? Yes, indeed, there are tests fit to break your arms and legs. Out of all these rascals you see here, there isn't one that hasn't been put through his paces. That fellow there went seven days without eating! Let's see if you can be an artist!"

He took one arm and raised it straight in the air; then he placed the other as if Joseph were about to strike somebody with his fist.

"We call that the telegraph test," said he. "If you stand so, without lowering or changing the position of your arms for fifteen minutes, why, you will have proved yourself to be a jolly blade."

"Come, little one, courage!" said the others. "Bless me! you have to suffer in order to be an artist."

Joseph, with the child-like faith of his thirteen years, stood without moving for about five minutes, and all the pupils began to regard him more seriously.

"Ah! you're lowering your arm," said one.

"*Saperlotte!* stick to it. The Emperor Napoléon

has stood for a whole month as you see him there,"
said another, pointing to Chaudet's fine statue of
Napoléon.

The Emperor was represented standing, with the
imperial sceptre in his hand; in 1814, the statue
was pulled down from the column it adorned so
well. At the end of ten minutes the perspiration
stood in drops on Joseph's forehead. At that
moment, a short, bald man, pale and sickly, entered
the room. The most respectful silence at once
reigned in the studio.

"Well, boys, what are you doing?" he said, looking at the martyr of the studio.

"This little fellow is posing," said the tall pupil
who had given Joseph his position.

"Aren't you ashamed of yourselves to torture a
poor child so?" said Chaudet, lowering Joseph's
arms. "How long have you been standing like
that?" he asked, patting the boy's cheek in a
friendly way.

"About a quarter of an hour."

"And what brings you here?"

"I want to be an artist."

"Where do you come from?"

"From mamma's house."

"Oh! mamma!" cried the pupils.

"Silence in the studio!" cried Chaudet.—"What
does your mamma do?"

"She's Madame Bridau. My papa, who is dead,
was the Emperor's friend. So the Emperor will pay
whatever you ask if you'll teach me to draw."

"His father was chief of division in the Department of the Interior," said Chaudet, as a sudden thought struck him.—"So you want to be an artist, already?"

"Yes, monsieur."

"Come here as often as you please, and we will amuse you! Give him a board and paper and pencils, and let him go ahead.—Understand, you rascals," said the sculptor, "that his father did me a service. Here, *Corde-à-puits*, go and buy some cakes and sweetmeats and candy," said he, handing some money to the pupil who had imposed on Joseph.—"We'll see whether you're an artist by the way you chew," he added, patting Joseph's chin.

Then he looked over the work of his pupils, accompanied by the child, who looked and listened and tried to understand. The refreshments arrived. The whole studio, as well as the sculptor and the child, attacked them. Thenceforward Joseph was petted as vigorously as he had been hoaxed.

This scene in which the merry humor and kind hearts of the artists made themselves manifest, and which he instinctively understood, made a profound impression on the child. The appearance of the sculptor Chaudet,—who was prematurely taken away by death, and whose renown was made secure by the Emperor's patronage,—was like a vision to Joseph. He said nothing to his mother of this escapade, but every Sunday and every Thursday he passed three hours in Chaudet's studio. La

Descoings, who smiled upon the whims of the two cherubs, from that time gave Joseph black and red pencils, prints and drawing paper. At the Imperial Lyceum the future artist sketched his masters and his comrades, made charcoal drawings of the dormitories, and was remarkably assiduous in his attendance at the drawing-class. Lemire, the professor of that branch at the Lyceum, was impressed not only with Joseph's aptness, but with his progress as well, and called upon Madame Bridau to inform her of her son's manifest vocation. Agathe, who, like a true provincial, knew as little of the arts as she knew much of housekeeping, was seized with terror. When Lemire had gone, the widow began to weep.

"Ah!" said she, when La Descoings arrived, "I am lost! Joseph, whom I expected to make a government clerk, and who had his road all marked out for him in the Department of the Interior, where, with the influence of his father's name, he would have become chief of bureau at twenty-five, wants to be a painter, a rag-and-tatters profession. I knew that child would never cause me anything but trouble!"

Madame Descoings confessed that she had been encouraging Joseph's passion for several months past, and had covered up his surreptitious visits to the Institute on Sundays and Thursdays. At the Salon, to which she had taken him, the profound scrutiny the little fellow bestowed on the pictures was something marvelous.

"If he understands painting at thirteen, my dear," said she, "your Joseph will be a man of genius."

"Yes, see what genius did for his father! dead from overwork at forty!"

In the last days of autumn, as Joseph was entering upon his fourteenth year, Agathe, despite La Descoings' entreaties, went to Chaudet to oppose his leading her son astray. She found the sculptor in a blue blouse, modeling his last statue; he was almost discourteous in his reception of the wife of the man who had come to his assistance years before on a critical occasion; but, feeling even then that death was upon him, he was working with the fierce energy that enables one to do in a few moments what it is difficult to do in months; he had found an idea of which he had long been in search, and he was handling his modeling-tool and his clay with sharp, abrupt movements that seemed to the ignorant Agathe to be those of a maniac. In any other mood, Chaudet would have begun to laugh; but when he heard this mother curse art in general, lament the destiny that was being forced upon her son, and request him not to admit him to his studio any more, he became righteously indignant.

"I was under obligations to your late husband, and I hoped to pay my debt by encouraging his son, by watching over little Joseph's first steps in the grandest of all careers!" he cried. "Aye, madame, let me tell you, if you do not know it, that a great artist is a king, more than a king; for in

IN CHAUDET'S STUDIO

———

"Go on, madame! make an idiot of him. ∗ ∗ ∗
I hope that, in spite of your efforts, he will persist
in being an artist. The vocation is stronger than
all the obstacles you can put in the way of its results! Vocation—the word means calling, that is,
selection by God! But you will make your child
unhappy!"

He threw the remaining clay into a pail, and said
to his model:

"Enough for to-day."

Cortazzo

ADecisy

the first place, he is happier, he is independent, he lives as he pleases; and he reigns in the world of fantasy. Now, your son has a glorious future! such qualities as his are rare, they are not revealed so early in life except in the Giottos, the Raphaels, the Titiens, the Rubenses, the Murillos; for it seems to me that he should be a painter rather than a sculptor. Good God! if I had such a son I should be as happy as the Emperor is over the birth of the King of Rome! However, you are the arbiter of your child's destiny. Go on, madame! make an idiot of him, a man who will do nothing but walk when he walks, a wretched scribbler; you will have committed murder. I hope that, in spite of your efforts, he will persist in being an artist. The vocation is stronger than all the obstacles you can put in the way of its results! Vocation—the word means calling, that is, selection by God! But you will make your child unhappy!"

He threw the remaining clay into a pail, and said to his model:

"Enough for to-day."

Agathe raised her eyes and saw a nude woman sitting on a stool in a corner of the studio on which her glance had not previously fallen; that sight drove her from the room in horror.

"You will not admit little Bridau again," said Chaudet to his pupils. "It annoys madame, his mother."

"Oho!" cried the pupils, when Agathe closed the door.

"And Joseph has been going to that place!" said the poor mother to herself, dismayed at what she had seen and heard.

As soon as the pupils in sculpture and painting learned that Madame Bridau did not want her son to become an artist, it was their greatest delight to entice Joseph to their rooms. Notwithstanding the promise his mother extorted from him, that he would not go to the Institute, the child often slipped into Regnauld's studio there and was encouraged to make daubs upon canvas. When the widow attempted to complain, Chaudet's pupils told her that Regnauld was not Chaudet; moreover, she had not given them monsieur her son to watch over, they said, with a thousand other jests. The mischievous *rapins* even composed and sang a *chanson* in a hundred and thirty-seven couplets upon the subject of Madame Bridau.

On the evening of that depressing day, Agathe refused to play at cards, and sat on the sofa, a prey to such profound melancholy, that at times the tears stood in her lovely eyes.

"What's the matter, Madame Bridau?" said old Claparon.

"She thinks her son will have to beg his bread, because he has the painter's hump," said La Descoings; "but, for my own part, I haven't the slightest anxiety for the future of my stepson, little Bixiou, who also has a rage for drawing. Men are made to get on in the world."

"Madame is right," said the spare, stern-faced

Desroches, who had never succeeded, despite his talents, in obtaining the post of deputy-chief clerk. "I have only one son, luckily; for, with my eighteen hundred francs and a wife who earns scarcely twelve hundred in the little shop where she sells stamped paper, I don't know what would become of me if I had more! I have put my boy out as a junior clerk to a solicitor, where he gets twenty-five francs a month and his luncheon; I give him as much more and he dines and sleeps at home; that's all he has, so he must push ahead, and he'll make his way! I cut out more work for him than he would have at school, and some day he'll be a solicitor; when I give him a ticket to the play, he's as happy as a king and always kisses me; oh! but I keep him straight and make him give me an account of the use he makes of his money. You're too indulgent to your children. If your son wants to follow a hard road, let him do it; it will make something of him."

"My son is only sixteen," said Du Bruel, an old chief of division who had just retired, "and his mother adores him; but I wouldn't listen to a vocation that declared itself so early. It's a mere caprice then, a whim that may pass away! According to my ideas, boys need to be guided."

"You are rich, monsieur," said Agathe, "and you are a man and have only one son."

"Faith," said Claparon, "children are our tyrants.—*Hearts.*—Mine drives me mad, he's brought me to want, and I have got to the point

where I don't bother myself about him at all.—
Independence.—Well, he's the happier for it, and so
am I. The rascal was partly responsible for his poor
mother's death. He's a traveling salesman now,
and he has found his proper place; he was no sooner
in the house than he wanted to be off again; he
couldn't sit still and he never wanted to learn anything; all that I ask of God is that I may die before
he dishonors my name! They who have no children miss many pleasures, but they also avoid much
suffering."

"That's like a father!" said Agathe to herself,
weeping afresh.

"What I say to you, dear Madame Bridau, is intended to convince you that you must let your son
become a painter; otherwise you will waste your
time—"

"If you were capable of forming his mind," said
the sour Desroches, "I would tell you to oppose his
inclinations; but you are so weak with them, that I
say, let him daub and draw."

"Lost!" exclaimed Claparon.

"How lost?" cried the poor mother.

"Why, *my independence in hearts ;** those spirited
outbursts of Desroches always make me lose."

"Console yourself, Agathe," said La Descoings,
"Joseph will be a great man."

After this discussion, which resembles all human

Independence—indépendance—is an expression used in the game of *boston*,
"derived," says Littré, "like the game itself, from the American War of Independence."

discussions, the widow's friends all veered around to the same opinion, and that opinion did not put an end to the widow's perplexities. They all advised her to let Joseph follow his vocation.

"If he turns out not to be a man of genius," said Du Bruel, who was paying court to Agathe, "you can still put him into the department."

La Descoings escorted the three old government clerks to the head of the stairs, calling them the *Wise Men of Greece*.

"She worries too much," said Du Bruel.

"She's only too fortunate to have her son want to do something," said Claparon.

"If God preserves the Emperor," said Desroches, "Joseph will be sure of his protection! So why need she be anxious?"

"She's afraid of everything where her children are concerned," La Descoings replied.—"Well, my dear girl," she said, as she returned to the salon, "you see they are unanimous; why are you crying still?"

"Ah! if Philippe were concerned, I should have no fear. You don't know what goes on in those studios! The artists have naked women there!"

"Well, they have a fire, I suppose," said La Descoings.

*

Not many days later, the news of the disastrous
retreat from Moscow burst upon France. Napoléon returned to organize new forces and to call
upon the nation for new sacrifices. The poor
mother thereupon fell a victim to anxieties of a
different sort. Philippe, who was disgusted with
the Lyceum, was determined to enter the service of
the Emperor. A review at the Tuileries—the last
that Napoléon ever held there—at which Philippe
was present, had turned his head. In those days,
military splendor, the sight of uniforms, the
authority of epaulets, exerted an irresistible fascination upon many young men. Philippe believed
that he had the same aptitude for military service
that his brother manifested for the arts. Without
his mother's knowledge, he wrote a petition to the
Emperor, in these words:

"Sire, I am the son of your Bridau; I am eighteen
years old, five feet six inches tall, with good legs, a good constitution, and a longing to be one of your soldiers. I claim
your protection to enable me to enter the army," etc.

The Emperor sent Philippe from the Imperial
Lyceum to Saint-Cyr within twenty-four hours, and
six months later, in November, 1813, he left that

4   (49)

establishment a sub-lieutenant in a cavalry regiment. Philippe remained at the depôt a portion of the winter; but, as soon as he could ride, he started for the front, overflowing with ardor. During the campaign in France he became lieutenant as the result of an affair of outposts, in which his impetuous courage saved his colonel's life. The Emperor made Philippe a captain at the battle of La Fère-Champenoise, and took him for an orderly. Encouraged by such rapid promotion, Philippe won the Cross at Montereau. He was present when Napoléon bade his army farewell at Fontainebleau, and, excited to fanaticism by that spectacle, refused to serve the Bourbons.

When he returned to his mother in July, 1814, he found her ruined. Joseph's scholarship at the Lyceum was taken from him during the vacation, and Madame Bridau, whose pension was paid from the Emperor's privy purse, begged in vain to have it continued as a charge upon the Department of the Interior. Joseph, who was more enthusiastic over his painting than ever, was overjoyed at these disasters; he asked his mother to allow him to go to Monsieur Regnauld's and promised that he could earn his living. He said that he was far enough advanced in the second class to drop his rhetoric. Philippe, a captain and decorated with the Cross of the Legion of Honor at nineteen, after having served as the Emperor's aide-de-camp on two battlefields, flattered his mother's self-esteem enormously; and although he was a vulgar, swaggering fellow, really possessed of no other merit than the ordinary bravado of the trooper, he was the man of genius in her eyes; while Joseph, stern of brow, small and slender and sickly, fond of peace and tranquillity, dreaming of artistic renown, seemed destined, according to her views, to cause her nothing but grief and anxiety. The winter of 1814-15 was a favorable season for Joseph, who, being secretly assisted by La Descoings and by Bixiou, the latter a pupil of Gros, was allowed to work in that famous studio, which sent forth so many men of talent in various lines; and there he became very intimate with Schinner.

The twentieth of March dawned and Captain Bridau, who joined the Emperor at Lyons and accompanied him to the Tuileries, was made captain of a company in the dragoons of the Garde Impériale. After the battle of Waterloo, at which he was slightly wounded, and where he earned the Cross of an officer of the Legion of Honor, he found himself with Maréchal Davout at Saint-Denis and not with the army of the Loire; so it was that, through the influence of Maréchal Davout, he retained his rank and his decoration; but he was put on half-pay. Joseph, being anxious concerning the future, studied throughout this period with an ardor that made him ill several times in the midst of that maëlstrom of exciting events.

"It's the smell of the paint," Agathe would say to Madame Descoings; "he ought to give up a trade so injurious to his health."

But all Agathe's anxiety at this time was centred upon her son, the lieutenant-colonel; in 1816, he had fallen from the salary of about nine thousand francs which a captain in the dragoons of the Garde Impériale received, to the half-pay of three hundred francs a month; she arranged the attic room over the kitchen for him, and expended some of her savings upon it. Philippe was one of the Bonapartists who were most assiduous in their attendance at the Café Lemblin, a genuine constitutional Bœotia; he acquired there the habits, the manners, the style and the mode of life of officers on half-pay; and, as any youth of twenty-one would have done, he carried them all to excess; in all seriousness he swore eternal hatred to the Bourbons and would not take the oath of allegiance; he even declined the opportunities that came to him of employment in the line with his old rank of lieutenant-colonel. In his mother's eye, Philippe was developing a grand character.

"His father could have done no better," she said.

His half-pay was enough for Philippe and he cost his mother nothing, while Joseph was entirely supported by the two widows. From that moment Agathe's preference for Philippe was manifest. Hitherto that preference had been a secret; but the persecution to which the faithful soldier of the Emperor was subjected, the memory of the wound received by that cherished son, his courage in adversity, which, albeit quite voluntary, seemed to her a noble adversity, caused Agathe's affection to

burst its bonds. The words: "He is unfortunate!"
justified everything.

Joseph, whose character was distinguished by
that simplicity which always abounds at the outset
of life in artistic souls; and who had been brought
up, moreover, to admire his older brother, was far
from being offended by his mother's preference, but
justified her in it by sharing to the full her adoration
of the gallant youth who had carried Napoléon's
orders in two battles, of a wounded veteran of Waterloo. How could he insinuate a doubt of the superiority
of his great brother whom he had seen in the beautiful
green and gold uniform of the dragoons of the guard,
commanding his company on the *Champ de Mai!*
Moreover, notwithstanding her preference, Agathe
showed herself an excellent mother; she loved
Joseph, but not blindly; she did not understand him,
that was all. Joseph adored his mother, whereas
Philippe allowed himself to be adored by her.
However, the dragoon toned down his military
brutality for her benefit; but he hardly concealed
his contempt for Joseph, although he expressed it
in a friendly way. Whenever he saw his brother,
with his powerful head, wasted by unremitting toil
and puny and sickly at seventeen, he called him:
"Ragamuffin!" His manner, always patronizing,
would have been insulting except for the indifference of the artist, who believed, too, in the kind-
liness supposed to be hidden beneath a soldier's
brutal exterior. Joseph did not know as yet, poor
child, that soldiers of real worth are gentle and

polished like other superior people. Genius always resembles itself under all circumstances.

"Poor boy!" Philippe would say to his mother, "you mustn't annoy him, let him amuse himself."

This contempt seemed to the mother a proof of brotherly affection.

"Philippe will always love and protect his brother," she thought.

In 1816, Joseph obtained his mother's permission to convert the garret adjoining his attic into a studio, and La Descoings gave him some money to procure the articles that were indispensable to the *painter's trade;* for, in the two widows' minds, painting was only a trade. With the intelligence and ardor which accompany a decided vocation, Joseph arranged everything himself in his poor studio. The landlord, at Madame Descoings' request, cut a hole in the roof and put in a window. The garret became a vast hall which Joseph painted a chocolate color; he hung a few sketches on the walls; Agathe, not without regret, contributed a small sheet-iron stove, and Joseph was able to work at home, without, however, neglecting Gros's studio or Schinner's.

The constitutional party, supported by half-pay officers and by the Bonapartist faction, stirred up émeutes around the Chamber in the name of the Charter, which no one wanted, and formed several conspiracies. Philippe, who was implicated in the disturbances, was arrested, but was soon released for lack of proof; but the Minister of War stopped his half-pay, putting his

name on what might be called a disciplinary list.
France was no longer a safe abiding-place, for
Philippe would surely end by falling into some
snare set by agents of the government. Government agents who were paid to incite disturbances
were much talked about in those days. While
Philippe was playing billiards in suspected cafés,
wasting his time and accustoming himself to sip
petits verres of different liqueurs, Agathe was in
mortal terror concerning the great man of the
family. The three Wise Men of Greece were too
well accustomed to making the same journey every
evening, ascending the staircase of the two widows,
finding them waiting for them all ready to ask them
their impressions of the day, ever to leave them,
and they still continued to come and play cards in
the little green salon.

The Department of the Interior, when it was
purged in 1816, had retained old Claparon, one of
the waverers who retailed the contents of *Le Moniteur* in an undertone, adding: "Don't betray me!"
—Desroches, who had gone on the retired list some
time after old Du Bruel, was still fighting for his
retiring pension. These three friends, witnesses of
Agathe's despair, advised her to send the colonel
abroad.

"There's much talk about conspiracies, and your
son, being the man he is, will fall into some trap
or other, for there are always traitors."

"What the devil! he's of the stuff that the Emperor made his marshals from," said Du Bruel in

an undertone, looking about him, "and he ought not to abandon his profession. Let him go and serve in the East, in the West Indies—"

"And what about his health?" said Agathe.

"Why doesn't he take an office?" said old Desroches. "There are so many special departments being organized! I propose to enter an insurance office as chief of a bureau, as soon as my pension is settled."

"Philippe's a soldier, he cares for nothing but war," said the bellicose Agathe.

"Then he ought to be sensible and apply for service under—"

"Those people?" cried the widow.

"Oh! I will never advise him to do that."

"You are wrong," rejoined Du Bruel. "My son has just been given a place by the Duc de Navarreins. The Bourbons are very kind to those who come over to them unreservedly. Your son would be appointed lieutenant-colonel in some regiment."

"They don't want any but nobles in the cavalry, and he will never be a colonel," cried La Descoings.

Agathe, in dismay, begged Philippe to go abroad and take service with some foreign government, for, she said, they would always welcome with favor one of the Emperor's orderlies.

"Take service with a foreign government?" cried Philippe in horror.

Agathe embraced her son effusively, saying:

"He is just like his father."

"He is right," said Joseph, "the Frenchman is

too proud of his Column to go and rear himself a
column elsewhere. And then perhaps Napoléon
will return again!"

To please his mother, Philippe thereupon conceived the magnificent idea of joining General
Lallemand in the United States, and of assisting in
the foundation of the Champ-d'Asile, one of the
most terrible of all the frauds that ever masqueraded
as national subscriptions. Agathe contributed ten
thousand francs from her savings, and spent a thousand francs to go to Havre with her son and see
him safely on board ship. At the end of 1817,
Agathe was able to live upon the six hundred francs
from her property in the Funds; then, by an inspi-
ration, she immediately invested the remaining ten
thousand francs of her savings, which yielded her
seven hundred francs more. Joseph desired to
assist in this work of devotion; he went about
dressed like a tipstaff; he wore heavy shoes and
blue stockings; he denied himself gloves, and
burned charcoal; he lived on bread and milk and
Brie cheese. The poor child received no encouragement except from old Descoings and Bixiou, his college and studio comrade, who was at that time
making his admirable caricatures, and at the same
time filling a minor place in one of the departments.

"How glad I was when the summer of 1818
came!" Bridau has often said, recounting his
woeful plight in those days. "The warm weather
made it unnecessary for me to buy charcoal."

Being already as strong as Gros in the matter of

coloring, he no longer saw his master except to consult him; he meditated breaking a lance with the classic school, shattering the old Greek conventions and the fetters that confined an art to which nature belongs as it is, in the omnipotence of its creations and its fantasies.   Joseph prepared for the struggle, which, from the day of his first appearance at the Salon, in 1823, never ceased.

It was a terrible year: Roguin, Madame Descoings' notary and Madame Bridau's, disappeared, carrying with him the sums laid aside out of the income of the life estate for seven years, which already amounted to enough to produce two thousand francs a year.   Three days after this catastrophe, a bill for one thousand francs, drawn by Colonel Philippe upon his mother, arrived from New York.   The poor boy, deceived like so many others, had lost everything in the Champ-d'Asile. The letter, which made Agathe, La Descoings and Joseph shed tears, spoke of debts contracted in New York, where the poor fellow's comrades had become surety for him.

"And it was I who forced him to go," cried the poor mother, always ingenious in finding an excuse for Philippe's faults.

"I don't advise you to force him to make journeys of that sort very often," said old Descoings to her niece.

Madame Descoings was heroic.   She continued to give a thousand crowns to Madame Bridau, but she also continued to cherish the same combination,

which had not won in the lottery since 1799. About
this time she began to suspect the good faith of the
management. She accused the government and
deemed it quite capable of holding the three numbers back in the urn in order to incite investors to
frantic plunges. After a hurried examination of
their resources, it seemed impossible to raise a
thousand francs without selling a part of their principal. The two women spoke of pawning the silver
plate, a portion of the linen, or such furniture as
they did not absolutely need. Joseph, dismayed at
these suggestions, sought out Gérard and described
his position, and the great painter obtained for him
an order for two copies of the portrait of Louis
XVIII., for the king's household, at five hundred
francs each. Although by no means generously inclined, Gros took his pupil to a dealer in colors and
told him to charge such supplies as Joseph needed
to his account. But the thousand francs were not
to be paid until the copies were delivered. So
Joseph painted four easel pictures in ten days, sold
them to dealers, and took the thousand francs to his
mother, who was thus able to take up the draft. A
week later came another letter wherein the colonel
advised his mother of his departure upon a packet-
boat, the captain of which took him upon credit.
Philippe announced that he should need at least a
thousand francs more on landing at Havre.

"All right!" said Joseph to his mother; "I shall
have finished my copies by that time, and you can
carry him the thousand francs."

"Dear Joseph!" cried Agathe, in tears, as she kissed him; "God will bless you. You do love the poor, persecuted boy, don't you? He is our glory and our whole future. So young and brave and unlucky! everything is against him, let us three at least be on his side."

"Painting is of some use, you see," cried Joseph, happy to obtain his mother's permission to be a great artist.

Madame Bridau hurried to meet her beloved son, Colonel Philippe. Once at Havre, she went every day beyond the round tower built by François I., awaiting the American packet-boat, and conceiving from day to day the most cruel anxiety. Mothers alone know how that species of suffering rekindles the mother-love. The packet-boat reached port safely on a lovely morning in October 1819, without having encountered so much as a squall. Upon the most inhuman of men the air of the fatherland and the sight of a mother never fail to produce a certain effect, especially after a long and uncomfortable journey. Philippe indulged himself therefore in an effusion of sentiment, which led Agathe to think: "Ah! how he loves me!" Alas! the young officer loved but one person in the wide world, and that person was Colonel Philippe. His misfortunes in Texas, his sojourn in New York,—a land where speculation and selfishness are carried to the highest pitch, where brutal indifference to the rights of others amounts to downright cynicism, where man, essentially isolated, finds himself compelled to march forward in his might and constantly to constitute himself judge of his own cause, where courtesy does not exist,—in a word, the incidents, even the most trivial, of his journey, had developed in Philippe the evil tendencies of the veteran soldier; he had become brutal in his manners, a great smoker and drinker, selfish and rude; poverty and physical suffering had depraved him. Moreover, the colonel looked upon himself as a persecuted man. The effect of that opinion is to make unintelligent men tyrannical and intolerant. For Philippe the universe began at his head and ended at his feet; the sun shone only for him. In fact, the spectacle of New York, as interpreted by this man of action, had removed his last remaining scruples in the direction of morality. With creatures of that type there are but two modes of existence; either they believe or they do not believe; either they have all the virtues of the honest man, or they yield to all the demands of necessity; in the latter case they accustom themselves to exalt their most trivial desires and every passing whim of their passions into a necessity. With this system one can go a long way.

The colonel had preserved, in appearance only, the straightforward bluntness, the off-hand manner of the soldier. For that reason he was an exceedingly dangerous man, for he seemed as ingenuous as a child; but, having to think only of himself, he never did anything without reflecting upon what it was for his interest to do, as a crafty attorney reflects upon some trick of Master Gonin; words cost him nothing, he would give you as many of them as you chose to believe. If, unluckily, anyone should venture not to accept the explanations by which he justified the contradictions between his language and his conduct, the colonel, who was a superior shot with the pistol, who could safely defy the most adroit fencing-master and who possessed the perfect *sang froid* of all those to whom life is indifferent, was ready to demand satisfaction for the slightest sharp word; but he seemed the very man to resort to acts of violence, pending the meeting, which would preclude the possibility of any adjustment. His imposing figure had become corpulent, his face had become bronzed during his stay in Texas; he retained his abrupt manner of speaking and the sharp tone of the man obliged to enforce respect for himself in the midst of the mixed population of New York. Thus equipped physically and morally, simply clothed, his body visibly hardened by his recent hardships, Philippe appeared to his poor mother like a hero; but he had simply become what the common people forcibly call a *chenapan* —scamp. Horrified by her beloved son's destitute condition, Madame Bridau procured him a complete wardrobe at Havre. As she listened to the story of his misfortunes, she had not the strength to prevent him from eating and drinking and merry-making as a man should eat and drink and make merry, who had just returned from the Champ-d'Asile. The idea of the conquest of Texas by the remains of the Imperial army was a fine conception, to be sure; but it fell through, less because of the subject-matter than because of the men concerned, for Texas to-day is a republic with a glorious future.

This experiment of liberalism under the Restoration proves most conclusively that its objects were purely selfish and in no sense national, that they aimed at power and nothing else. Neither men nor places nor ideas nor devotion were wanting, but the money and the assistance of that hypocritical party which had enormous sums at its disposal but gave nothing when there was a prospect of recovering an empire. Housekeepers of the Agathe type have a sound commonsense that enables them to fathom this sort of political trickery. The poor mother caught a glimpse of the truth from her son's story; for, in the exile's interest, she had listened, during his absence, to the pompous manifestoes of the constitutional journals and followed the progress of that famous subscription, which yielded barely a hundred and fifty thousand francs when five or six millions would have been required. The leaders of the liberal party soon perceived that they were serving Louis the Eighteenth's purposes by sending away from France the glorious remnants of our armies, and they abandoned the most devoted, the most ardent, the most enthusiastic of their adherents, those who were the first to come forward. Agathe could not explain to her son that he was a dupe rather than a persecuted man. In her belief in her idol, she accused herself of ignorance, and deplored the unhappy times which caused Philippe's misfortunes. In truth, she said, thus far in all his trials he had been rather a victim of his generous disposition, of his energetic character, of the downfall of the Emperor, of the vindictiveness of the Bourbons against the Bonapartists, than blameworthy on his own account. She did not dare during that week at Havre—a terribly expensive week—to suggest a reconciliation with the royal government and that he should call upon the Minister of War; she had enough to do to induce him to leave Havre and to take him back to Paris, when she had only enough money left for the journey. La Descoings and Joseph, who were awaiting the exile in the courtyard of the Messageries Royales, were deeply impressed by the change in Agathe's face.

"Your mother has aged ten years in two months," said La Descoings to Joseph, in the midst of the embracing, while the two trunks were being unloaded.

"Good morning, Mother Descoings," was the colonel's affectionate greeting to the old grocer, whom Joseph called affectionately "Mamma Descoings."

"We have no money for the cab," said Agathe in a sorrowful voice.

"I have," replied the young painter.—"My brother has a superb color!" he cried, looking at Philippe.

"Yes, I'm colored like a pipe. But you haven't changed, little one."

Joseph at this time was twenty-one years old; his merit was appreciated by the few friends who stood by him in his days of trial, and he felt his strength and was conscious of his talent. He represented painting in a club composed of young men whose lives were devoted to the sciences, letters, politics and philosophy. He was wounded therefore by the gesture with which his brother still expressed his contempt: Philippe pulled his ear as if he were a mere boy. Agathe noticed the sort of coldness that succeeded the first effusion of affection on the part of La Descoings and Joseph; but she set everything right by telling them of the hardships undergone by Philippe during his exile. La Descoings was determined to make a holiday of the son's return—she called him the prodigal son under her breath—and had prepared the best dinner imaginable, to which old Claparon and the elder Desroches were invited. All the friends of the family were expected to come and did come during the evening. Joseph had asked Léon Giraud, D'Arthez, Michel Chrestien, Fulgence Ridal and Bianchon, his friends of the club. La Descoings told Bixiou, her pretended stepson, that there would be a game of écarté for the young men. Desroches the younger, who had taken his certificate as a law student in obedience to his father's unbending will, was also of the evening party. Du Bruel, Claparon, Desroches and Abbé Loraux made a study of the exile, whose coarse manners and bearing, whose voice thickened by constant drinking, whose speech

5

interlarded with slang expressions and whose eva-
sive glance alarmed them.   While Joseph was
arranging the card-tables, the most devoted of
Agathe's old friends gathered about her.

"What do you expect to do with Philippe?" they
asked.

"I don't know," she replied, "but he is still unwilling to serve the Bourbons."

"It is very hard to find a place for him in France.
If he doesn't re-enter the army, he won't find a berth
in the departments very soon," said old Du Bruel.
"Certainly it's enough to hear him talk to know
that he won't have the resource of writing plays for
the stage, as my son has."

By the movement of the eyes with which Agathe
replied, they all understood how anxious were her
thoughts concerning Philippe's future; and as none
of her friends had anything to suggest, they all
kept silent.   The exile, Desroches junior and
Bixiou played at écarté, a game which was then all
the rage.

"Mamma Descoings, my brother has no money
to play with," Joseph whispered in the kindly, excellent woman's ear.

The investor in the royal lottery went and got
twenty francs and handed them to the artist, who
slipped them secretly into his brother's hand.
Everybody arrived.   There were two tables of boston and the party became very animated.   Philippe
showed himself a wretched player.   After winning
a good deal at first, he lost; about eleven o'clock he

owed the young Desroches and Bixiou fifty francs. The loud voices and quarreling at the écarté table filled the ears of the peaceful players of boston more than once, and they looked at Philippe on the sly. The exile gave proof of such an evil temper, that, in his last dispute, in which Desroches, who was none too gentle himself, was involved, Desroches senior, although his son was in the right, blamed him and forbade his playing. Madame Descoings took the same course with her grandson, who was beginning to indulge in such bright remarks that Philippe did not understand them, to be sure, but, in case one of the poisoned arrows had pierced the colonel's thick skull, the merciless wag might have found himself in danger.

"You must be tired," said Agathe in Philippe's ear; "why don't you go to bed?"

"Traveling forms young men," said Bixiou, smiling, when the colonel and Madame Bridau had left the room.

*

Joseph, who rose at dawn and went to bed early, did not see the close of the party. The next morning, as Agathe and La Descoings were preparing breakfast in the kitchen, they could not avoid the thought that evening parties would be very expensive, if Philippe continued to play that game, as La Descoings expressed it. The old lady, who was at this time seventy-six years of age, suggested that she should sell her furniture, give up her apartment on the second floor to the landlord, who asked nothing better than to have it given up, take Agathe's salon for her bedroom, and use the dining-room for a salon as well. In this way they would save seven hundred francs a year and could allow Philippe fifty francs a month until he should find a position. Agathe accepted this sacrifice.

When the colonel came down and his mother had asked him if he had been comfortable in his little room, the two widows set before him the position of the family. By combining their resources, Madame Descoings and Agathe possessed fifty-three hundred francs a year, of which the former's four thousand were for her life only. La Descoings allowed six hundred francs a year to Bixiou, whom she had acknowledged as her grandson for six months past, and six hundred to Joseph; the remainder of her income was employed, as Agathe's was, in rent and household expenses. All the savings had been consumed.

"Never fear," said the lieutenant-colonel, "I am going to look for employment, and I shall not be a burden to you; I only ask for a crust and a corner for the moment."

Agathe embraced her son and La Descoings slipped a hundred francs into his hand to pay his gambling debt of the previous night.

Within ten days the furniture had been sold, the apartment given up and the changes made in Agathe's apartment with the rapidity that is seen nowhere but in Paris. During those ten days Philippe regularly disappeared after breakfast, returned to dinner, went out in the evening again, and did not come home to bed until toward midnight. These are the habits which this disbanded trooper contracted, almost mechanically, and which took deep root; he had his boots polished on Pont Neuf for the two sous he would have had to pay if he had gone by Pont des Arts, on his way to the Palais-Royal, where he consumed two small glasses of eau-de-vie while he read the newspapers, an occupation which filled up the time until noon; about that hour he strolled through Rue Vivienne to the Café Minerve, where liberal politics were brewed at this time, and played billiards with old officers. Whether he won or lost, Philippe always drank three or four *petits verres* of divers liqueurs, and smoked ten government cigars, sauntering about through the streets. After smoking several pipes during the evening at the Estaminet Hollandais, he went up to the card-room about ten o'clock, and the attendant gave him a card and a pin; he would inquire of some expert gamblers how the red and the black were running, and would stake ten francs at what seemed an opportune moment. He never played more than three times, whether he won or lost. When he won, which was almost always the case, he would consume a bowl of punch and return to his attic; but he would talk about slaughtering the ultras and the bodyguards, and sing on the stairs: *Let us guard the welfare of the Empire!* His poor mother when she heard him, would say:

"Philippe is very lively this evening."

And she would go upstairs to kiss him good-night, heedless of the odors of punch, liqueurs and tobacco, with which he was reeking.

"You ought to be satisfied with me, my dear mother," he said to her toward the end of January. "I am leading the most regular life you can imagine."

Philippe had dined five times at a restaurant with some of his former comrades. These old soldiers had mutually exchanged confidences as to the state of their affairs, as they talked of the hopes aroused by the construction of a submarine boat to be used for the rescue of the Emperor. Among his former comrades, Philippe particularly affected the society of an old captain in the dragoons of the guard, named Giroudeau, in whose company he had first seen service. This former dragoon was the cause of Philippe's completing what Rabelais called the equipage of the devil, adding a fourth wheel to the *petit verre*, the cigar, and the card-table. One evening, early in February, Giroudeau took Philippe, after dinner, to the *Gaîeté*, in a box allotted to a small theatrical newspaper belonging to his nephew Finot, where he kept the books and the cash-box and made up and verified the subscription lists. Clad, according to the custom of Bonapartist officers belonging to the constitutional opposition, in ample frockcoats with square collars buttoned to the chin and falling to their heels, decorated with the rosette and armed with canes with leaded knobs which they swung by a cord of plaited leather, the two ex-troopers had got a little tipsy, and were mutually opening their hearts to each other as they entered the box. Through the vapors of a large number of bottles and *petits verres* of various liqueurs, Giroudeau pointed out to Philippe a short, plump, agile *figurante* named Florentine, whose good graces and affection fell to his lot, as did the box, through the omnipotence of the newspaper.

"But," said Philippe, "how far do her good graces go for an old, scarred, grizzled trooper like you?"

"Thank God," Giroudeau replied, "I have never abandoned the time-honored doctrines of our glorious uniform! I have never spent two farthings on a woman."

"What's that?" cried Philippe, putting a finger to his left eye.

"It's true," replied Giroudeau. "But, between ourselves, the paper has a good deal to do with it. To-morrow we shall put in a couple of lines advising the management to give Mademoiselle Florentine an opportunity to dance. Faith, my dear boy, I am very lucky."

"Well!" thought Philippe, "if this venerable Giroudeau with his bald pate, as smooth as my knee, with his forty-eight years, his big belly, his vinedresser's face and his potato-shaped nose, is the friend of a *figurante*, I ought to be the friend of the finest actress in Paris. Where do you find her?" he said aloud to Giroudeau.

"I'll show you Florentine's establishment to-night. Although my Dulcinea has only fifty francs a month at the theatre, thanks to a retired silk-merchant named Cardot, who allows her five hundred francs a month, she's very nicely fixed!"

"Yes, but—" the jealous Philippe began.

"Bah!" said Giroudeau, "true love is blind."

After the play Giroudeau escorted Philippe to Mademoiselle Florentine's, two steps from the theatre, on Rue de Crussol.

"We must be careful," said Giroudeau. "Florentine has a mother with her; you understand that I haven't the money to provide her with one, and this good woman is really her mother. She was a concierge once, but she knows a thing or two, and her name is Cabirolle; call her 'madame'; she's very particular about that."

Florentine had a friend with her that evening,

one Marie Godeschal, lovely as an angel, cold as a
ballet-dancer, and a pupil of Vestris, who predicted
for her a most exalted choregraphic destiny. Mademoiselle Godeschal, who was anxious to make
her début at the Panorama-Dramatique, under the
name of Mariette, relied upon the patronage of one
of the first gentlemen of the Chamber, to whom
Vestris was to have presented her long before.
Vestris, who was still in her prime, did not think
that her pupil knew enough. The ambitious Marie
Godeschal made her pseudonym of Mariette famous,
and her ambition was a very laudable one. She
had a brother, a clerk in Derville's office. The
brother and sister being orphans and wretchedly
poor, but devotedly attached to each other, had seen
life as it is in Paris; the brother was anxious to
become a solicitor in order to make a home for his
sister, and he lived on ten sous a day; the sister
had coolly determined to become a dancer, and to
make the most of her beauty as well as of her
shapely limbs, in order to purchase an office for her
brother. Outside of their regard for each other,
their common interests and their common life,
everybody was a barbarian, a stranger, an enemy
to them, as to the Romans and Hebrews centuries
ago. This touching affection, which nothing could
diminish, explained Mariette's personality to those
who knew her intimately. The brother and sister
lived at this time on the eighth floor of a house on
Rue Vieille-du-Temple. Mariette had begun to
study at the age of ten, and now counted sixteen

summers. Alas! for lack of a little care with her dress, her beauty, which appeared to be mediocre, hidden under a rabbit's-fur shawl, mounted upon iron clogs, dressed in calico and badly groomed, could be divined only by Parisians accustomed to hunting grisettes and keen on the scent of beauty in distress.

Philippe fell in love with Mariette. Mariette saw in Philippe the captain in the dragoons of the guard, the Emperor's orderly, the young man of twenty-seven, and the pleasure of showing herself superior to Florentine by virtue of Philippe's manifest superiority to Giroudeau. Florentine and Giroudeau, he to give pleasure to his comrade, she to provide her friend with a protector, urged Mariette and Philippe to arrange a marriage *en détrempe*. This Parisian expression is equivalent to the expression *morganatic marriage* applied to kings and queens. Philippe, as they left the house, confided his poverty to Giroudeau; but the old rake reassured him to a great extent.

"I will speak to my nephew Finot about you," said Giroudeau. "You see, Philippe, the reign of civilians and palaver has arrived and we must submit. To-day the writing desk does everything. Ink takes the place of powder and words are substituted for bullets. After all, these little devils of managing editors are very shrewd and very good fellows. Come and see me to-morrow at the office; I will say a couple of words about your position to my nephew, in the meantime. Before long you shall have a place on some paper or other. Mariette takes you just now—don't make any mistake on that point—because she has nothing, no engagement and no possibility of making her début; I told her that you were going to be on a newspaper, like me; she'll prove to you that she loves you for yourself alone and you'll believe her! Do as I do, keep her a *figurante* as long as possible! I was so in love that, as soon as Florentine wanted an opportunity to dance, I asked Finot to request them to let her make her début; but my nephew said: 'She has talent, hasn't she? Very good, the day she begins to dance, she'll dance you out of the door.' Oh! that's just like Finot. You'll find him a very shrewd boy."

The next day, at four o'clock, Philippe found himself in a little entresol on Rue du Sentier, where he saw Giroudeau caged up like a wild animal in a sort of hencoop, which contained a small stove, a small table, two small chairs and some small pieces of firewood. This retreat was dignified by the magic words: *Subscription bureau,* printed on the door in black letters, and by the word: *Cashier,* written on a piece of paper and fastened above the grated wicket. Along the wall facing the captain's establishment was a bench, on which a one-armed veteran, called *Coloquinte* by Giroudeau, presumably because of the Egyptian hue of his face, was then breakfasting.

"A pretty place!" said Philippe, examining the apartment. "What are you doing here,—a man who was in Colonel Chabert's charge at Eylau? *Nom de nom!* superior officers!—"

"Well, yes!—*broum! broum!*—a superior officer receipting bills for a newspaper," said Giroudeau, pulling his black silk cap down over his forehead. "And what's more, I am the responsible publisher of this stuff," he added, pointing to the newspaper.

"And I, who have been in Egypt, am going to the *Stamp Office*," said the veteran.

"Silence, Coloquinte!" said Giroudeau, "you are in the presence of a brave officer who carried the Emperor's orders at the battle of Montmirail."

"Present arms!" said Coloquinte; "I lost my missing arm there."

"Coloquinte, watch the shop; I am going up to my nephew."

The two ex-troopers went up to the fourth floor and into an attic at the end of a corridor, where they found lying on a wretched couch a young man with a pale, colorless eye. The civilian did not change his position as he offered cigars to his uncle and his uncle's friend.

"My friend," said Giroudeau in a mild and humble tone, "this is the gallant captain in the Garde Impériale, of whom I spoke to you."

"Well?" said Finot, eying Philippe, who lost all his courage, as Giroudeau did, in presence of the diplomatist of the press.

"My dear boy," said Giroudeau, trying to pose as the uncle, "the colonel has just returned from Texas."

"Aha! so you went into the Texas business, the Champ-d'Asile? You were very young, I should say, to turn *soldier laborer.*"

The acerbity of this jest will be understood only by those who remember the deluge of engravings, screens, clocks, bronzes and plaster casts which had their origin in the idea of the *soldier laborer,* a grandiloquent image of the fate of Napoléon and his gallant troops, which eventually furnished the theme of several comic operas. That idea produced at least a million. You will still find *soldier laborers* on wall-papers in the provinces. If this young man had not been Giroudeau's nephew, Philippe would have boxed his ears.

"Yes, I went into it, and I lost twelve thousand francs and my time," he rejoined, trying to force a smile.

"And you are still devoted to the Emperor?" queried Finot.

"He is my god," replied Philippe Bridau.

"You are a liberal?"

"I shall always belong to the constitutional opposition! Oh! Foy! oh! Manuel! oh! Laffitte! there are men! they will rid us of these wretches who skulked back to France at the heels of foreigners!"

"Well," rejoined Finot coolly, "we must make the most of your misfortunes, for you are a victim of the liberals, my dear man! Remain a liberal, if you are wedded to your opinions; but threaten the liberals with the unmasking of the Texas idiocy.

You didn't get two farthings of the national subscription, did you? Very good, you're in an excellent position to demand an account of the money
subscribed. This is what will happen to you: a
new opposition newspaper will be founded under
the patronage of certain deputies of the Left; you
will be the cashier, a permanent place, with a salary
of a thousand crowns. You will not have to furnish
bonds for more than twenty thousand francs; find
them and you will have the berth in a week. I
will advise the council to get rid of you by causing
the place to be offered you; but you must make a
noise and a loud noise too!"

Giroudeau allowed Philippe, who was profuse in
his thanks, to go down a few stairs, and said to his
nephew:

"Well, what a villain you are, still!—you keep
me here at twelve hundred francs—"

"The paper won't last a year," replied Finot.
"I have something better than that for you."

"*Nom de nom!*" said Philippe to Giroudeau,
"your nephew's nobody's fool! I hadn't thought
of taking advantage of my position, as he says."

That evening, at the Café Lemblin and the Café
Minerve, Colonel Philippe declaimed against the liberal party, which took up subscriptions, which sent
you to Texas, which talked hypocritically about
soldier laborers, which left brave men in want, without assistance, after eating up their twenty thousand francs and keeping them on the move for two
years.

"I propose to demand an account of the subscriptions to the Champ-d'Asile," he said to one of the habitués of the Café Minerve, who repeated it to divers journalists of the Left.

Philippe did not return to Rue Mazarine, but went to Mariette's to inform her of his future co-operation in a newspaper which was to have ten thousand subscribers, and in which her choregraphic claims would be warmly upheld. Agathe and La Descoings sat up for Philippe, almost dead with terror, for the Duc de Berri had just been murdered. The next morning the colonel made his appearance a few moments after breakfast; when his mother told him how anxious his absence had made her, he flew into a passion and asked if he was not of age.

"*Nom de nom!* I bring you good news and you're as glum as gravestones. The Duc de Berri is dead, you say? Well, so much the better; there's one less of 'em. I am going to be cashier of a newspaper with a salary of a thousand crowns, so you see you needn't worry any more so far as I am concerned."

"Is it possible?" said Agathe.

"Yes, if you can let me have twenty thousand francs to put up as security; you need only deposit your certificates of stock in the Funds, and you'll draw your thirteen hundred francs a year, semi-annually just the same."

The two widows, who had been wearing themselves out for nearly two months trying to ascertain what Philippe was doing, and where and how they could find a place for him, were so overjoyed at this prospect, that they forgot the various disasters of the moment. That evening, old Du Bruel, Claparon, who was failing fast, and the inflexible Desroches senior, these *Wise Men of Greece*, were unanimous in advising the widow to furnish the security for her son. The paper, which very luckily was founded before the assassination of the Duc de Berri, avoided the blow which was thereupon aimed by Monsieur Decazes at the press. Widow Bridau's certificate of thirteen hundred francs was accepted as security for Philippe, who became cashier. That exemplary son at once promised to give the two widows a hundred francs a month for his board and lodging, and was proclaimed the best of children. Those people who had augured ill of him, congratulated Agathe.

"We misjudged him," they said.

Poor Joseph, in order not to be behind his brother, tried to earn his own living, and succeeded. Three months passed, and the colonel, who ate and drank enough for four, who was very hard to please and led the two widows into large outlays for the table, on the pretext that he was paying for his board, had not contributed one sou. Neither his mother nor La Descoings cared to remind him of his promise. The year passed, and not one of those pieces, so graphically called by Léon Gozlan *tigers with five claws*, had found its way from Philippe's pocket into the family treasury. To be sure, the colonel

6

had allayed the scruples of his conscience in that respect by seldom dining at home.

"At all events he is happy," said his mother, "his mind is at rest, he has employment!"

Through the influence of the *feuilleton* edited by Vernou, a friend of Bixiou, Finot and Giroudeau, Mariette made her début, not at the Panorama-Dramatique, but at the Porte-Saint-Martin, where she achieved some success beside La Bégrand. Among the directors of that theatre at the time was a rich and ostentatious general officer, who was in love with an actress and had become an *impresario* on her account. At Paris one constantly meets men who are enamored of actresses, ballet-dancers or singers and who become theatrical managers for love. This general officer knew Philippe and Giroudeau. With the assistance of Finot's little sheet and Philippe's, Mariette's début was the more promptly arranged between the three officers because, as it would seem, the passions are all at one in point of folly. The mischief-making Bixiou soon informed his grandmother and the pious Agathe that Philippe the cashier, the paragon of paragons, loved Mariette, the famous *danseuse* at the Porte-Saint-Martin. This old news was like a thunderbolt to the two widows; in the first place, Agathe's religious sentiments led her to look upon all stage women as brands from hell; and in the second place, it seemed to them both that such women lived on gold, drank pearls and wrecked the handsomest fortunes.

"Nonsense," said Joseph to his mother; "do you

suppose my brother is idiotic enough to give money to his Mariette? Those women ruin only the rich."

"They are already talking of engaging Mariette at the Opéra," said Bixiou. "But don't be afraid, Madame Bridau, the diplomatic corps frequents the Porte-Saint-Martin and this lovely girl won't be long with your son. They say an ambassador is madly in love with Mariette already. Another piece of news! Père Claparon is dead, he's to be buried to-morrow, and his son, now a banker and rolling in gold and silver, has ordered a first-class funeral. That boy lacks education. They don't do things so in China!"

Philippe, with mercenary views, proposed marriage to the *danseuse;* but on the eve of her first appearance at the Opéra, Mademoiselle Godeschal, either because she had fathomed the colonel's intentions or because she understood how necessary her independence was to her fortune, refused him. During the remainder of that year, Philippe saw his mother twice a month at most. Where was he? At his office, at the theatre, or at Mariette's? No information as to his mode of life reached the little household on Rue Mazarine. Giroudeau, Finot, Bixiou, Vernou and Lousteau saw that he was leading a life of pleasure. Philippe was at all the parties given by Tullia, one of the leading performers at the Opéra; by Florentine, who replaced Mariette at the Porte-Saint-Martin; by Florine and Matifat, Coralie and Camusot. From four o'clock, when he left his office, he amused himself until

midnight; for there was always a party planned
from the night before; a good dinner given by
somebody, a card-party or a supper. Philippe was
in his element. This carnival, which lasted eighteen months, was not wholly untroubled by cares.
The fair Mariette, at the time of her début at the
Opéra, in January, 1821, brought to her feet one of
the most gorgeous dukes of Louis the Eighteenth's
court. Philippe tried to hold his own against the
duke; but, although he had some luck at play, at
the time of the renewal of her engagement, in the
month of April, he was compelled by the exigencies
of his passion, to draw upon the funds of the newspaper. In May, he owed eleven thousand francs.
In that fatal month, Mariette traveled to London, to
exploit the noblemen there while they were preparing a temporary home for the Opéra in the Hôtel
Choiseul on Rue Le Peletier. The unfortunate
Philippe had come to love Mariette, as frequently
happens, despite her open infidelities; but she had
never seen in him aught but a brutish, unintelligent
soldier, a first rung of the ladder, upon which she
did not propose to remain long. And so, foreseeing
the time when Philippe's money would be exhausted, the girl had been clever enough to secure
supporters in the journalistic world, who would
make it unnecessary for her to retain Philippe;
nevertheless, she had for him the gratitude which
women of her sort feel for the man who was the
first to smooth away the obstacles, so to speak, that
lay in her path in the lamentable career of the stage.

*

Forced to allow his redoubtable mistress to go to London and leave him behind, Philippe went into winter quarters once more—to use his own expression—and returned to his attic on Rue Mazarine; he indulged in gloomy reflections there, night and morning. He had a feeling that it was impossible for him to live otherwise than he had lived for a year past. The luxury that reigned in Mariette's apartments, the dinners and suppers, the evenings in the wings, the enlivening companionship of clever men and journalists, the constant bustle about him, and all the resulting flattery to his vanity and his sensations; this sort of life, which is found nowhere but at Paris, and which has something new to offer every day, had become more than a habit to Philippe; it constituted a necessity, like his tobacco and his *petits verres.* So it seemed to him that he could not live without these constant diversions. The idea of suicide passed through his mind, not because of the deficit in his cash account that was sure to be discovered, but because he could no longer live with Mariette and in the atmosphere of pleasure in which he had been basking for a year. With his mind full of these depressing thoughts, he went for the first time to his brother's studio, where he found him at work, in a blue blouse, copying a picture for a dealer.

(85)

"So this is how pictures are made?" said Philippe, hesitating how to open the conversation.

"No," replied Joseph, "but this is how they are copied."

"How much do they pay you for that?"

"Oh! never enough—two hundred and fifty francs; but I have an opportunity to study the style of the great masters, I pick up a good deal of useful knowledge and discover the secrets of the profession. There's one of my pictures," he added, pointing with the end of his brush to a sketch on which the colors were still moist.

"And how much do you pocket a year?"

"Unfortunately I am not known yet to anyone but painters. I am backed by Schinner, who will probably get me some work to do at the Château de Presles, where I expect to go about October to paint arabesques and interior decorations generally, for all of which I shall be well paid by the Comte de Sérizy. With a few such trifles as that and orders from the dealers, I may thereafter make eighteen hundred to two thousand francs, all expenses paid. Bah! at the next Exposition I shall exhibit yonder picture; if it takes, my business is done; my friends are satisfied with it."

"I don't know anything about such things," said Philippe, in a soft voice that compelled Joseph's attention.

"What's the matter?" he asked, when he saw that his brother was as pale as death.

"I would like to know how long it will take you to paint my portrait."

"Why, by working steadily, if the weather is bright, I can do it in three or four days."

"That's too long a time, I have only to-day to give you. My poor mother loves me so dearly that I would like to leave my likeness with her. Let's say no more about it."

"Why, are you going away again?"

"I am going away, never to return," said Philippe with an air of feigned gayety.

"Come, come! Philippe, my dear boy, what's the matter with you? If it's anything serious, I am a man and not an idiot, and I am all ready for a hard fight; or, if you require secrecy, I will hold my tongue."

"Sure?"

"On my honor."

"You won't say a word to anybody on earth?"

"Nobody."

"Well, I am going to blow out my brains."

"You! Are you going to fight?"

"I am going to kill myself."

"What for?"

"I have taken eleven thousand francs belonging to the paper, and I must hand in my accounts to-morrow; my security will be cut down one-half and our poor mother will be reduced to six hundred francs a year. That is nothing, for I could make a fortune for her later; but I am dishonored! I cannot live in dishonor."

"You won't be dishonored if you make restitution, but you will lose your place; you will have remaining to you only the five hundred francs that go with your Cross, but you can live on five hundred francs."

"Adieu!" said Philippe, and he rushed hastily downstairs, refusing to listen to anything more.

Joseph left his studio and went down to breakfast with his mother; but Philippe's disclosure had taken away his appetite. He took La Descoings aside and told her the shocking news. The old woman uttered an exclamation of horror, dropped a bowl of milk she had in her hand and threw herself on a chair. Agathe ran to her. From exclamation to exclamation the fatal truth was made known to the mother.

"He! dishonored! Bridau's son take money that was entrusted to him!"

The widow trembled in every limb, her staring eyes seemed to increase in size, became fixed; she sat down and burst into tears.

"Where is he?" she cried amid her sobs. "Perhaps he has thrown himself into the Seine!"

"You mustn't despair," said La Descoings, "because the poor boy fell in with a bad woman and she made him do foolish things. God knows that happens often enough. Philippe had so much bad luck before his return, and he has had so few opportunities to be happy and loved, that we mustn't wonder at his passion for that creature. All passions tend to excess! I have reason to reproach

myself for something of the same sort in my past
life, and yet I consider myself an honest woman!
A single slip doesn't make vice! And then, after
all, it's only those who do nothing that never make
mistakes!"

Agathe was so overwhelmed by her despair that
La Descoings and Joseph had no choice but to make
light of Philippe's wrong-doing by telling her that
such things happened in all families.

"But he is twenty-eight years old," cried Agathe,
"he's no longer a child."

A crushing rejoinder, which showed how much
the poor woman's mind dwelt upon her son's conduct.

"I assure you, mother, that he thinks of nothing
but your suffering and the wrong he has done you,"
said Joseph.

"Oh! my God, let him return! let him live, and
I will forgive everything!" cried the poor mother,
with the horrible picture of Philippe taken from the
water, a corpse, constantly before her eyes.

For some moments a depressing silence reigned.
The day passed in most cruel alternations of hope
and fear. All three rushed to the window of the
salon at the slightest sound, and abandoned themselves to countless conjectures.

While his family was thus torn with despair,
Philippe was calmly putting everything in order at
his office. He had the audacity to tender his accounts, saying that he had the eleven thousand
francs at his rooms, to guard against accident. The

rascal left the office at four o'clock, taking five hundred francs more from the till, and coolly betook
himself to the gaming-table, which he had not visited since he had held his position, for he realized
that a cashier cannot afford to haunt gambling dens.
The fellow did not lack the instinct of calculation.
His subsequent conduct will prove, moreover, that
he resembled his grandfather Rouget more than his
virtuous father. Perhaps he would have made a
good general, but in his private life he was one of
those deep villains who shelter their undertakings
and their evil deeds behind the screen of legality
and under the discreet family roof. Philippe retained all his self-possession in this supreme enterprise. He won at first and at one time had six
thousand francs to his credit; but he allowed himself to be dazzled by the desire to put an end to his
uncertainty at a single stroke. He left the *trente-
et-quarante* table when he heard that at roulette the
black had come up sixteen times in succession; he
staked five thousand francs on the red, and the black
came up for the seventeenth time. The colonel
thereupon placed his last thousand-franc note on
the black and won. Despite this astonishing good
understanding with chance, his head was tired;
and, although he was conscious of it, he was determined to continue; but the divinatory sense to
which gamblers listen, and which comes in flashes,
was impaired already. When it becomes intermit-
tent the gambler is lost. Lucidity of thought, like
the sun's rays, has no effect unless it shines in an

absolutely straight line; its power of divination
exists only on condition that its glance is not interrupted; it becomes uncertain when exposed to the
vagaries of chance.   Philippe lost everything.
After such cruel tests as this, the most reckless as
well as the most intrepid heart weakens.   Philippe,
as he returned home, thought the less of his threat
of suicide in that he had never really intended to
kill himself.   He no longer thought of his lost place,
or of his impaired security, or of his mother, or of
Mariette, the cause of his ruin; he walked through
the streets mechanically.   When he entered the
house, his weeping mother, La Descoings and his
brother leaped upon his neck, kissed him, and joy-
fully led him to a seat by the fire.

"Aha!" he thought, "the threat has produced its
effect."

The monster assumed the more easily an expression adapted to the occasion because his experience
at play had moved him very deeply.   Seeing her
wicked Benjamin before her, pale and dejected, the
poor mother knelt at his feet, kissed his hands,
pressed them to her heart and gazed long and
earnestly at him with eyes filled with tears.

"Philippe," she said in a choking voice, "promise
not to kill yourself and we will forget everything!"

Philippe glanced at his brother's sympathetic face
and at La Descoings, who had a tear in her eye; he
said to himself:

"They are good people!"

Thereupon he raised his mother, took her upon

his knee, pressed her to his heart, and said in her ear as he kissed her :

"You give me life a second time !"

La Descoings found the materials for an excellent dinner, and added to it two bottles of old wine and a little Curaçoa, a part of her former stock in trade.

"Agathe, we must let him smoke," she said at dessert.

And she produced cigars and offered them to Philippe.

The two poor creatures imagined that if they allowed the young man to take his ease in every respect, he would grow to love the house and would stay at home, so they both tried to accustom themselves to tobacco-smoke, which they loathed. This immense sacrifice was not even noticed by Philippe.

The next day Agathe seemed to have grown ten years older. When her anxiety was once allayed, reflections came, and the poor mother was unable to close her eyes during that horrible night. Her income was to be reduced to six hundred francs. La Descoings, like all stout, gormandizing women, was getting to be very slow and heavy in her movements, and she suffered from an obstinate catarrhal cough; her footsteps resounded on the stairs like blows with a club; she might die at any moment, and with her the four thousand francs would disappear. Was it not absurd to count upon them any longer? What could she do? what would become of them? Having made up her mind to go out as a nurse rather than be a burden to her children,

Agathe did not think of herself. But what would
Philippe do when he was reduced to the five hundred francs appurtenant to his officer's Cross of the
Legion of Honor? In the last eleven years La Descoings, by putting aside a thousand crowns each
year, had paid her debt almost twice over, and she
continued to sacrifice her grandson's interests to
those of the Bridau family. Although all Agathe's
sternly upright principles were wounded in this
shocking calamity, she said to herself:

"Poor boy, is it his fault? he is faithful to his
oaths. I have done wrong not to find a wife for him.
If I had done so, he wouldn't have taken up with
that dancing girl. He has such a vigorous constitution!—"

The old tradeswoman had also reflected during
the night upon the best means of saving the honor
of the family. At daybreak she left her bed and
went to her friend's room.

"It isn't your place or Philippe's to arrange this
delicate matter," she said. "Although our two
old friends Claparon and Du Bruel are dead,
Père Desroches is left; he has good judgment, and
I will go and see him this morning. Desroches will
say that Philippe fell a victim to his confidence in
a friend, that his weakness in such matters makes
him altogether unfit to have the care of funds.
The same thing may happen again. So Philippe
prefers to resign and he won't be discharged."

Agathe, seeing a hope of sheltering her son's
honor behind this ingenious falsehood, at least so

far as strangers were concerned, kissed La Descoings, who left the house to adjust the painful affair. Philippe had slept the sleep of the just.

"The old lady is very cunning!" he said with a smile, when Agathe told him why their breakfast was delayed.

Old Desroches, the last remaining friend of the two poor women, who, despite the natural harshness of his disposition, never forgot that he owed his place to Bridau, acquitted himself of the delicate mission La Descoings entrusted to him like a consummate diplomatist. He came to dine with the family, to tell Agathe to go the next morning to the Treasury on Rue Vivienne, to sign the transfer of the consols that were to be sold, and to receive the certificate for the six hundred francs a year that would still be hers. The old clerk did not leave that abode of sorrow until he had induced Philippe to sign a petition to the Minister of War, praying that his name might be restored to the army list. Desroches promised the two women that he would follow the petition into the offices of the War Department, and would take advantage of the duke's triumph over Philippe in the matter of the *danseuse* to obtain that great nobleman's protection for him.

"Within three months, he will be a lieutenant-colonel in the regiment of the Duc de Maufrigneuse, and you will be rid of him."

Desroches went away, laden with the blessings of the two widows and of Joseph. As to the

newspaper, two months late, as Finot had predicted,
it ceased to appear.   Thus Philippe's offence made
no noise in the world.   But Agathe's mother-love
had received the most cruel of wounds.   Her faith in
her son once shaken, she lived thenceforth in constant dread, lightened by satisfaction when her apprehensions of evil proved to be unfounded.

When men endowed with physical courage, but
cowardly and base in their moral nature, as Philippe
was, see affairs resuming their natural course around
them after a catastrophe in which their moral character has almost gone by the board, such complaisance on the part of their family and friends is to
them a sort of premium to encourage them in their
evil courses.   They rely upon impunity; their perverted minds, their gratified passions, lead them to
study the methods by which they have succeeded in
circumventing the laws of society, and they become
woefully adroit.

A fortnight later Philippe was once more the idle,
discontented man he had been; he resumed his
fatal café life with its stations embellished by *petits
verres*, his long games of billiards accompanied by
bowls of punch, his night sessions at the gaming-
table, where he risked a trifling stake and realized
a trifling profit which sufficed to support him in his
disorderly life.   To keep up an appearance of economy, the better to deceive his mother and La Descoings, he wore a hat that was almost dirty, and
was worn shiny on the crown and brim, patched
boots, a threadbare coat, on which his red rosette

made but little show, discolored as it was by its
long sojourn in his buttonhole, and stained by drops
of liquor or coffee; his greenish kid gloves lasted
him a long while; he did not lay aside his satin
stock until it resembled wadding.   Mariette was his
only love; so it was that that ballet-girl's treachery
did much to harden his heart.   When it happened
that his winnings were unexpectedly large, or when
he supped with his old friend Giroudeau, Philippe
resorted to street-corner Venuses with a sort of
brutal contempt for the whole sex.   He was quite
regular in his habits, breakfasted and dined at
home, and came in every night about one o'clock.

Three months of this horrible life restored poor
Agathe's confidence in some degree.   Meanwhile
Joseph, who was at work upon the magnificent picture to which he owes his reputation, lived in his
studio.   La Descoings, who believed in Joseph's
future glory on the strength of what her grandson
told her, lavished a mother's care upon the painter;
she carried him his breakfast in the morning, she
did his errands, she cleaned his boots.   The painter
rarely showed himself until dinner, and his evenings belonged to his friends of the club.   He also
read much, and acquired that profound and serious
learning which one always owes to one's self, and
to which all talented men and women devote their
energies between twenty and thirty.   Agathe, seeing Joseph but little and having no anxiety on his
account, lived only in Philippe, who alone caused
her those alternations of fear aroused and allayed,

which in some degree give life to the emotions and are as essential to maternal affection as to love. Desroches, who came about once a week to see the widow of his old friend and chief, gave her ground for hope: the Duc de Maufrigneuse had asked to have Philippe assigned to his regiment and the Minister of War had ordered a report to be made to himself; as the name of Bridau appeared upon no police list and upon no documents at the Palais de Justice, Philippe would receive his certificate of restoration to the army list and his assignment to service early in the next year. Desroches had set all his acquaintances at work, in order to ensure success; his investigations at the prefecture of police afforded the information that Philippe frequented gambling-houses every evening, and he deemed it necessary to confide that intelligence to La Descoings only, urging her to keep an eye on the future lieutenant-colonel, for the fact, if made public, might ruin everything. For the moment, the Minister of War was not likely to inquire whether Philippe was a gambler, and when he was once enrolled, he would soon abandon a passion born of his idleness.

Agathe, who no longer had her regular evening visitors, read her prayer-book in the chimney corner, while La Descoings conned over the cards, seeking an explanation of her dreams and applying the rules of the *cabala* to her lottery combinations. This obstinate gambler never missed a drawing; she clung to her combination, which had not yet

7

won.   The combination would soon be twenty-one
years old; it was approaching its majority.   The
old shareholder based a deal of hope on that trivial
circumstance.   One of the numbers had remained
at the bottom of all the wheels since the foundation
of the lottery; so La Descoings plunged very heavily
upon that number and upon all the combinations of
its three figures.   The lower mattress of her bed
was the poor old soul's place of safe-keeping for her
savings; she would rip it open, put in the gold
piece, carefully wrapped in paper, which she had
succeeded in putting aside, over and above the
necessary expenditures, and sew it up again.   She
intended to venture all her savings upon her cherished combination at the last Paris drawing of the
year.   This passion, which is so universally con-
demned, has never been fairly studied.   No one
has detected in it the opium of poverty.   Did not
the lottery, the most powerful fairy in the world,
arouse magic hopes?   The turn of the roulette
wheel, which gave the gamblers a glimpse of heaps
of gold and untold enjoyment, lasted only as long
as a flash of lightning; while in the lottery the
brilliant gleam lasted five days.   What social
power to-day will give you five days' happiness for
forty sous and bestow upon you in fancy all the
joys of civilization?   Tobacco, which is a thousand
times more immoral than gambling, destroys the
body, impairs the intellect, stupefies a whole nation;
whereas the lottery did not cause the slightest difficulty of that sort.   Moreover, the passion was

compelled to put restraint upon itself, as well by the
length of time between the drawings as by the fact
that everyone had a predilection for some particular
wheel. La Descoings would not invest in any
other wheel than the one in Paris. In the hope of
witnessing at last the triumph of the combination
she had cherished for twenty years, she had subjected herself to very great privations in order that
she might be perfectly free to make her investment
for the last drawing of the year. When she had
cabalistic dreams—for all dreams do not refer to
numbers in the lottery—she would go and tell them
to Joseph, for he was the only one who would listen,
not merely without scolding her, but with the kindly
words with which true artists console the vagaries
of the mind. All great talents understand and respect genuine passions, they can explain them to
themselves, and they find their roots either in the
heart or in the head. According to Joseph, his
brother loved tobacco and liqueurs, his old Mamma
Descoings loved combinations, his mother loved
God, Desroches junior loved lawsuits, Desroches
senior loved angling; everybody, he said, loved
something. He himself loved the ideally beautiful in everything; he loved Byron's poetry, Géri-
cault's painting, Rossini's music and Walter Scott's
novels.

"Everyone to his taste, mamma," he would say,
"but your combination doesn't combine."

"It will come out, and you will be rich, and so
will my little Bixiou!"

"Give it all to your grandson," replied Joseph.
"But of course you will do what you please."

"Ah! but if it comes out, I shall have enough for
everybody. In the first place, you shall have a fine
studio, you shall not stay away from the *Italiens* to
save money to pay your models and your dealer in
colors. Do you know, my boy," said she, "it's not
a pleasant part you make me play in that picture?"

For economy's sake, Joseph had requested La
Descoings to pose for his superb picture of a young
courtesan led before a Venetian senator by an old
woman. That picture, one of the masterpieces of
modern painting, taken by Gros himself for a
Titian, served excellently to prepare the younger
artists to recognize and proclaim Joseph's superiority
at the Salon of 1823.

"Those who know you, know who you are," he
replied gayly, "and why should you worry about
those who don't know you?"

For ten years or more, La Descoings' complexion
had taken on the ripe tint of a *pomme de reinette* at
Easter. Wrinkles had formed in the folds of her
flesh, which had become lifeless and flabby. Her
eyes were full of life and seemed to be animated by
thoughts still youthful and vivacious, thoughts which
might be deemed to be inspired by avarice with the
more reason because there is always a touch of
avarice in the gambler. Her fat face bore traces of
profound dissimulation and of a secret thought
buried in the bottom of her heart. Her passion demanded secrecy. In the movement of her lips, there

was some indication of gluttony. And so, although she was the upright and excellent woman you know, the eye might be misled. Thus she was admirably adapted for a model of the old woman that Bridau wished to paint. Coralie, a young actress who died in the very prime of life, mistress of a young poet, a friend of Bridau, Lucien de Rubempré, had given him the idea of this picture. The beautiful canvas was sneered at as a copy,—although it was a splendid setting of three portraits. Michel Chrestien, one of the young men of the club, had lent his republican head for the senator, and Joseph made the face a touch more mature, just as he forced La Descoings' expression a little.

This great picture, which was destined to create such a sensation and to arouse so much hatred and jealousy and admiration of Joseph, was at this time merely sketched; as he was constantly compelled to suspend work upon it in order to execute commissions to obtain money to live on, he copied the pictures of the old masters, saturating himself with their methods; so that he is one of the most thoroughly informed of artists. His artist's good sense bade him conceal from his mother and La Descoings, the small profits he was beginning to harvest, when he saw that Philippe and the lottery were an unfailing cause of ruin to them. The species of indifference displayed by the soldier in his catastrophe, the scheme which Joseph detected beneath the pretended suicide, the remembrance of the wrong he had done in a career he should not have abandoned, in a word, the most trivial details of his brother's conduct had at·last opened Joseph's eyes.   Painters rarely lack perspicacity of that sort; occupied as they are for whole days at a time, in the silence of their studios, upon work that leaves their minds free to a certain extent, they somewhat resemble women; their minds are in a position to scrutinize the petty incidents of life and detect their hidden meaning.

Joseph had purchased one of those magnificent chests, then entirely unknown to the world of fashion, to adorn a corner of his studio where the light that sparkled in the bas-reliefs was reflected, imparting all its lustre to that masterpiece of the sixteenth century workmanship.   He discovered a secret compartment therein, and accumulated a little hoard there in case of emergency.   With the instinctive confidence of true artists, he usually placed the money set aside for the month's expenses in a skull that stood upon one of the compartments of the chest.   After his brother's return to the house, he found a constant disagreement between the sum in the skull and the balance that should have been there.   The hundred francs a month disappeared with incredible rapidity.   When he found the skull empty after he had spent only forty or fifty francs, he said to himself:

"It seems that my money has taken wings!"

The next time he noted his expenses carefully; but it availed him nothing to count, like Robert Macaire, sixteen and five make twenty-three; that

did not solve the difficulty. When, for the third
time, he noticed a still greater discrepancy, he
communicated this subject of perplexity to old Madame Descoings, who, he knew, loved him with
that motherly, trustful, credulous, enthusiastic,
tender love, which he missed in his mother, kind
though she was to him, and which was quite as
necessary to the first essays of the artist as the
mother-hen's care to her little ones until their
feathers have grown. To her alone could he confide
his ghastly suspicions. He was as sure of his
friends as of himself; La Descoings certainly would
not take anything to invest in the lottery—at the
mere suggestion the poor woman wrung her hands;
Philippe alone therefore could have committed this
petty domestic theft.

"Why doesn't he ask me for what he needs?"
cried Joseph, taking paint from his palette and
blurring his picture without heeding what he was
doing. "Would I refuse him money?"

"Why, it's like robbing a child!" cried La Descoings, whose features expressed the most profound
horror.

"No," said Joseph, "he can do it, he is my
brother, my purse is his; but he ought to tell me."

"Put a certain sum in the skull this morning and
don't touch it," said La Descoings; "I shall know
who goes to your studio, and if he's the only one,
why you will be certain."

The next day Joseph secured proof in that way
of the involuntary loans he was making his brother.

Philippe entered the studio when Joseph was not there and took such small sums as he needed. The artist trembled for his little treasure.

"Wait! wait! I'll catch you, my boy!" said he to La Descoings with a laugh.

"And you will do well; we ought to teach him a lesson, for I can't be sure now that I may not find a deficit in my purse. But the poor boy must have his tobacco, he's so used to it."

"Poor boy! poor boy!" rejoined the artist. "I am inclined to the opinion of Fulgence and Bixiou: Philippe is pulling our legs all the time; first he gets mixed up in the *émeutes* and we have to send him to America; he costs our mother twelve thousand francs then; he doesn't succeed in finding anything in the forests of the New World, and his return costs as much as his setting out. Because he repeated a couple of words from Napoléon to some general, Philippe fancies himself a great soldier and obliged to make faces at the Bourbons; meanwhile he amuses himself, he travels, he sees the world; for my part, I don't believe in this humbug of his misfortunes—he doesn't look like a man who wouldn't have the best of everything everywhere! We find my gentleman an excellent place, he leads the life of a Sardanapalus with a girl from the Opéra, devours the funds of a newspaper and costs our mother another twelve thousand francs. As far as I myself am concerned, I don't care a fig for it; but Philippe will bring the poor woman to beggary. He looks upon me as of no account, because I never

was in the dragoons of the guard! And I may be
the one to support our dear good mother in her old
age, while our swashbuckler, if he goes on in this
way, will end I don't know how. Bixiou said to
me: 'Your brother's an infernal fool!' And, do
you know, your grandson is quite right; Philippe
will get into some difficulty in which the family
honor will be compromised, and we shall have to
find ten or twelve thousand francs more for him!
He gambles every evening, and when he comes
home, drunk as a lord, he drops on the stairs the
pricked cards he has used to mark the times the red
and black come up. Père Desroches is doing his
best to get Philippe into the army, and I should
think, upon my word! that he would be willing to
do anything to enter the service again. Would you
have believed that a fellow with such beautiful clear
blue eyes and the air of a Chevalier Bayard, would
turn out a sneak?''

*

Despite the prudence and *sang-froid* with which
Philippe laid his stakes in the evening, he experienced from time to time what gamblers call being
cleaned out. At such times, impelled by an irresistible desire to procure the wherewithal to play
the next evening—ten francs—he made a descent
upon his brother's money, upon that that La Descoings left lying about, or upon Agathe's slender
store. One night the poor widow had, in her first
nap, a horrible vision. Philippe entered her room,
and took from the pocket of her dress all the money
that was there. Agathe pretended to be asleep, but
she wept the rest of the night. Her eyes were
opened. "A single slip is not vice," La Descoings
had said; but, after constant repetitions, the vice
was beyond question. Agathe could no longer doubt
that her oldest son had neither delicacy nor honor.

On the morning following that ghastly vision,
after breakfast, and before Philippe left the house,
she took him into her room and begged him, in a
supplicating tone, to ask her for such money as he
needed. Thereupon the requests were renewed so
often that, within a fortnight, Agathe had exhausted
all her savings. She was left without a sou and
began to think of working; for several evenings,
she discussed with La Descoings the different
methods of earning money with her hands. The

poor mother went so far as to apply for embroidery
to do at the *Père de Famille*—work that yields about
twenty sous a day. Notwithstanding her niece's
profound silence, La Descoings had divined the explanation of this longing to earn money by her
handiwork. The change in Agathe's countenance,
too, was sufficiently eloquent: her fresh complexion
became sallow, the skin was drawn tightly over the
temples and cheekbones, and the forehead was fur-
rowed with wrinkles; the eyes lost their limpidity;
it was evident that some internal fire was consum-
ing her, that she passed her nights in weeping; but
the one thing that caused the greatest havoc was
the necessity of keeping silent as to her grief, her
sufferings, her apprehensions. She never went to
sleep until Philippe had returned, she listened for
his footsteps in the street. She had studied the
variations of his voice, of his gait, the language of
his cane upon the pavement; there was nothing she
did not know, even to the degree of intoxication at
which he had arrived, and she trembled as she heard
him stumbling on the stairs. One night she had
picked up several gold pieces that he had dropped.
When he had been drinking heavily and had won,
his voice was hoarse and his cane dragged; but,
when he had lost, there was something sharp and decided and furious about his gait; he sang aloud and
held his cane aloft at the carry arms. At breakfast,
when he had won, his bearing was gay and almost
affectionate; he joked, coarsely to be sure, but still he
joked with his mother and La Descoings and Joseph;

but on the contrary, when he had lost, he was sullen and frowning, and his short, abrupt sentences, his stern glance and his depression terrified them all.

This dissipated life and the drinking habit caused marked changes from day to day, in the features that were once so fair to see. The veins of the face were injected with blood, the features grew coarser, the eyes lost their lashes and seemed to become dry. He paid little heed to his person and exhaled the miasmatic odors of the tap-room, and the smell of muddy boots which, to a stranger, would have seemed the seal of vulgar debauchery.

"You ought to fit yourself out with new clothes from head to feet," La Descoings said to him early in December.

"Who will pay for them, I should like to know?" he rejoined sourly. "My poor mother hasn't a sou; I have five hundred francs a year. It would take one whole year's pension to buy clothes, and I have pledged it for three years—"

"What for?" said Joseph.

"A debt of honor. Giroudeau borrowed a thousand francs of Florentine to lend me.—I am no dandy, it is true; but when you think that Napoléon is at Saint Helena and is selling his silver plate to buy bread, the soldiers who remain faithful to him can afford to walk on their uppers," he said, pointing to his heelless shoes.

And he left the room.

"He's not a bad boy," said Agathe; "his heart's in the right place."

"A man can love the Emperor and still dress decently," said Joseph. "If he took care of himself and his clothes, he wouldn't look so much like a vagabond!"

"Joseph, you must be indulgent to your brother," said Agathe. "You follow your own bent, while he certainly is not in his proper place."

"Why did he leave it?" demanded Joseph. "What difference does it make whether Louis the Eighteenth's bugs or Napoléon's cuckoo are on the flag, so long as the bunting is French? France is France! I would paint for the devil, so far as I am concerned! A soldier, if he's a true soldier, should fight for love of the art. And if he had remained quietly in the army he would be a general to-day—"

"You are unjust to him," said Agathe. "Your father, who adored the Emperor, would have applauded him. But, at all events, he has consented to go back to the army! God knows the sorrow it causes your brother to do what he looks upon as treason."

Joseph rose to go up to his studio; but Agathe seized his hand and said:

"Be kind to your brother, he is so unfortunate!"

When the artist returned to his studio, followed by La Descoings, who was urging him to spare his mother's feelings, and remarking how she had changed, and how great an inward suffering that change betrayed, to their great amazement they found Philippe there.

"Joseph, my boy," said he, carelessly, "I am

much in need of money. Damme! I owe thirty francs for cigars at my tobacco shop, and I don't dare pass the infernal place without paying them. I've promised them a dozen times."

"I should prefer that," said Joseph; "take them out of the skull."

"But I took all there was there last night after dinner."

"There were forty-five francs—"

"Yes! that agrees with my account," replied Philippe; "I found them. Did I do wrong?" he added.

"No, my dear fellow, no," said the artist. "If you were rich, I would do the same; only, before I took it, I'd ask you if you were willing."

"It's very humiliating to ask," said Philippe. "I would rather have you take it as I do, without saying anything; it shows more confidence. In the army, if a comrade dies and has a pair of good boots while you have bad ones, you change with him."

"True, but you don't take them from him when he's alive!"

"Oh! nonsense," retorted Philippe with a shrug. "So you have no money?"

"No," said Joseph, who did not choose to disclose the hiding-place of his treasure.

"In a few days we shall be rich," said La Descoings.

"Oh! yes, you think your combination will come out on the twenty-fifth at the Paris drawing. You

will have to put in a lot of money if you expect to
enrich us all."

"Two hundred francs on a simple combination
will win three millions, without counting the complicated variations."

"At fifteen thousand times the investment—yes,
you need just two hundred francs," cried Philippe.

La Descoings bit her lip; she saw that she had
been imprudent.   In fact, Philippe, as he went
downstairs, was asking himself:

"Where can that old witch hide the money for her
lottery tickets?   It's money wasted, and I could use
it to such good advantage!   With four stakes of fifty
francs each, a fellow might win two hundred thousand francs! and it's a little more reliable than the
success of a combination!"

He cudgeled his brains to discover La Descoings'
probable hiding-place.   On the eve of all church
festivals, Agathe went to church and remained there
a long while, confessing, in all probability, and preparing for the communion.   It was the day before
Christmas and La Descoings must necessarily go
out and purchase some little dainties for the midnight meal; but perhaps she would make her investment in the lottery at the same time.   The lottery
had a drawing every five days, at the wheels
of Bordeaux, Lyon, Lille, Strasbourg and Paris
successively.   The Paris drawing took place
on the twenty-fifth of each month, and the lists
were closed on the twenty-fourth, at midnight.
The soldier studied out all the circumstances

and awaited developments. About noon he returned to the house, La Descoings having gone
out; but she had taken the key. That was not a
serious obstacle. Philippe pretended to have forgotten something, and requested the concierge to go
herself for a locksmith, who lived only a few steps
away, on Rue Guénégaud, and who came and
opened the door. The trooper's first thought was of
the bed; he pulled back the clothes and felt the
mattresses before trying the bedstead; and in the
lowest mattress he felt the gold pieces wrapped in
paper. He ripped open the ticking in very short
measure and took out twenty napoléons; then,
without taking the trouble to sew up the mattress,
he remade the bed with sufficient neatness to make
it improbable that La Descoings would notice anything.

The gambler hurried away, light of foot, proposing
to play at three different times, three hours apart,
and for only ten minutes each time. The genuine
gamblers, after 1786, when the public gaming-tables
were invented, the great gamblers whom the management dreaded, and who ate up the bank's
money, to use a gambling-house expression, never
played in any other way. But, before experience
taught them the lesson, fortunes were lost. All
the philosophy of the bankers, and their profits,
came from the stability of their capital, from the
equal hands, called *draws*, when half of the stakes
belonged to the bank, and from the notorious bad
faith authorized by the government, which consisted

8

in accepting and paying the stakes of the players
only at its option.   In a word, the bank, which declined the game of the rich and self-possessed
player, devoured the fortune of the player who was
so insanely infatuated as to allow himself to be
carried away by the rapid movement of the machine.
The dealers at *trente-et-quarante* moved almost as
quickly as the roulette wheel.

Philippe had succeeded in acquiring the self-possession of a commanding general, which enables a
man to retain a clear eye and keen perception when
everything is in a turmoil about him.   He had attained that eminence in the science of gambling,
which, let us observe in passing, supported a mul-
titude of people in Paris whose heads were strong
enough to look into an abyss without having the
vertigo.   With his four hundred francs, he determined to make his fortune that day.   He placed two
hundred in his boots as a reserve fund, and kept
two hundred in his pocket.   At three o'clock he
went to the establishment, now occupied by the
Théâtre du Palais-Royal, where the play was
highest.   He left the place half an hour later with
seven thousand francs.   He went to see Florentine,
to whom he owed five hundred francs, gave them to
her and suggested that they should take supper at
the *Rocher de Cancale* after the play.   Thence he
went to the office of the newspaper on Rue du
Sentier to inform his friend Giroudeau of the pro-
jected entertainment.   At six o'clock Philippe won
twenty-five thousand francs and played only ten

minutes, as he had determined. In the evening, at ten o'clock, he had won seventy-five thousand francs. After the supper-party, which was a magnificent affair, Philippe returned to the game about midnight, tipsy and confident. In utter disregard of the law he had imposed upon himself, he played an hour, and doubled his winnings. The bankers, from whom he had extorted a hundred and fifty thousand francs by his style of play, looked at him with deep interest.

"Will he go away? will he stay?" they asked one another with a glance. "If he stays, he is lost."

Philippe believed that he had struck a vein of good luck, and he stayed. By three o'clock in the morning, the hundred and fifty thousand francs had returned to the bank. The officer, who had consumed a large amount of grog as he played, left the establishment in a state of intoxication, which the cold air of the street aggravated to the last degree; but a waiter followed him out, picked him up and took him to one of those vile houses, at whose doors these words may be read upon a lantern: *Lodging for the night.* The waiter paid for the ruined gambler, who was placed fully dressed upon a bed, where he remained until the evening of Christmas Day. The management of the gaming-tables had great consideration for their regular patrons and for great gamblers. Philippe did not wake until seven o'clock; his mouth was parched, his head swollen, and he was in a high nervous fever. By sheer force he succeeded in walking to his mother's house, upon which he had unintentionally brought mourning, desolation, misery and death.

The night before, when their dinner was ready, La Descoings and Agathe waited for Philippe about two hours. They did not sit down at the table until seven o'clock. Agathe almost always went to bed at ten; but as she intended to be present at the midnight mass, she lay down immediately after dinner. La Descoings and Joseph remained alone in front of the hearth in the little salon which was used for every purpose, and the old woman begged him to reckon up the chances of her wondrous investment, her monstrous investment upon the celebrated combination. She intended to play the complicated variations of the combination in order to take all possible chances. After she had thoroughly relished the fascination of the stake, after she had emptied the two horns of plenty at her adopted son's feet, and had told him her dreams, pointing out the certainty of winning, and worrying only over the difficulty of bearing such good fortune, of waiting from midnight until ten o'clock the next day, Joseph, who did not see the four hundred francs she proposed to risk, asked where they were. The old woman smiled and led him into the former salon, now her bedroom.

"I'll show you!" she said.

She hurriedly removed the bedclothes, and got her scissors to rip open the mattress; she took her spectacles, examined the ticking, saw the condition

of affairs and dropped the mattress.   When he heard
the old woman utter a sigh that came from the
lowest depths of her being and seemed to be
strangled by the blood rushing back to her heart,
Joseph instinctively held out his arms to catch the
old lottery shareholder and placed her, fainting, in
a chair, calling to his mother to come.   Agathe
rose, put on her dressing-gown, and hurried to the
room; by the light of a candle she applied the
ordinary remedies to her aunt; eau de Cologne on
the temples and cold water on the forehead; she
burned a feather under her nose, and at last saw
that her consciousness was returning.

"They were there this morning; but *he* took
them, the monster!"

"What?" said Joseph.

"I had twenty louis in my mattress, my savings
for two years.   No one but Philippe could have
taken them—"

"But when?" cried the poor mother, utterly
overwhelmed.   "He hasn't come home since breakfast."

"I wish I could be mistaken," replied the old
woman.   "But in Joseph's studio this morning,
when I was talking about the lottery, I had a presentiment; I did wrong not to come down at once
and take my little all and make my investment
right away. I meant to do it, and I am sure I don't
know what prevented me.   Oh! *mon Dieu!* I
went out to buy cigars for him!—"

"But the apartment was locked," said Joseph.

"Besides, it's such a detestable thing that I can't believe it. Philippe spy upon you, cut your mattress open, plan the theft?—No!"

"I felt them when I made my bed this morning, after breakfast," repeated La Descoings.

Agathe, in dire dismay, went downstairs and inquired if Philippe had returned during the day, and the concierge told her of his exploit. The mother, pierced to the heart, ascended the stairs entirely changed. She was as white as the linen of her chemise and walked as ghosts are supposed to walk, noiselessly and slowly, as if impelled by a superhuman power, and almost mechanically. She held in her hand a candle, which shone full on her face and showed her eyes transfixed with horror. Unknown to herself, she had disarranged her hair as she passed her hands across her forehead, and this circumstance imparted to her face such a ghastly beauty that Joseph stood rooted to the spot by the apparition of her remorse, by that vision of Terror and Despair.

"Take my silver covers, aunt," said she, "I have six of them; that will make up what you want, for I took it to give Philippe; I thought I should be able to put it back before you discovered it. Oh! I have suffered so!"

She sank into a chair. Her dry, staring eyes wavered a little.

"It was he who did it," said La Descoings to Joseph in an undertone.

"No, no," rejoined Agathe. "Take my covers

and sell them; they're of no use to me, we can use yours."

She went into her room, took down the box that contained the covers, found it very light, opened it and found in it nothing but a pawn-ticket. The poor mother uttered a horrible shriek. Joseph and La Descoings ran to her, looked into the box, and the mother's sublime falsehood availed her nothing. All three remained silent, avoiding one another's glance. At that moment, with an almost insane gesture, Agathe placed a finger on her lips to urge the keeping of a secret that no one was inclined to divulge. They all returned to the salon and sat in front of the fire.

"Look you, my children," cried La Descoings, "I am struck to the heart; my combination will come out, I am sure. I am not thinking of myself now, but of you two!—Philippe," she said to her niece, "is a monster; he doesn't love you, in spite of all you do for him. If you don't take precautions against him, the miserable wretch will bring you to beggary. Promise me to sell your consols, take the money and invest it in an annuity. Joseph has a good profession at which he can make a living. By taking this course, my dear, you will never be a burden to Joseph. Monsieur Desroches intends to set his son up in business. Little Desroches"—he was then twenty-six—"has found a practice. He will take your twelve thousand francs and pay you an annuity."

Joseph seized his mother's candlestick and rushed

up to his studio, returning almost immediately with three hundred francs.

"Here, Mamma Descoings," he said, offering her his little hoard, "it is none of our business what you do with your money; we owe you what you lack, and here is almost the full amount."

"What! take your little store, the fruit of your privations, which make me so unhappy! Are you mad, Joseph?" cried the aged investor in the royal lottery of France, visibly in sore perplexity between her unreasoning faith in her combination and an act which seemed sacrilegious to her.

"Oh! do what you please with it," said Agathe, moved to tears by her true son's impulsive action.

La Descoings took Joseph's face in her hands and kissed him on the forehead.

"My child," she said, "don't tempt me. I might lose again, you know. The lottery is all folly!"

Never was so heroic a sentence uttered in the unseen dramas of private life. Was it not the triumph of affection over an inveterate vice? At that moment, the bells rang for the midnight mass.

"It's too late now anyway," said La Descoings.

"Give me your cabalistic calculations," said Joseph.

The generous artist seized the numbers, darted into the hall and rushed away to place the money. When he was no longer in the room, Agathe and La Descoings burst into tears.

"He has gone, dear love," cried the gambler. "But it shall be all for him, it's his money!"

Unfortunately Joseph had no idea of the location of the lottery offices, which the regular investors were as familiar with, in those days, as the smokers of the present day are with the government tobacco agencies. The painter rushed about like a madman, looking at the lanterns. When he asked the passers-by to direct him to a lottery-office, someone answered that they were closed, but that Perron's, at the Palais-Royal, sometimes remained open a little later. He at once flew to the Palais-Royal, but found the office closed.

"Two minutes earlier and you could have put in your money," said one of the ticket vendors who stood in front of Perron's, shouting these strange words: "Twelve hundred francs for forty sous!" and offering tickets all prepared.

By the rays of the lantern and the lights from the Café de la Rotonde, Joseph looked to see if, by chance, there were any of La Descoings' numbers on the tickets they offered; but he could not find a single one, and he returned home with the chagrin of having done to no purpose all that it was in his power to do to gratify the old woman, whom he told of his failure. Agathe and her aunt went together to the midnight mass at Saint-Germain des Prés. Joseph went to bed. The midnight repast was not served. La Descoings had lost her head and Agathe had a never-ending sorrow in her heart. The two women rose late. Ten o'clock was striking when La Descoings tried to exert herself to prepare breakfast, which was not ready until half-past eleven.

About that time, oblong frames were hung above the doors of the lottery offices, containing the lucky numbers. If La Descoings had had her ticket, she would have gone at half-past nine to Rue Neuve-des-Petits-Champs to learn her fate, which was decided in a building adjoining the Treasury Department, the site of which is now occupied by the Théâtre and Place Ventadour. On the day of every drawing, those interested in strange sights could see about the door of that building a motley crowd of old men and women and cooks, who, in those days, presented as interesting a spectacle as that of the long line of bondholders on the day interest is paid at the Treasury.

"Well, well, you are the richest of the rich at last!" cried old Desroches, entering the room just as La Descoings had taken her last spoonful of coffee.

"What do you mean?" cried poor Agathe.

"Her combination has won," he said, producing a list of the numbers written on a little slip of paper, of the sort that the sellers of tickets kept by the hundred in wooden bowls on their counters.

Joseph read the list, Agathe read the list. La Descoings read nothing; she was as completely crushed as if she had been struck by lightning; at the change that took place in her features, at the cry she uttered, old Desroches and Joseph carried her to her bed. Agathe ran to fetch a doctor. The poor woman was stricken with apoplexy and did not recover consciousness until about four o'clock in the afternoon. Old Haudry, her physician, informed her that, notwithstanding this apparent improvement, she must think about putting her affairs in order and preparing to meet her Maker. She had said only these two words:

"Three millions!"

Desroches senior, having been informed by Joseph as to the circumstances—but with the necessary reservations—cited several examples of gamblers who had missed making their fortunes on the day when fatality had willed that they should forget to place their money; but he understood how likely to be fatal was such a blow after twenty years of perseverance. At five o'clock, when the most absolute silence reigned in the little apartment, while the invalid, attended by Joseph and his mother, one sitting at the foot and the other at the head of the bed, was awaiting the arrival of her grandson, whom Desroches had gone out to find, the sound of Philippe's footsteps and cane were heard on the stairs.

"There he is! there he is!" cried La Descoings, sitting up in bed and succeeding in moving her paralyzed tongue.

Agathe and Joseph were deeply impressed by the feeling of repulsion that stirred the invalid to such intense excitement. Their painful suspense was fully justified by the aspect of Philippe's distorted, livid face, by his staggering walk, by the horrible condition of his deeply sunken, lifeless and yet haggard eyes; he was shaking with fever and his teeth chattered.

"Misery in Prussia!" he cried. "No bread to eat or water to drink and my gullet is on fire!—Well, what's the matter? The devil's always meddling in our affairs. My old Descoings in bed and staring at me with eyes as big as saucers."

"Hush, monsieur," said Agathe, rising, "and at least respect the misery you have caused."

"Oho! *monsieur?*—" he exclaimed, looking at his mother. "That is not kind of you, my dear little mother—do you no longer love your boy?"

"Are you worthy to be loved? do you forget what you did yesterday? You may look for other apartments; you shall live with us no longer.—After to-morrow," she added, "for, in your present condition, it would be very hard—"

"To turn me out, eh?" he retorted. "Ah! so you are playing the melodrama of the *Banished Son?* Well! well! so this is the way you take a joke? Very good, you are a pack of fine idiots. What wrong have I done, pray? I cleaned out the old lady's mattress a bit. Money shouldn't be kept in wool, deuce take me! And where's the crime? Didn't she take twenty thousand francs from you? Aren't we her creditors? I have reimbursed myself just so much, that's all!"

"O my God! my God!" cried the dying woman, clasping her hands and praying.

"Be quiet!" exclaimed Joseph, leaping upon his brother and putting his hand over his mouth.

"Left wheel, march, booby of a painter!" retorted

Philippe, bringing his strong hand down upon Joseph's shoulder and throwing him heavily upon a sofa. "The moustache of a captain in the dragoons of the Garde Impériale is not to be pulled like that!"

"But she has paid back all she owed me," cried Agathe, with an angry glance at her son. "Besides, that's nobody's concern but mine; you are killing her. Go, my son," she said, with a gesture that exhausted her strength, "and never let me see your face again. You are a monster."

"I am killing her?"

"Why, her combination won," cried Joseph, "and you stole the money for her ticket."

"If she's dying because a certain combination won, I'm not killing her," retorted the drunkard.

"Leave the room, I say!" exclaimed Agathe. "You make me shudder. You have all the vices! —My God, can he be my son?"

A hollow rattle in La Descoings' throat had aggravated Agathe's indignation.

"I love you still, my mother, although you are the cause of all my misfortunes!" said Philippe. "You turn me out of doors, on Christmas Day, the birthday of—what's his name?—Jesus! What did you do to Grandpa Rouget, your father, to make him turn you out and disinherit you? If you hadn't done something to displease him, we should have been rich and I shouldn't have been reduced to the last extremity. What did you do to your father, good woman that you are? You see that I may be a good boy and still be turned out of doors,—I, the glory of the family!"

"The shame!" cried La Descoings.

"You will leave this room, or you will kill me!" cried Joseph, rushing upon his brother with the fury of a lion.

"My God! my God!" shrieked Agathe, trying to separate the brothers.

At that moment, Bixiou and Haudry the physician entered.   Joseph had overturned his brother and stretched him out upon the floor.

"He's a downright wild beast," he said.   "Not a word! or I'll—"

"I will remember this," whined Philippe.

"A family quarrel?" queried Bixiou.

"Take him up," said the doctor; "he's as sick as the good woman here.   Take off his boots, undress him and put him to bed."

"That's easy to say," cried Bixiou; "but his boots will have to be cut off, his legs are so swollen."

Agathe took a pair of scissors.   When she had slit the boots, which in those days were worn over tight-fitting trousers, ten gold pieces rolled on the floor.

"There's her money!" muttered Philippe.   "Infernal fool that I am, I forgot the reserve.   And I have missed my chance too!"

The high fever from which Philippe was suffering made him delirious and he began to rave.   Joseph, assisted by Desroches senior, who arrived opportunely, and by Bixiou, succeeded in carrying the

poor wretch to his chamber.   Doctor Haudry was
obliged to write a line to the officials at the Charity
Hospital, asking for the loan of a strait waistcoat,
for the delirium reached a point where there was
serious danger that he would kill himself : he was
like a raving maniac.   At nine o'clock the household was once more tranquil.   Abbé Loraux and
Desroches tried to console Agathe, who wept un-
ceasingly at her aunt's pillow; she listened, but
shook her head and maintained an obstinate silence ;
only Joseph and La Descoings knew the depth and
extent of her internal wound.

"He will reform, mother," said Joseph at last,
when Desroches and Bixiou had gone.

"Oh!" cried the widow, "Philippe is right; my
father cursed me.   I have no right to—Here's the
money," she said to La Descoings, putting together
Joseph's three hundred francs and the two hundred
found upon Philippe.   "Go and see if your brother
doesn't need his draught," she said to Joseph.

"Will you keep a promise made to a dying
woman ?" said La Descoings, who felt that her mind
was failing.

"Yes, aunt."

"Then promise me on your oath to give your
money to little Desroches and take an annuity.
You will have to do without my income, and from
what I have heard you say I know you would allow
that villain to screw your last sou out of you."

"I swear, aunt."

The old grocer died on the thirty-first of December,

five days after receiving the horrible blow that the elder Desroches had innocently dealt her. The five hundred francs, the only money there was in the house, hardly sufficed to pay the funeral expenses of Widow Descoings. She left only a little silver plate and furniture, the value of which was given by Madame Bridau to her grandson. Reduced to an annuity of eight hundred francs paid her by Desroches junior, who was in treaty for what was called a *naked title*, that is to say, an office with no clientage attached, and who gladly took Agathe's capital of twelve thousand francs, Agathe abandoned her apartment on the third floor to the landlord, and sold all unnecessary furniture. When the invalid became convalescent, at the end of a month, Agathe coldly informed him that the expenses of his sickness had absorbed all the ready money, and that she should be compelled thenceforth to work for her living; she urged him therefore in the most affectionate way to re-enter the service and try to take care of himself.

"You might have spared your sermon," said Philippe, looking at his mother with eyes which perfect indifference made cold. "I have seen clearly enough that neither you nor my brother loves me any more. I am now alone in the world; I prefer that!"

"Make yourself worthy of affection," replied the poor mother, moved to the bottom of her heart, "and we will give you ours once more."

"Nonsense!" he interposed.

He took his old hat, worn shiny at the brim, and his cane, placed his hat over his ear and went downstairs whistling.

"Philippe! where are you going without money?" cried his mother, unable to restrain her tears. "Here—"

She handed him a hundred francs in gold, wrapped in paper. Philippe retraced his steps and took the money.

"Well, won't you kiss me?" said she, bursting into tears.

He pressed his mother to his heart, but without that effusion of sentiment which alone gives value to a kiss.

"Where are you going?" said Agathe.

"To Florentine, Giroudeau's mistress. They are friends!" he replied brutally.

He went downstairs. Agathe returned to the apartment with trembling limbs, eyes blinded with tears and a sore and oppressed heart. She fell upon her knees, prayed to God to take her unnatural child under His protection, and resigned her burdensome motherhood.

*

In February, 1822, Madame Bridau had taken up her quarters in the room formerly occupied by Philippe, situated over the kitchen of her former apartment. The studio and the painter's bedroom were opposite, on the other side of the landing.

When he found his mother reduced to that point, Joseph determined that she should at least be as comfortable as possible. After his brother's departure, he took the arrangement of the attic into his own hands and impressed the true artistic stamp upon it. He placed a carpet on the floor. The bed, which was arranged simply but with exquisite taste, was monastic in its plainness. The walls, covered with cheap percaline, judiciously selected, of a color that harmonized with the renovated furniture, gave an air of neatness and refinement to the room. He added a double door on the landing, and a portière inside. The window was hidden by a shade that admitted a pleasant light. Although the poor mother's life was reduced to the simplest expression that a woman's life can assume in Paris, Agathe was, at all events, in better state than any other woman in a similar situation, thanks to her son. To spare his mother the most wearisome part of Parisian housekeeping, Joseph took her every day to dine at a table-d'hôte on Rue de Beaune, frequented by fashionable women, deputies and

titled individuals, and costing ninety francs a
month for each person.   With nothing but the
breakfast to provide, Agathe resumed for her son
her habit of the old days when his father was
living.

Despite Joseph's pious falsehoods, she found out
at last that her dinner cost nearly a hundred francs
a month.   Horrified at the enormity of the sum, and
having no idea that her son could earn much money
by painting naked women, she obtained, through
the efforts of Abbé Loraux, her confessor, a position
at seven hundred francs a year in a lottery office
belonging to the Comtesse de Bauvan, widow of a
former leader of the Chouans.   The lottery offices,
which were the prerogative of widows under government protection,   ordinarily provided for the
support of the families which undertook to carry
them on.   But, under the Restoration, the difficulty
of rewarding, within the bounds of constitutional
government, all the services rendered, led to the
practice of allotting to unfortunate women of title
not one, but two lottery offices, the receipts of
which amounted to from six to ten thousand francs.
In that case, the general's or nobleman's widow who
was thus provided for, did not carry on the offices
herself, but had managers with an interest in the
profits.   When these managers were unmarried
men, they could not dispense with the services of a
clerk; for the office must be open from morning
until midnight, and the reports required by the
Ministry of Finance also called for considerable

writing. The Comtesse de Bauvan, to whom Abbé Loraux explained the widow Bridau's plight, promised, in case her manager should leave her employ, that Agathe should succeed him, and, meanwhile, she stipulated that the widow should receive a salary of six hundred francs. Poor Agathe was obliged to be at the office at ten o'clock in the morning and hardly had time for dinner. She returned to the office at seven in the evening and remained till midnight. For two years, Joseph did not once fail to go after his mother at night to bring her home, and he often went to take her out to dinner; his friends saw him leave the Opéra, the Italiens and the most fashionable salons in order to be at Rue Vivienne before midnight.

Agathe soon fell into the monotonous regularity of existence, in which those who are afflicted with crushing sorrow find a sort of comfort. In the morning, after she had arranged her own room, where there were no longer any cats or little birds, and had prepared the breakfast at the fire on the hearth, she carried it into the studio and breakfasted there with her son. She arranged Joseph's room, put out her own fire, and carried her work into the studio beside the little sheet-iron stove, but went out as soon as one of his comrades came, or a model. Although she understood nothing of his art or its methods, the profound silence of the studio was pleasant to her. She made no progress in an artistic way, she indulged in no hypocritical pretences, she was astonished beyond measure at the importance he attached to coloring, to composition, to design.   When some of the members of the club, or some painter friend of Joseph's,—Schinner, for instance, Pierre Grassou, or Léon de Lora, a very young *rapin*, who was called *Mistigris* in those days, —were engaged in one of their discussions, she would watch and listen closely, unable to discover anything that called for such long words and such hot disputes.   She laundered her son's linen, mended his stockings and underclothes; she even went so far as to clean his palette, hunt up cloths to wipe his brushes, and put everything in order in the studio.   When he saw that his mother had grasped those petty details, Joseph overwhelmed her with attentions.   If the mother and son did not understand each other in matters of art, they were wonderfully united in affection.   The mother had a little project of her own.

One morning, when Agathe had been fawning over Joseph as he was sketching an immense picture, which was afterwards painted but not understood, she ventured to say, aloud:

"*Mon Dieu!* what is he doing?"

"Who?"

"Philippe."

"Oh! that fellow's having a hard time.   He will be a man if he live long enough."

"But he has already known what want is, and perhaps it is want that has changed him in our eyes. If he were fortunate, he would be kind—"

"You think, dear mother, that he suffered terribly

when he was in America, don't you? But you are
mistaken; he enjoyed himself at New York just as
he is doing here."

"But if he should really be suffering, close by us
here, it would be frightful—"

"Yes," replied Joseph. "As far as I am concerned I would gladly give him money, but I don't
want to see him. He killed poor Mamma Descoings."

"Then you wouldn't paint his portrait?" said
Agathe.

"For you, mother, I would suffer martyrdom. I
will remember only one thing—that he is my
brother."

"His portrait as a captain of dragoons on horseback?"

"Yes, I have a beautiful horse here, after Gros,
and I don't know what use to make of him."

"Very well, then, go and ask his friend what has
become of him."

"I will go."

Agathe rose; her scissors, everything fell to the
ground; she kissed Joseph on the head and concealed two tears in his hair.

"That boy is your passion," he said; "each of
us has his own unhappy passion."

That evening, about four o'clock, Joseph went to
Rue du Sentier and found his brother there in
Giroudeau's place. The old captain of dragoons
had become the cashier of a weekly newspaper
undertaken by his nephew. Although Finot was

still the proprietor of the small paper, which he had
made into a stock company, keeping all the shares
in his own hands, the visible proprietor and editor-
in-chief was one of his friends named Lousteau, the
son of that subdelegate at Issoudun upon whom
Bridau's grandfather had attempted to take vengeance, and consequently Madame Hochon's
nephew. To please his uncle, Finot had given
his place to Philippe, but had cut down the salary
one-half. And every day, at five o'clock, Giroudeau
verified the cash and took away the money received
during the day. Coloquinte, the veteran who acted
as office-boy and did the errands, kept his eye upon
Colonel Philippe more or less, and Philippe behaved
very well. Six hundred francs salary and the five
hundred francs of his allowance as an officer of the
Legion of Honor enabled him to live with reasonable comfort; for he had a warm place to sit in during the day and passed his evenings at the theatres
at no expense to himself, so that he had only to
think of food and lodging. Coloquinte was just
starting out with a bundle of papers on his head and
Philippe was brushing his green baize false sleeves
when Joseph entered.

"Hallo, here's the ragamuffin," said Philippe.
"Well, we will dine together and you shall come to
the Opéra. Florine and Florentine have a box. I
am going with Giroudeau and you shall come along
and make Nathan's acquaintance!"

He took his loaded cane and moistened his cigar.

"I cannot accept your invitation, for I have to

take mother out to dinner; we dine at table d'hôte."

"And how is the poor dear woman?"

"Why, she's very well," the painter replied. "I have touched up our father's portrait and the one of Aunt Descoings. I have finished my own and I would like to give mother one of you in the uniform of the dragoons of the Garde Impériale."

"Good!"

"But you must come and pose—"

"I have to be in this chicken-coop every day from nine o'clock till five—"

"Two Sundays will be enough."

"Agreed, little one," rejoined Napoléon's ex-orderly, lighting his cigar at the porter's lamp.

When Joseph described Philippe's position to his mother as they went to Rue de Beaune to dine, he felt her arm tremble in his and a gleam of joy lighted up the faded face; the poor woman breathed like a person relieved of an enormous weight. The next day, she lavished upon Joseph little attentions inspired by her happiness and her gratitude to him; she placed flowers in his studio and purchased two jardinières for him. On the first Sunday that Philippe was to come for a sitting, Agathe took pains to prepare a delicious breakfast in the studio. She placed everything on the table, not forgetting a decanter of eau-de-vie, which was only half full. She remained behind a screen in which she had made a hole. The ex-dragoon had sent his uniform the day before and she could not refrain from kissing it. When he was all dressed and sitting astride one of the stuffed horses that saddlers have for hire and which Joseph had borrowed, Agathe was obliged, in order not to betray herself, to mingle the sound of her tears with the conversation of the brothers.

Philippe posed two hours before and two hours after breakfast. At three in the afternoon he resumed his ordinary clothes, lighted a cigar and, for the second time, proposed to his brother that they should dine together at the Palais-Royal. He rattled gold in his pocket.

"No," Joseph replied, "you frighten me when I see you have money."

"Oho! so you still have a bad opinion of me in this house?" cried the lieutenant-colonel in a voice of thunder. "A man can't save money, I suppose!"

"No, no," interposed Agathe, emerging from her hiding-place and embracing her son. "Let us go and dine with him, Joseph."

Joseph did not dare to scold his mother, so he dressed, and Philippe escorted them to the *Rocher de Cancale* on Rue Montorgueuil, where he gave them a splendid dinner that cost a hundred francs.

"The devil!" said Joseph uneasily, "with eleven hundred francs a year you seem to save enough to buy real estate, like Ponchard in *La Dame Blanche.*"

"Pshaw! I am in the mood for it," retorted the dragoon, who had drunk an enormous quantity.

When he said that, they were standing in the doorway, about to take a carriage to go to the play, for Philippe proposed to take his mother to the

Cirque-Olympique, the only theatre her confessor permitted her to attend.   Joseph pressed his mother's arm and she at once feigned a sudden indisposition and declined to go to the theatre. Philippe thereupon returned to Rue Mazarine with them.   When the mother and Joseph were alone once more, she had nothing to say.

On the following Sunday, Philippe came for his second sitting.   This time his mother was present openly.   She served the breakfast and was able to question the dragoon.   She learned that the nephew of old Madame Hochon, her mother's friend, played quite a prominent part in literature.   Philippe and his friend Giroudeau were members of a coterie of journalists, actresses and booksellers, and were highly considered there in the quality of cashiers. Philippe drank kirschwasser exclusively during his sitting after breakfast, and his tongue was unloosed. He boasted that he should be somebody again before long.   But when Joseph questioned him as to his pecuniary resources, he said nothing.   As it happened, the paper was not to appear the next day, because it was a holiday, and Philippe proposed to sit again then, in order to have done with the business.   Joseph informed him that the time for the opening of the Salon was approaching, that he had no money to buy frames for his two pictures, and could not procure it except by finishing a copy of a Rubens for a dealer in pictures named Magus.   The original belonged to a rich Swiss banker, who had lent it for ten days only, and the next day was the

last; it was absolutely necessary, therefore, to postpone the sitting to the following Sunday.

"Is that it?" said Philippe, looking at the Rubens
which stood on an easel.

"Yes," Joseph replied.   "It is worth twenty
thousand francs.   That is what genius can do.
There are pieces of canvas that are worth hundreds
of thousands of francs."

"For my part, I prefer your copy," said the
dragoon.

"It's younger," laughed Joseph; "but my copy is
worth only a thousand francs.   I must have to-morrow to give it all the tones of the original and make
it look old so that people can't distinguish them."

"Adieu, mother," said Philippe, kissing Agathe.
"Until next Sunday."

The next day Elie Magus came to get his copy.
A friend of Joseph, Pierre Grassou, who was working for the same dealer, was anxious to see the copy
finished.   When he heard his knock, Joseph, in
order to play a little trick upon him, placed his
copy, varnished with a special varnish of his own,
in the place of the original and put the original on
his easel.   He completely mystified Pierre Grassou
of Fougères, who was amazed beyond measure at
his performance.

"Could you deceive old Elie Magus?" he said.

"We shall see," said Joseph.

The dealer did not come; he was very late.
Agathe was dining with Madame Desroches, who
had just lost her husband.   So Joseph proposed to

Pierre Grassou to dine at the table d'hôte in her place. As he went out, he left the key of his studio with the concierge, as was his custom.

"I am to have a sitting this evening," said Philippe to the concierge, an hour after his brother left the house. "Joseph is coming back very soon and I am to wait in the studio."

The concierge gave him the key; Philippe went up, took the copy, supposing it to be the original, went downstairs again, returned the key to the concierge, saying that he had forgotten something, and went off to sell the Rubens for three thousand francs. He had taken the precaution to send word to Elie Magus, in his brother's name, not to come until the next day.

In the evening, when Joseph returned with his mother, whom he had been to fetch from Madame Desroches', the concierge told him of the peculiar actions of his brother, who had no sooner come than he went away again.

"I am lost if he didn't have the decency to take the copy only," cried the painter, instinctively divining the theft.

He ran rapidly up the three flights, rushed into his studio, and said:

"God be praised! he has shown himself once more what he always will be, a mean rascal!"

Agathe, who had followed Joseph, did not understand what he said; but when her son had explained the condition of affairs, she stood like a statue, without a tear in her eye.

"I have but one son now!" she said in a feeble voice.

"We have done our best not to dishonor him in the eyes of strangers," said Joseph; "but now we must put the concierge on his guard. Henceforth we will keep our keys. I will finish his accursed face from memory; it is almost done."

"Leave it as it is, it would hurt me too much to look at it," replied the mother, wounded to the bottom of her heart and fairly dazed by such cowardly villainy.

Philippe knew the destined use of the money for the copy, he knew the dilemma into which his action forced his brother, but he had no thought for anything. After this last crime, Agathe ceased to speak of Philippe, her face assumed the cold, concentrated expression of bitter despair; a single thought was killing her.

"Some day," she said to herself, "we shall see Bridau before the courts!"

Two months later just about the time that Agathe was to enter upon her duties at the lottery office, an old soldier, who said he was a friend of Philippe, made his appearance one morning, asking to see Madame Bridau on urgent business.

When Giroudeau gave his name, the mother and the son trembled more than they might have done had not the ex-dragoon presented a by no means inviting sea-wolf's physiognomy. His two dead-gray eyes, his piebald moustache, the scattered remnants of hair upon his butter-colored cranium, gave him

an indescribably dilapidated and libidinous air.
He wore an old iron-gray redingote, adorned with
the rosette of an officer of the Legion of Honor,
which could hardly be made to meet over a genuine
cook's paunch, that harmonized with his mouth, extending from ear to ear, and his broad shoulders.
His trunk was supported by a pair of meagre little
legs.   He exhibited on his cheek bones a vivid color
that told of a joyous life.   His wrinkled chops hung
down in folds over a worn black velvet stock.
Among other embellishments the ex-dragoon wore
enormous gold earrings.

"What a *jolly blade!*" said Joseph to himself, resorting to a slang expression that had found its way
into the studios.

"Madame," said Finot's uncle and cashier, "your
son finds himself in such an unfortunate plight, that
it is impossible for his friends not to request you to
share the very heavy burdens he imposes upon
them; he can no longer perform his duties on the
newspaper, and Mademoiselle Florentine, of the
Porte-Saint-Martin, allows him to occupy a wretched
attic in her house in Rue de Vendôme.   Philippe is
dying; if you and his brother cannot pay the doctor
and the bill for medicines, we shall be obliged, in
the interest of his recovery, to have him carried to
the Capuchins; but for three hundred francs we
would keep him.   It is absolutely necessary that he
should have a nurse; he goes out in the evening,
when Mademoiselle Florentine is at the theatre, and
eats and drinks things that irritate and aggravate

his disease and interfere with the treatment; and, as we are fond of him, it makes us unhappy. The poor fellow has assigned his pension for three years, his place is filled provisionally at the office, and he hasn't anything; but he will kill himself, madame, if we don't send him to Doctor Dubois's hospital. That is a very respectable place and it will cost ten francs a day. Florentine and I will make up half the month, if you will pay the rest—Come, it will hardly last more than two months!"

"It is hard, monsieur, for a mother not to be everlastingly grateful for what you are doing for her son," Agathe replied; "but that son has been torn from my heart; and, as for money, I have none. In order not to be a burden to my son here, who works day and night, who is killing himself, and who earns all his mother's love, I am going to enter a lottery-office to-morrow as sub-manager. At my age!"

"And what about you, young man?" said the old dragoon to Joseph. "Won't you do as much for your brother as a poor dancer at the Porte-Saint-Martin and an old soldier are doing?"

"Look you," said Joseph sharply, "do you want me to express in artist's language the purpose of your visit? Well, you came here to pull the wool over our eyes."

"To-morrow, then, your brother will go to the Hôpital du Midi."

"He will be very comfortable there," retorted Joseph. "If I should ever be in the same condition, I would go!"

Giroudeau withdrew, sorely disappointed, but also sorely humiliated to have to send to the Capuchins a man who had carried the Emperor's despatches at the battle of Montereau.

Three months later, toward the end of July, as Agathe was on her way to her lottery office one morning, crossing the Pont Neuf in order to avoid the payment of a sou on Pont des Arts, she saw in front of the shops on the Quai de l'Ecole, as she walked along the parapet, a man wearing the livery of destitution of the second order, the sight of whom caused her to turn giddy; she detected some resemblance to Philippe. It is a fact that there are in Paris three orders of destitution. In the first place, the destitution of the man who keeps up appearances, and to whom the future belongs; the destitution of young men, of artists, of men of the world momentarily embarrassed. The outward signs of this sort of destitution are visible only to the microscope of the most experienced observer. Such people belong to the equestrian order of destitution, they still ride in carriages. In the second order are old men to whom everything is indifferent, who wear the cross of the Legion of Honor on an alpaca redingote in June. Such is the destitution of old annuitants, old government clerks who live at Sainte-Périne, and who have ceased to think of their external appearance. Lastly, there is destitution in rags, the destitution of the common people, the most poetic of all—the destitution that Callot, Hogarth, Murillo, Charlet, Raffet, Gavarni,

Meissonier, aye, Art itself, adores and cultivates, especially during the carnival!

The man in whom poor Agathe thought that she recognized her son was astride upon the two last-named orders.   She saw a horribly threadbare stock, a mangy hat, patched boots down at the heel, a shiny redingote with buttons minus their shells whose gaping or shriveled coverings were in perfect harmony with torn pockets and a soiled collar. White marks upon his coat indicated plainly enough that if it contained anything, it could only be dust. The man withdrew hands as black as a navvy's, from a pair of shabby iron-gray trousers.   Over his chest was a knitted woolen undervest, dingy from long wear, which reached below his sleeves, came out over his trousers, was visible everywhere, and was worn, doubtless, as a substitute for linen.   Philippe wore an eye shade of green silk and brass wire. His almost bald head, his color, his haggard face, were sufficiently convincing testimony that he was just out of the horrible Hôpital du Midi.   His blue coat, worn white at the seams, was still decorated with the rosette.   The people in the street looked after *the gallant fellow*,—a victim of the government doubtless—with mingled curiosity and sympathy; for the rosette disturbed their eyes, and aroused doubts that were honorable to the Legion of Honor in the minds of the most ferocious ultra.   At this time, although there had been an attempt to cast discredit on the order by promotions without limit, there were not fifty-three thousand persons decorated

in France.   Agathe trembled in her whole being.
Although it was impossible for her to love her son,
she could still suffer terribly through him.   Assailed
by a last outburst of maternity, she wept when she
saw the once brilliant orderly of the Emperor start
to enter a tobacco agency to buy a cigar : and stop
short in the doorway ; he had felt in his pocket and
found nothing there.   Agathe walked swiftly across
the quay, slipped her purse into Philippe's hand and
hurried away as if she had committed a crime.
For two days she could not eat : she had always
before her eyes the horrible vision of her son dying
of hunger in Paris.

"After he has spent the contents of my purse,
who will give him any more ?" she thought.   "Giroudeau did not deceive us ; Philippe is just out of
the hospital."

She no longer saw in him her poor aunt's murderer, the family scourge, the household thief, the
gambler, the drunkard, the depraved sot ; she saw a
convalescent dying of hunger, a smoker without a
cigar.   At forty-seven she became like a woman of
seventy.   Her eyes lost their animation in weeping
and in prayer.   But this was not the last blow that
this son was destined to deal her, and her most horrible presentiment was realized.   An officers' conspiracy was discovered in the heart of the army,
and the extract from *Le Moniteur* giving the details
of the arrests was cried through the streets.

Agathe, in her little cage in the lottery office on
Rue Vivienne, heard the name of Philippe Bridau.

She fainted, and the manager, who understood her trouble and the necessity of doing something, gave her leave of absence for a fortnight.

"Ah! my dear, we drove him to it, with our harsh treatment," she said to Joseph, as she went to bed.

"I will go and see Desroches."

While the artist was placing his brother's interests in the hands of Desroches, who was considered to be the shrewdest and most astute of Parisian solicitors, and who had made himself useful to several persons of prominence, among others Des Lupeaulx, at that time general secretary of one of the great departments, Giroudeau called once more upon the widow, who on this occasion gave him her confidence.

"Madame," he said, "find twelve thousand francs and your son will be released for lack of evidence. It's a matter of purchasing the silence of two witnesses."

"I will get them," said the poor mother, not knowing where or how.

Inspired by the imminence of the danger, she wrote to her godmother, old Madame Hochon, and requested her to ask Jean-Jacques Rouget for the necessary amount to save Philippe. If Rouget refused, she begged Madame Hochon to lend her the amount, promising to repay it in two years. At the earliest possible moment, she received the following reply:

" MY DEAR GIRL,

" Although your brother has forty thousand francs a year, without counting the money he has saved these seventeen

years, which Monsieur Hochon reckons at more than six
hundred thousand francs, he won't give two sous to help
nephews he never saw. As for myself, you do not know
that I shall not have six francs at my own disposal until my
husband dies. Hochon is the greatest miser in Issoudun. I
don't know what he does with his money; he doesn't give
twenty francs a year to his grandchildren; in order to borrow,
I should have to obtain his sanction and he would refuse it.
I haven't even tried to send word to your brother, who has a
concubine in his house, whose very humble servant he is.
It's pitiful to see how the poor man is treated at home, when
he has a sister and nephews. I have tried to make you understand, again and again, that your presence at Issoudun
might save your brother and rescue a fortune of forty, or, it
may be, sixty thousand a year from that reptile's claws for
the benefit of your children; but you never reply and do not
seem to have understood me. And so I am obliged to write
you to-day without any epistolary precautions. I am very
sorry for the disaster that has befallen you, but I can only
pity you, my dear love. This is why I can be of no service
to you: at eighty-five years of age, Hochon eats his four
meals a day, eats salad with hard-boiled eggs at night, and
runs about like a rabbit. I shall have passed my life—for
he will live to write my epitaph—without having ever seen
twenty francs in my purse. If you conclude to come to Issoudun to combat the concubine's influence over your brother,
as there are reasons why Rouget should not receive you at
his house, I shall have difficulty enough in obtaining my husband's permission to have you visit me. But you may come,
he will yield to me on that point. I know one way of obtaining what I want from him, and that is to mention my will.
It seems to me such a ghastly thing that I have never resorted
to it, but for you I will attempt the impossible. I trust that
your Philippe will get out of the difficulty, especially if you
hire a good lawyer; but come to Issoudun as soon as possible.
Remember that at fifty-seven your imbecile brother is more
sickly and older than Monsieur Hochon. So there is need of

haste. There is already some talk of a will which would deprive you of the succession ; but, as Monsieur Hochon says,
there is still time to have it revoked. Adieu, little Agathe,
may God help you ! and count also upon your loving godmother,

   "MAXIMILIENNE HOCHON, *née* LOUSTEAU.

   "P. S.—Has my nephew Etienne, who writes for the newspapers, and who is very intimate, they say, with your son
Philippe, been to pay his respects to you? But come to me,
and we will talk about him."

This letter made a profound impression upon
Agathe; she necessarily showed it to Joseph, to
whom she was forced to repeat Giroudeau's proposition. The artist, who became very prudent, as
soon as there was any question of his brother, suggested to his mother that she should tell Desroches
everything.

Impressed by the good sense of that suggestion,
the mother, accompanied by her son, went to Desroches' office on Rue de Buci at six o'clock the
next morning. The solicitor, a dried-up little man
like his late father, with a shrill voice, a sallow
complexion, pitiless eyes, and the face of a weasel
who wets his lips in the blood of chickens, leaped
like a tiger when he learned of Giroudeau's visit
and proposition.

"Ah! Mère Bridau," he cried in his thin, cracked
voice, "how long will you be hoodwinked by your
infernal brigand of a son? Don't give two farthings! I'll answer to you for Philippe; it's for the
purpose of saving his future from wreck that I

believe in letting him be tried by the Court of Peers;
you are afraid of seeing him convicted, but I say,
God grant that his advocate allows a conviction to
be obtained against him! Go to Issoudun and save
the fortune of your children. If you don't succeed,
if your brother has made a will in this woman's
favor, and if you can't find any way to make him
revoke it,—why, you can at least collect material
for disputing the validity of the will on the ground
of undue influence, and I will manage the suit for
you. But you're too honest a woman to succeed in
finding grounds for a suit of that sort! In the vacation I will go myself to Issoudun—if I can."

The words "I will go myself!" made the artist
tremble in his skin. Desroches winked at him to
bid him let his mother leave the room first, and he
detained him for a moment.

"Your brother is a great rascal," he said; "voluntarily or involuntarily, he was the cause of the
discovery of the conspiracy; the villain is so sly
that it's impossible to find out the truth on that
point. Between idiot and traitor, choose whichever
part you please for him. He will be put under police
surveillance undoubtedly, but that is all. Have no
fear, I am the only one who knows this secret.
Hurry to Issoudun with your mother; you're a
bright fellow, try to rescue that inheritance."

"Desroches is right, my dear mother," said
Joseph, joining Agathe on the stairs; "I have sold
my two pictures; let us start for Berri, as you have
a fortnight to yourself."

*

After writing to Madame Hochon to announce their arrival, Agathe and Joseph started the next afternoon for Issoudun, abandoning Philippe to his fate. The diligence passed through Rue d'Enfer to take the Orléans road. When Agathe saw the Luxembourg, to which Philippe had been transferred, she could not restrain the words:

"If it hadn't been for the Allies, he wouldn't have been there!"

Many children would have made an impatient movement, would have smiled pitifully; but the artist, who was alone with his mother in the forward compartment, put his arms about her and pressed her to his heart, saying:

"Oh! mother, you are as a mother what Raphael was as a painter!" he said. "And you will always be an idiot of a mother!"

Soon diverted from her sorrow by the distractions of the journey, Madame Bridau was constrained to think of the purpose for which she was making the journey. Naturally, she re-read Madame Hochon's letter, which had so excited the solicitor Desroches. Impressed by the words *concubine* and *reptile*, which a septuagenarian as pious as she was respectable had employed to describe the woman who was in the act of devouring the fortune of Jean-Jacques Rouget, himself dubbed *imbecile*, she asked herself how, by her presence at Issoudun, she could rescue an inheritance. Joseph, poor, unselfish artist that he was, knew very little about the Code and his mother's exclamation caught his attention.

"Before sending us to rescue an inheritance, our friend Desroches would have done well to explain the method of laying hold of it," he cried.

"So far as my poor head, which is still giddy at the thought of Philippe's being in prison, perhaps without tobacco, and on the point of appearing before the Court of Peers, remembers anything at all," said Agathe, "it seems to me that young Desroches told us to collect evidence on which to contest my brother's will in case he should have made one in favor of that—that—woman."

"He is right there!" cried the painter. "Bah! if we don't understand how to go about it, I will ask him to go himself."

"Let's not cudgel our brains to no purpose," said Agathe. "When we reach Issoudun, my godmother will tell us what to do."

This conversation, which took place as they were entering Sologne after changing carriages at Orléans, displays sufficiently the unfitness of the painter and his mother to play the part which the redoubtable Master Desroches had assigned to them. But Agathe found such great changes in the manners and customs of Issoudun, upon returning thither after an absence of thirty years, that it is necessary, in a few words, to draw a picture of the town. Otherwise the reader would find it hard to understand the heroism exhibited by Madame Hochon in offering her assistance to her stepdaughter, and the strange position of Jean-Jacques Rouget. Although the doctor had taught his son to look upon Agathe as a stranger, there was something a little too extraordinary in a brother remaining thirty years without giving his sister the slightest reason to think that he was alive. This silence was evidently based upon some unusual circumstances which any relatives other than Joseph and Agathe would have sought long since to discover. Indeed, there were certain points of contact between the condition of the town and the affairs of the Bridaus, which will be made manifest in the course of the narrative.

With due deference to Paris, be it said, Issoudun is one of the oldest towns in France. Despite the historical prejudices which make of the Emperor Probus, the Noah of the Gauls, Cæsar mentions the excellent wine of Champ-Fort—*Campo Forti*—one of the best vineyards of Issoudun. Rigord expresses himself on the subject of this town in terms that leave no doubt as to its great population and its extensive commerce. But these two witnesses would assign a very modest length of life to the town in comparison to its great antiquity. Indeed, explorations recently made by a learned archæologist of the town, Monsieur Armand Pérémet, have led to the discovery of a basilica of the fifth century under the famous tower of Issoudun—probably the only one in France. This church bears, in the very materials of which it is constructed, the sign-manual of an anterior civilization, for its stones were part of a Roman temple which it replaced. Thus, in the light of this antiquary's researches, Issoudun, like all the towns in France whose ancient or modern termination is DUN—*dunum*—offers, in its name, the certificate of its existence in the days of the aborigines. The word *Dun*—applied to every eminence consecrated to the Druidical worship—would denote a military and religious establishment of the Celts. The Romans must have built under the Dun of the Gauls a temple to Isis. Thence, according to Chaumon, the name of the town: *Is-sous-Dun!* Is being an abbreviated form of Isis. It is quite certain that Richard Cœur-de-Lion built the famous tower, in which he coined money, above a basilica of the fifth century, the third monument of the third religion of that ancient town. He used the church as a convenient support for his ramparts, and preserved it intact, covering it with his feudal fortifications as with a cloak. Issoudun was at that time the seat of the ephemeral power of the bands of mercenaries and freebooters, the *condottieri* whom Henri II. opposed to his son, Richard, at the time of his rebellion as Comte de Poitou.

The history of Aquitaine, which was not written by the Benedictines, will probably never be written at all, as there are no Benedictines now. Therefore one cannot throw too much light into these archæological dark corners in the history of our manners, whenever occasion offers.

There exists another testimony to the former
supremacy of Issoudun in the opening to navigation
of the Tournemine, a small stream that flows
through a considerable extent of country, several
metres above the level of the Théols, the river that
surrounds the town.   That work is attributable,
doubtless, to the genius of Rome.   Indeed, the
suburb that lies north of the château is traversed by
a street that has been called Rue de Rome for nearly
two thousand years.   The suburb itself is called
Faubourg de Rome.   The natives of this suburb,
who seem to bear the stamp of a distinct race in
their faces and their blood, claim to be descended
from the Romans.   They are almost all vinedressers,
and remarkably strait-laced in point of morals, because of their origin without doubt, and perhaps
also because of their victory over the mercenaries
and freebooters, whom they exterminated on the
plain of Charost in the twelfth century.   After the
insurrection of 1830, France was too intensely
excited to pay any heed to the rising of the vinedressers of Issoudun, terrible though it was, so that
its details have never been published, and for good
cause.   In the first place, the bourgeois of Issoudun
did not allow the troops to enter their town.   They
preferred to undertake the whole responsibility for
the defence of their homes, in accordance with the
manners and customs of the bourgeoisie in the Middle Ages.   The constituted authorities were compelled to yield to a rabble supported by six or seven
thousand vinedressers, who had burned all the

archives and the offices for the collection of imposts, and who dragged from street to street a clerk in the customs service, crying at each lantern they passed: "Let us hang him up there!" The poor fellow was rescued from the infuriated mob by the National Guard, who saved his life by taking him to prison on the pretext of prosecuting him. The general entered the town only by virtue of a capitulation with the vinedressers, and it required great courage to go in among them; for, when he appeared at the town hall, a man from Faubourg de Rome dealt a blow at his neck with his *volant*—the *volant* is the large bill-hook attached to a rod, which is used for pruning trees—and cried: *Pu d'commis, ou y a rin d'fait!** The vinedresser would have laid in the dust the head that sixteen years of war had respected, except for the swift interposition of one of the leaders of the uprising, to whom a promise was given *that the Chambers should be asked to suppress the rats de cave !*†

In the fourteenth century Issoudun still had sixteen to seventeen thousand inhabitants, the remnant of a population that was twice as large in Rigord's time. Charles VII. owned a mansion there, which is still in existence, and was known as late as the eighteenth century as the King's House. This town, then the centre of the woolen trade, supplied a large part of Europe, and manufactured cloths, hats and excellent kid gloves, on a

* Down with the clerks, or there's nothing done.

† *Rats de cave,*—popular expression for *excise officers.*

large scale. Under Louis XIV. Issoudun, to which
we owe Baron and Bourdaloue, was still quoted as
a centre of refined manners, courtly language, and
pleasant society. In his *Histoire de Sancerre* the
curé Poupart maintained that the people of Issoudun
were noteworthy above all the other inhabitants of
Berri for their shrewdness and their *natural wit.*
To-day all that splendor, and the wit as well, have
entirely disappeared. Issoudun, whose extensive
territory bears witness to its old-time importance,
contains twelve thousand souls, including the vinedressers of four enormous faubourgs : Saint-Paterne,
Vilatte, Rome and Les Alouettes, which are small
cities in themselves. The bourgeoisie, like that
of Versailles, lives in the streets. Issoudun still
retains the wool-market of Berri, a trade threatened
by the many improvements in sheep-breeding which
are being introduced everywhere, but which Berri
does not adopt. The vinedressers of Issoudun produce a wine that is drunk in two departments,
which, if it were made as Bourgogne and Gascogne
make theirs, would become one of the best wines in
France. But alas ! *to do as our fathers did*, to frown
upon all innovations, is the law of the province.
The vinedressers continue, therefore, to leave the
stalks on during the fermentation, thereby imparting a detestable flavor to a wine which might be
the source of increased wealth and renewed life for
the province. Thanks to the acidity imparted by
the stalk,—which is said, by the way, to be softened
by age,—this wine will last a century ! This fact,

given by the *Vignoble*, is of sufficient importance in œnology to be published.   Guillaume le Breton, too, has devoted a few lines in his *Philippide* to this peculiarity of the Issoudun vintage.

The decadence of Issoudun is explained therefore by the spirit of immobility carried to the point of absurdity; a single fact will serve to illustrate. When the building of the road from Paris to Toulouse was in contemplation, the natural route was from Vierzon to Châteauroux through Issoudun. It would have been materially shorter than the route through Vatan, which was finally selected. But the notables of the province and the municipal council of Issoudun, the record of whose deliberations is said to be still extant, requested that the Vatan route be adopted, giving as their reasons that, if the high road should pass through their town, the price of provisions would rise and they would be in danger of having to pay thirty sous for chickens. Nothing analogous to such a performance can be found except in the wildest regions of Sardinia, a country once so wealthy and thickly peopled and to-day so utterly deserted.   When King Charles Albert, with the laudable purpose of extending civilization, desired to connect Sassari, the second capital of the island, with Cagliari by a magnificent, finely built road, the only one that exists in that prairie called Sardinia, the plans required that it should pass through Bonorva, a district inhabited by savages, who could fittingly be compared to our Arab tribes as they are, like them, descendants of

the Moors.   When they found that they were on
the point of being invaded by civilization, the savages of Bonorva, without taking the trouble to
deliberate, signified their opposition to the proposed
line.   The government paid no heed to the warning.
The engineer who planted the first stake received a
bullet in his brain and died on his stake.   The
matter was not investigated, and the road described
a curve which increased its length eight leagues!

At Issoudun, the increasing fall in the price of the
wines sold for home consumption, thus gratifying
the desire of the bourgeoisie to live cheaply, is preparing the ruin of the vinedressers, who are more
and more overburdened with the expense of raising
their crops and with the taxes; just as the ruin of
the woolen trade of the province is made inevitable
by the impossibility of adopting modern methods of
breeding sheep.   Country people have a deep-rooted
horror of every sort of change, even of that which
seems likely to benefit themselves.   A Parisian
found in the country a laboring man who ate for
dinner an enormous quantity of bread, cheese and
vegetables; he proved to him that, if he should
substitute a reasonable portion of meat for that
diet, it would afford him more nourishment, he
would be able to live more cheaply, to work more,
and would not draw so heavily upon his capital
of vitality.   The Berrichon admitted the justness of
the demonstration.   "But," he said, "the *gossips*,
monsieur! The *gossips ?*"—"Why, yes, what would
people say?—He would be the talk of the whole

11

province," observed the landowner on whose estates
this scene took place; "they would think he was as
rich as a bourgeois; in short, he's afraid of public
opinion, he's afraid of being pointed at, of being
considered a weak or sickly man.—That's the kind
of men we are in this province!"—Many bourgeois
utter this last phrase with a secret feeling of pride.
If ignorance and routine are invincible in the rural
districts, where the peasantry are left to themselves, the town of Issoudun has reached a point of
complete social stagnation.   Being compelled to
combat the diminution of fortune by the closest
economy, each family lives within itself.   Moreover, society there is forever deprived of the antagonism that gives tone to manners.   The town no
longer knows aught of that opposition of two forces
to which the Italian republics owed their existence
in the Middle Ages.   There are no noble families in
Issoudun now.   The mercenaries, the freebooters,
the *jacquerie*, the religious wars and the Revolution
have totally suppressed the nobility there.   The
town is very proud of that triumph.

Issoudun has constantly refused to encourage high
prices for provisions or to support a garrison.   It
has declined that method of keeping in touch with
the age, losing at the same time the profits to be
made out of the soldiery.   Before 1756, Issoudun
was one of the pleasantest of garrison towns.   A
legal drama that attracted the attention of all France,
—the affair of the lieutenant-general of the baili-
wick against the Marquis de Chapt, whose son, an

officer of dragoons, was, justly perhaps, but treach-
erously put to death in connection with a love in-
trigue,—deprived the town of its garrison about that
time. The sojourn of the forty-fourth demi-
brigade, quartered there during the civil war, was
not calculated to reconcile the inhabitants to the
military caste. Bourges, whose population shows a
constant decrease from decade to decade, is afflicted
with the same social malady. Vitality is departing
from those great bodies. Certainly the government
is chargeable with this unfortunate state of affairs.
It is the duty of a government to detect these blem-
ishes upon the body politic, and to remedy them by
sending energetic men to the infected localities to
change the face of affairs. But alas! far from it—
the government congratulates itself upon this ominous and deplorable tranquillity. And then, how is
it possible to send new officials or more capable
magistrates? Who, in our day, is anxious to go
and bury himself in departments where whatever
good work he may do brings him no renown? If,
by chance, an ambitious stranger to the province is
planted there, he soon succumbs to the force of in-
ertia, and accommodates himself to the tone of this
atrocious provincial life. Issoudun would have
put Napoléon to sleep.

As a result of this peculiar condition of affairs,
the arrondissement of Issoudun was in 1822 governed entirely by Berrichons. The constituted
authorities therefore were entirely disregarded
there, or were without any sort of power, except in

the cases, naturally very rare, in which the law is compelled to act because of their undisguised gravity. The king's attorney, Monsieur Mouilleron, was everybody's cousin, and his deputy belonged to a family in the town. The president of the court, before attaining that dignity, made himself famous by one of those remarks which, in the provinces, place a fool's cap on a man's head for the rest of his life. After completing the preliminary examination of a criminal charge that involved the death penalty, he said to the accused: "My poor Pierre, it's a clear case against you and you will lose your head. Let this be a lesson to you!" The commissioner of police, appointed since the Restoration, had relatives throughout the arrondissement. Lastly, not only did religious influence amount to nothing, but the curé enjoyed no consideration whatsoever. The radical, penurious, ignorant bourgeoisie told many more or less amusing tales concerning the poor man's relations with his maid-servant. And still the children attended the catechism and partook of their first communion; there was, moreover, a college there; mass was said regularly and all the church feasts were duly observed; the people paid their taxes, the only thing that Paris requires from the provinces and the mayor pronounced decrees; but these acts of ordinary social life were performed as matters of routine. Thus the mildness of the government harmonized admirably with the moral and intellectual condition of the province. The incidents of this narrative will set forth the effects of this state of affairs, which is not so anomalous as one might think. Many towns in France, particularly in the South, resemble Issoudun. The condition in which the triumph of the bourgeoisie has left that principal town of its arrondissement is the condition which awaits all France, Paris included, if the bourgeoisie continues in control of the internal and external policy of our country.

Now, a word as to the topography. Issoudun runs north and south upon a hillside that rises toward the Châteauroux road. At the foot of this slope, to supply the needs of the factories or to fill the moats of the ramparts in the days of the town's prosperity, a canal was built long ago, now called the *Rivière-Forcée*, its water being drawn from the Théols. The Rivière-Forcée forms an artificial arm which empties into the river beyond the Faubourg de Rome, at the point where the Tournemine and some other small streams also flow into it. These small streams of running water and the two rivers water meadows of considerable extent, which are surrounded on all sides by white or yellowish hills, dotted with black spots. Such is the appearance of the vineyards of Issoudun during seven months of the year. The vinedressers cut the vines to the ground every year, leaving only ugly stumps, without poles, and having a funnel-shaped appearance. When you come from Vierzon, Vatan or Châteauroux, the eye, wearied by a long succession of monotonous fields, is agreeably surprised at the sight of the meadows of Issoudun, the oasis of this part of Berri,

which furnishes the province with vegetables for
ten leagues around. Below the Faubourg de Rome
is a vast tract of marshland entirely given over to
kitchen gardens and divided into two districts
which bear the names of Upper and Lower Baltan.
A long, broad avenue with two rows of poplars leads
from the town, across the meadows, to a former convent called Frapesle, whose English gardens, unlike
anything else in the arrondissement, have received
the ambitious name of Tivoli. On Sundays,
amorous couples exchange their confidences there.

Traces of the former grandeur of Issoudun necessarily reveal themselves to a careful observer, and
the most noticeable are the divisions of the town.
The château, which formerly formed a little town
by itself with its walls and its moats, constitutes a
distinct quarter, to which there is no access to-day except by the ancient gates, from which there is no
egress except by the three bridges thrown across the
arms of the two rivers, and which alone has the
aspect of an ancient town. The ramparts still
show here and there the formidable abutments upon
which houses now stand. Above the château rises
the tower, which was its fortress. When one had
made himself master of the town that lay stretched
about those two fortified points, he had still to take
both the tower and the château. Even the possession of the château did not give possession of the
tower. The Faubourg of Saint-Paterne, which lies
beyond the tower in the shape of a palette and en-
croaches upon the meadow, is of so great an extent

that it must have been in remote ages the town itself. Since the Middle Ages, Issoudun, like Paris, must have climbed its hill and have concentrated itself beyond the tower and the château. This opinion derived a sort of certainty, up to 1822, from the existence of the charming church of Saint-Paterne, recently demolished by the heir of the person who purchased it from the nation. This church, which was one of the most attractive specimens of Romance architecture that France could boast, was demolished, and no one copied the design of the main door, which was in a perfect state of preservation. The only voice that was raised to save the edifice found no echo, either in the town or in the department. Although the château of Issoudun resembles an ancient town, with its narrow streets and its venerable houses, the town properly so-called, which was taken and burned several times at different epochs, notably during the Fronde, when it was entirely destroyed by fire, has a modern appearance. Streets of unusual width, compared with those in other towns, and well-built houses offer a striking contrast to the aspect of the château —a contrast which has procured for the town, in some geographies, the name of Jolie.

*

In a town thus constituted, devoid of activity in any direction, even in that of trade, with absolutely no taste for the arts, with no occupations into which learning enters—a town where everyone passed his time in his own house—it was certain to happen, and did happen, in 1816, after the Restoration, when the war was at an end, that among the young men of the town there were many who had no career marked out for them to follow, and who knew not what to do pending marriage or their succession to their parents' property. Bored to distraction at home, these young men found no means of diversion in the town; and as *young men must work off their evil humors,* as they say in the province, they amused themselves at the expense of the town. It was very difficult for them to work in the daylight, for they would have been recognized; and when the cup of their crimes was once filled to overflowing, they would have ended by being haled before the police court for the first peccadillo that was a little too outrageous; therefore they wisely selected the hours of darkness to play their naughty tricks. Thus, among those ancient relics of so many diverse vanished civilizations, a vestige of the spirit of drollery that distinguished the manners of the olden time gleamed like a last expiring flame. The young men amused themselves as Charles IX. and

his courtiers and Henri IV. and his boon companions used to amuse themselves, and as people used
to amuse themselves in many provincial towns.
Once bound together by the necessity of assisting
and defending one another and of inventing amusing pranks, there developed among them, by the
contact of their ideas, the sum total of mischief-
making which is characteristic of youth, and which
is noticed even in animals.   The confederation
afforded them, moreover, the petty pleasures due to
the mystery of a permanent conspiracy.   They
called themselves *Knights of Idleness.*   During the
day, the young monkeys were little saints, they
pretended, one and all, to be extremely well-
behaved; and they were accustomed to sleep very
late after the long nights they devoted to their un-
holy works.   The Knights of Idleness began with
commonplace tricks, such as unhanging and changing signs, ringing door-bells, rolling with a great
crash a cask that someone had left outside his door,
into his neighbor's cellar, awakening the aforesaid
neighbor with a noise that made him think a mine
had exploded.   At Issoudun, as in many other
towns, the cellar is commonly entered through a
trap door, the opening of which is beside the front
door and is covered with heavy wooden planking,
swung on hinges and fastened by a great bolt.
These new "bad boys" had not, toward the close of
the year 1816, gone beyond the practical jokes to
which urchins and young men throughout the provinces are addicted.   But in January, 1817, the Order

of Idleness had a grand master, and distinguished itself by exploits which, up to 1823, caused a sort of panic terror in Issoudun, or at least kept artisans and bourgeoisie in a constant state of alarm.

This grand master was a certain Maxence Gilet, called Max for short, whom his antecedents, no less than his youth and physical strength, marked out for that rôle. Maxence Gilet was commonly reputed in Issoudun to be the natural son of the subdelegate Lousteau, brother of Madame Hochon, whose gallant propensities gave rise to much gossip, and who had, as we have seen, drawn upon himself the hatred of old Doctor Rouget, in connection with the birth of Agathe. But the intimacy between the two men before their rupture was so close, that, as the saying went in the province at that time, they delighted to travel by the same roads. And so it was maintained by some that Max might be the doctor's son as well as the subdelegate's; but in fact he belonged to neither, for his father was a fascinating officer of dragoons in garrison at Bourges. Nevertheless, as a result of their subsequent enmity, and very fortunately for the child, the doctor and the subdelegate were constantly disputing over his paternity. Max's mother, the wife of a poor cobbler of the Faubourg de Rome, was, to her soul's perdition, wondrously beautiful, of the true Transtévérine type of beauty, the only property that she transmitted to her son. Madame Gilet brought Max into the world in 1788; she had long desired that blessing from heaven, which people were so unkind as to ascribe to the dissolute habits of the two friends, doubtless for the purpose of inflaming them against each other. Gilet, an old toper, a six-bottle man, smiled upon his wife's irregularities with a collusive complaisance not without precedent among the lower classes. In order to secure influential protectors for her son, La Gilet was careful not to enlighten the supposititious fathers. In Paris she would have been a millionaire; in Issoudun she was sometimes in comfortable circumstances, sometimes miserably poor, and, generally speaking, looked down upon.

Madame Hochon, Lousteau's sister, contributed some ten crowns a year to pay for Max's schooling. This liberality, which Madame Hochon was in no position to indulge in, on account of her husband's penuriousness, was naturally attributed to her brother, then at Sancerre. After Doctor Rouget, who was not happy as a widower, had noticed Max's beauty, he paid the board of the *young rascal,* as he called him, at the collegiate school until 1805. As the subdelegate died in 1800, and as the doctor, in paying Max's board for five years, seemed to be obeying a selfish sentiment, the question of paternity remained undecided. Moreover, Maxence Gilet, the theme of innumerable jests, was soon forgotten. And this is how it came about. In 1806, a year after Doctor Rouget's death, the youth, who seemed to have been created for an adventurous life and was endowed with remarkable strength and agility, indulged in a great number of rascalities

more or less dangerous to commit. He conspired
with Monsieur Hochon's grandson to drive the
grocers of the town to frenzy, he gathered the fruit
in advance of its owners, thinking nothing of
scaling high walls. The imp had not his equal in
violent outdoor exercises; he was unapproachable
at the game of prison-bars, and he could have out-
stripped a hare in running. Having a keenness of
sight worthy of Leatherstocking himself, he was
already passionately fond of hunting. Instead of
studying, he passed his time firing at a target. He
used the money extorted from the old doctor in the
purchase of powder and balls for a wretched pistol
that Père Gilet, the cobbler, had given him. During the autumn of 1806, Max, at that time seventeen years of age, committed an involuntary murder
by frightening a young woman far advanced in
pregnancy, whom he surprised, after nightfall, in
her garden, where he was proposing to pilfer fruit.
Threatened with the guillotine by his father, the
cobbler, who was doubtless anxious to be rid of him,
Max fled, without taking breath, to Bourges, over-
took a regiment under marching orders for Spain,
and enlisted in it. The affair of the young woman's
death had no serious consequences.

A youth of Max's character was certain to distinguish himself, and he did distinguish himself to
such good purpose that after three campaigns he became a captain, for the little education he had received served him well. In Portugal, in 1809, he
was left for dead in an English battery into which

his company had forced its way, but was unable to hold what it had gained. Max was taken by the English and sent aboard the Spanish hulks at Cabrera, the most horrible of all. The Cross of the Legion of Honor and the rank of major were solicited for him, but the Emperor was then in Austria; he reserved his favors for the brilliant actions that were performed before his eyes; he looked askance at those who allowed themselves to be taken and was by no means pleased with the condition of affairs in Portugal. Max remained on the hulks from 1810 to 1814. During those four years he became completely demoralized, for the hulks were the galleys, minus the crime and disgrace. In the first place, in order to maintain his freedom of action and to defend himself from the corruption that ran riot in those vile prisons, unworthy of a civilized people, he killed in duels—the duels were fought in a space six feet square—seven *bretteurs* or bullies, exterminating them from his hulk to the great joy of their victims. Max became a sort of king among his fellow-prisoners, thanks to the prodigious skill he acquired in the management of his weapons, to his physical strength and his address. But he, too, in time committed arbitrary acts, he had sycophants who worked for him and became his courtiers. In that school of misery, where embittered natures dreamed of naught but vengeance, where the sophistries that blossomed in those crowded brains legitimized evil thoughts, Max became altogether depraved. He listened to the views of those who dreamed of winning fortune at any price, nor did he recoil from the suggestion of criminal acts, provided that they were performed without witnesses. And when peace was declared he emerged from prison thoroughly perverted, although innocent; capable of becoming a great statesman in an exalted sphere, or a villain in private life, according to his destiny.

On his return to Issoudun he learned of the deplorable end of his father and mother. Like all those who abandon themselves to their passions and who make their lives short and sweet, as the saying is, the Gilets had died in the most horrible destitution at the hospital. Almost immediately, the news of Napoléon's landing at Cannes spread throughout France. Max could think of no wiser course to pursue than to go to Paris and solicit his commission as major and his Cross. The marshal who then held the War portfolio remembered Captain Gilet's gallant conduct in Portugal; he placed him in the Guard as captain, which gave him the rank of major in the line, but he could not obtain the Cross for him.

"The Emperor said you would find a way to earn it in the first battle," said the marshal.

In fact, the Emperor designated the brave captain as one of those to be decorated on the evening after the battle of Fleurus, in which Gilet made himself conspicuous. After the battle of Waterloo, Max retired upon the Loire. When the army was disbanded, the Maréchal Duc de Feltre refused to recognize Gilet's rank or his decoration. The soldier of Napoléon returned to Issoudun in a state of exasperation easy to imagine; he refused to serve unless with the rank of major and the cross. The department deemed those conditions exorbitant on the part of a nameless young man of twenty-five, who might in that way become a colonel at thirty. And so Max sent in his resignation. The commandant—for the Bonapartists recognized among themselves the honors acquired in 1815—thus lost the slender emolument, called half-pay, which was allotted to the officers of the Army of the Loire. At the sight of this handsome youth, whose whole property consisted of twenty napoleons, considerable sympathy was aroused in Issoudun, and the mayor gave him a place in his office with a salary of six hundred francs. Max held the place about six months, then voluntarily abandoned it and was succeeded by a Captain Carpentier, who had, like himself, remained true to Napoléon.

Having ere this become grand master of the Order of Idleness, Gilet had adopted a mode of life which caused him to lose the esteem of the first families of the town, although the change of feeling was not openly displayed; for he had a violent temper and was feared by everybody, even by the officers of the old army, who had followed his example in refusing to serve, and had returned to Berri to a life of retirement.

From what has been said, it will be seen that there is nothing surprising in the lack of affection for the Bourbons by the natives of Issoudun.

Indeed, there were more Bonapartists in that small town, relatively to its importance, than anywhere else in France. Almost all Bonapartists became liberals, as we know. In Issoudun or its immediate neighborhood there were a dozen officers in the position of Maxence, who selected him for their leader, they were so pleased with him; always excepting, however, Carpentier, his successor at the mayor's office, and a certain Monsieur Mignonnet, ex-captain of artillery in the Guard. Carpentier, a parvenu cavalry officer, was married and belonged to one of the most considerable families in the town, the Borniche-Héreaus. Mignonnet, a pupil at the Ecole Polytechnique, had served in an arm of the service that assumes a sort of superiority over the others. There were two shades of distinction among the soldiers in the imperial armies. A great majority held the bourgeois, the *pékin*—civilian—in contempt equal to that of the nobles for their serfs, of the victor for the vanquished. They did not always observe the laws of honorable dealing in their relations with civilians, or reprobate too severely those who sabred unoffending bourgeois. The others, and especially the artillery, as a result of its republicanism perhaps, did not adopt that doctrine, which tended to nothing so much as to make two Frances: a military France and a civilian France. And so, although Commandant Potel and Captain Renard, two officers of the Faubourg de Rome, whose opinions as to *pékins* never varied, were fast friends to Maxence Gilet, Commandant Mignonnet

12

and Captain Carpentier took the side of the bourgeoisie, deeming Max's conduct unbecoming a man
of honor.   Commandant Mignonnet, a short, slim
man, full of dignity, busied himself with the prob-
lems that the steam-engine offered for solution, and
lived very quietly, his only intimate friends being
Monsieur and Madame Carpentier.   His mild manners and scientific pursuits won for him the regard
of the whole town.   So it was said that Messieurs
Mignonnet and Carpentier were *a very different
sort* from Commandant Potel and Captain Renard,
Maxence and the other frequenters of the Café
Militaire, who retained the bluff military manners
and divers other traces of the Empire.

So it was that when Madame Bridau returned to
Issoudun, Max was shut out from the bourgeois society there.   The young man was wise enough, by
the way, never to claim admission to the social set
called the Circle, and never to complain of the de-
plorably low esteem in which he was held, although
he was the most fashionable and best dressed young
man in all Issoudun, although he spent money very
freely, and although he owned a horse, a phenomenon as rare at Issoudun as Lord Byron's at Venice.
We shall see in due time how it came about that
Maxence, poor and without apparent resources, was
placed in a position to be the dandy of Issoudun;
for the shameful methods which earned for him the
contempt of scrupulous or pious folk, were connected with the interests that brought Joseph and
Agathe to Issoudun.   To judge by his insolent

bearing and the expression of his face, Max cared very little for public opinion; he expected, in all probability, to take his revenge some day and to hold sway over the very people who now despised him. Moreover, although the bourgeoisie had a low opinion of Max, the admiration that his character aroused among the common people formed a counterpoise to that opinion; his courage, his activity, his decision were certain to please the masses, to whom his depravity was unknown— indeed, the bourgeois themselves had no suspicion of its extent. Max played at Issoudun a part almost identical with that of the Smith in the *Fair Maid of Perth;* he was the champion of Bonapartism and the Opposition. They relied upon him as the burgesses of Perth relied upon Smith on all important occasions. One affair in particular displayed in bold relief the hero and the victim of the Hundred Days.

In 1819, a battalion commanded by royalist officers, young men from the Maison Rouge, passed through Issoudun on its way to go into garrison at Bourges. Not knowing how to employ their time in so constitutional a town as Issoudun, the officers found their way to the Café Militaire. In all provincial towns there is a Café Militaire. That at Issoudun, located in a corner of the fortifications on the Place d'Armes, and kept by an officer's widow, was naturally used as a club by the Bonapartists of the town, officers on half-pay, or those who shared Max's opinions and whom the prevalent sentiment

in the town permitted to give expression to their
adoration of the Emperor. From 1816 there was a
banquet at Issoudun every year, to celebrate the anniversary of Napoléon's coronation. The first three
royalists who appeared asked for the newspapers,
La Quotidienne and *Le Drapeau Blanc* among others.
Public opinion at Issoudun, especially at the Café
Militaire, did not favor royalist journals. The
café took in only *Le Commerce*, a name which *Le
Constitutionnel*, after it was suppressed by royal
decree, was obliged to assume for some years. But
as it began its Paris Notes, on its first appearance
under that title, with these words: "*Le Commerce
is essentially Constitutionnel*," people continued to
call it *Le Constitutionnel*. All the subscribers
grasped the meaning of the pun, overflowing with
the spirit of opposition and with mischievous meaning, by which they were requested to pay no attention to the sign, as the same wine would still be
served. From the vantage-ground of her counting-
room, the stout lady informed the royalists that she
had not the papers they sought.

"What papers do you take, pray?" said one of
the officers, a captain.

The waiter, a diminutive youth in a blue cloth
jacket and a coarse cotton apron, brought *Le Commerce*.

"Ah! that's your paper, is it? Haven't you any
other?"

"No," said the waiter, "that's the only one."

The captain tore the organ of the Opposition into

small pieces, threw them on the floor and spat upon them, saying:

"Dominoes!"

Within ten minutes the news of the insult paid to the constitutional opposition and to the liberal cause in the person of its sacrosanct journal, which assailed priests with the courage and wit that are familiar to us all, had spread through the streets and found its way into the houses like a flash of lightning; everyone told it to his neighbor. The same words came at once to everybody's lips: "We must tell Max!" It was not long before Max knew of the incident. The officers had not finished their game of dominoes when he entered the café, accompanied by Commandant Potel and Captain Renard, and followed by thirty young men, curious to see the end of the affair, almost all of whom remained in a group on the Place d'Armes. The café was soon full.

"Waiter, *my* paper," said Max in a mild voice.

He was playing a little comedy. The stout woman said, in a frightened, conciliatory tone:

"I have lent it, captain."

"Go and get it," cried one of Max's friends.

"Can't you get along without the paper?" said the waiter. "We haven't got it now."

The young officers laughed and cast sidelong glances at the bourgeois.

"They tore it up!" cried a young townsman, looking at the young royalist captain's feet.

"Who took the liberty to tear up the newspaper,

I pray to know?" demanded Max in a voice of
thunder, rising to his feet with folded arms and
eyes flashing fire.

"And we spat upon it," replied the three young
officers, rising and looking Max in the face.

"You have insulted the whole town," said Max,
who had become perfectly white.

"Very good,—and then?"—queried the youngest
officer.

With an address, an impetuosity and a rapidity
that the young men could not provide against,
Max struck the first officer in the line two blows
across the face, and said to him:

"Do you understand French?"

They fought in the avenue at Frapesle, three
against three.   Potel and Renard absolutely refused
to allow Gilet to demand satisfaction alone from all
three officers.   Max killed his man.   Commandant
Potel wounded his so severely that the unfortunate
fellow, a young man of good family, died the next
day at the hospital to which he was carried.   The
third escaped with a sword-thrust and wounded
Captain Renard.   The battalion left for Bourges
in the night.   This affair, which made a great
noise in Berri, exalted Maxence definitively into a
hero.

The Knights of Idleness, all young men,—the
oldest was less than twenty-five,—admired Maxence.
Some of them, far from sharing the prudery and
rigid morality of their families with regard to their
leader, envied his position and deemed him very

fortunate. Under such a leader, the order accomplished marvels. From the month of January, 1817, not a week passed that the town was not stirred to its centre by some fresh exploit. Max made it a point of honor to demand certain conditions from the knights. The statutes of the order were promulgated. The young devils thereupon became as active as pupils of Amoros, bold as kites, skilful at all exercises, strong and adroit as evil-doers. They perfected themselves in the art of climbing upon roofs, scaling walls, jumping, walking without noise, mixing mortar and walling up doors. They had a veritable arsenal of ropes, ladders, tools and disguises. Thus the Knights of Idleness attained the beau ideal of mischief, not only in the execution, but in the conception of their tricks. They came at last to have the genius for evil that so delighted Panurge, that provokes laughter and makes the victim so ridiculous that he dares not complain. These well-born youths had accomplices within the houses, too, which fact enabled them to obtain information that was very useful in the perpetration of their pranks.

One very cold night the incarnate devils carried a stove from a man's living-room into his courtyard, and stuffed it so full of wood that the fire was still burning in the morning. Thereupon it was reported through the town that Monsieur So-and-so— a miser!—had been trying to heat his courtyard.

Sometimes they all lay in ambush on Grand' Rue or Rue Basse, two streets which are the main

arteries of the town and into which many narrow
cross streets run.   Crouching in the angles of the
walls, each at the corner of one of these small
streets, with eyes and ears open, just as each family
was in its first sound sleep, they would begin to cry
out, in frightened tones, from door to door, and from
one end of the town to the other: "Oh! what is
it?—what is it?"   These questions, repeated again
and again, awoke the bourgeois, who would appear
at their windows in their shirts and cotton night-
caps, lamp in hand, all questioning one another,
holding the strangest conversations and making the
most curious faces imaginable.

There was a poor bookbinder, very old, who believed in evil spirits.   Like almost all provincial
artisans, he worked in a little low shop.   The
knights, disguised as devils, invaded his shop at
night, placed him in his box of shavings and left
him alone, yelling like three men at the stake.
The poor man awoke his neighbors and told them of
the appearance of Lucifer, and they were hardly
able to undeceive him.   The bookbinder nearly
went mad.

In the midst of a severe winter, the knights demolished the chimney of the tax-collector's office,
and rebuilt it in one night, so that no difference
could be detected, and without leaving the slightest
trace of their work.   Their chimney, however, was
so arranged within as to fill the room with smoke.
The collector passed two months in discomfort before he discovered why it was that his chimney,

which formerly worked so well and was so satisfactory, played him such base tricks, and he was obliged to build it over.

One day they stuffed three bunches of straw dipped in brimstone and a quantity of greasy paper into the chimney of a pious old lady's house. In the morning, upon lighting her fire, the poor woman —a gentle, peaceful creature, a friend of Madame Hochon—thought that she had set fire to a volcano. The fire engines arrived, the whole town rushed to the spot, and as there were several Knights of Idleness among the firemen, they deluged the old woman's house with water, and put her in fear of death by drowning, after frightening her with fire. She was ill from the fright.

When the fancy seized them to make some person pass the whole night under arms and in mortal anxiety, they would send him an anonymous letter to warn him that his house was to be robbed; then they would pass along his garden wall or under his windows, one by one, whistling to one another.

One of their neatest tricks, which entertained the town for a long time and is still talked of there, was to send to all the heirs of an extremely miserly old woman, who was likely to leave a large estate, a line announcing her death and requesting them to be on hand promptly at the time appointed for placing seals upon her property. About eighty of the heirs arrived, from Vatan, Saint-Florent, Vierzon and the neighboring places, all in deep mourning but in the best of spirits, some with their wives, widows with their sons, children with their fathers, in jaunting cars and wicker cabriolets and rickety wagons. Imagine the scenes between the old lady's maidservant and the first arrivals! and the subsequent consultations at notaries' offices! There was something like a revolution in Issoudun.

At last the sub-prefect awoke one day to the fact that this state of things was intolerable, particularly as it was impossible to discover the perpetrators of these practical jokes. Suspicion hovered over the young men of the town; but, as the National Guard was a mere name at Issoudun, as there was no garrison, as the lieutenant of gendarmerie had only eight gendarmes under his orders and as they made no patrols, it was impossible to obtain proofs. The sub-prefect was placed on the black list, and was at once set down as a *bête noire*. This functionary was in the habit of breakfasting upon two fresh eggs. He kept hens in his courtyard, and combined with his mania for eating fresh eggs a mania for cooking them himself. Neither his wife nor his servant nor anybody else, according to his idea, knew how to cook an egg properly; he would look at his watch and boast that he was superior to the whole world in that respect. For two years he had cooked his own eggs with a success which called forth innumerable jests. Every night, for one whole month, the eggs laid by his hens were taken away and hard ones substituted. The sub-prefect was at his wit's end and lost his reputation as the *sub-prefect à l' œuf*. He eventually adopted a different

breakfast.   But he did not suspect the Knights of
Idleness, who covered their tracks too well.   Max
conceived the idea of coating his stove-pipes every
night with oil saturated with such fetid odors that
it was impossible to remain in his house.   Nor was
that enough.   One day his wife, proposing to go to
mass, found her shawl covered on the inside with
some sticky substance, and had to go without it.
The sub-prefect asked to be transferred.   That
functionary's cowardly submission definitively established the burlesque, occult authority of the
Knights of Idleness.

Between Rue des Minimes and Place Misère there
existed at this time a district bounded by the arm
of the Rivière-Forcée below and by the fortifications
above, and reaching from the Place d'Armes to the
Pottery Market.   This sort of irregular square was
crowded with houses of wretched appearance, hud-
dled close together, and divided by streets so narrow that it was impossible for two to walk abreast.
This part of the town, a sort of Court of Miracles,
was occupied by the very poor and by people engaged in unprofitable occupations, who lived in the
hovels and in buildings picturesquely called in
familiar language one-eyed houses.   At all periods
of the town's history, this was indubitably an un-
savory quarter, the resort of those who lead evil
lives, for one of the streets is called *Rue du Bour-*
riau.   That is evidence that the town executioner
had his house *with the red door* there for more than
five centuries.   The assistant to the executioner of

Châteauroux lives there to this day, if we may believe common report, for the bourgeoisie never see him. Only the vinedressers have any relations with this mysterious being, who has inherited from his predecessors the power to cure fractures and wounds. In former times, when the town put on the airs of a capital, the prostitutes had their headquarters there. There were second-hand dealers, too, whose articles it would seem were not likely to find purchašers, pawnbrokers whose wares poisoned the atmosphere, in a word, the apocryphal population that is found in similar places in almost all towns, usually dominated by one or two Jews.

At the corner of one of these dark streets, in the most animated portion of the quarter, there existed, from 1815 to 1823, and perhaps later, a tavern kept by a woman known as Mère Cognette. This tavern was a one-story-and-a-half structure, reasonably well built of white stone in courses, with the spaces between filled with rubble and mortar. Over the door gleamed an enormous branch of pine like Florentine bronze. As if that symbol were not eloquent enough, the eye was caught by a bright blue placard affixed to the door-jamb, whereon, beneath the words: GOOD MARS' BEER, was the figure of a soldier offering a very *décolletée* woman a stream of foamy fluid falling from the jug into the glass she held, describing a graceful curve, all of a color to make Delacroix faint. The ground floor consisted of an immense room used both as kitchen and dining-room, with the provisions necessary for the business of the establishment hanging from nails fixed in the beams. Behind this room, a narrow, steep staircase led to the upper floor; at the foot of the stairs was a door opening into a long, narrow room, with a window looking on one of those provincial courtyards which resemble the flue of a chimney, they are so narrow and long and black. Concealed by a lean-to and hidden from all eyes by high walls, this little room was used by the wild youth of Issoudun as the seat of their plenary court. Ostensibly Père Cognet furnished entertainment for the country people on market days; but, secretly, he was the host of the Knights of Idleness.

Père Cognet, once a groom in some wealthy family, had married La Cognette, formerly a cook in some aristocratic household. The Faubourg de Rome continues the practice, still in vogue in Italy and Poland, of feminizing the husband's name for the wife, in the Latin fashion. By combining their savings, Père Cognet and his wife had purchased the house in question to begin business as innkeepers. La Cognette, a woman of about forty years, tall and plump, with a nose *à la Roxelane*, tanned complexion, jet-black hair, brown eyes, round and animated, and an intelligent, affable expression, was selected by Maxence Gilet to be the Léonarde of the order, because of her disposition and her talents as a cook. Père Cognet was something like fifty-six years of age, short, thickset, submissive to his wife, and, as she was never tired of saying, he could see things with only one good eye, for he was one-eyed. In seven years, from 1816 to 1823, neither husband nor wife ever gave the slightest hint as to what took place nightly beneath their roof or as to the plots that were hatched there, and they always entertained the warmest affection for all the knights; their devotion was absolute, but it may perhaps seem a little less worthy of admiration if we remember that their selfish interests were the guaranty of their silence and their affection. 'At whatever hour of the night the knights descended upon La Cognette, they had but to knock in a certain way and Père Cognet, recognizing the signal, would rise, light a fire and candles, open the door, and fetch from the cellar the wines purchased expressly for the order, and La Cognette would cook them an exquisite supper, sometimes before, sometimes after the expeditions resolved upon the night before or during the day.

*

While Madame Bridau was traveling from Orléans to Issoudun, the Knights of Idleness were maturing one of their most notable exploits. An old Spaniard, a former prisoner of war, who had remained in the province at the time of the peace and now carried on a small business in grain, came early to the market and left his empty wagon at the foot of the tower of Issoudun. Maxence, who was the first to arrive at the rendezvous appointed for that night at the foot of the tower, was soon assailed with this question, asked in a low voice:

"What shall we do to-night?"

"Père Fario's wagon is over yonder," he replied, "I nearly broke my neck over it; let's put it up on the platform of the tower first and then we'll see."

When Richard built the tower of Issoudun, he planted it, as has been said, upon the ruins of the basilica on the site of the Roman temple and the Celtic Dun. These different ruins, each of which represented a long period of centuries, formed a mountain big with monuments of three ages. Richard Cœur-de-Lion's tower stands therefore at the summit of a cone whose slope is equally steep at all points, so that it can be reached only by escalade. To describe in a few words the position of the tower, we may compare it to that of the obelisk of

Luxor on its pedestal.   The pedestal of the tower of
Issoudun, which concealed at this time so many unknown archæological treasures, is about eighty feet
high on the side toward the town.   In an hour, the
cart was taken to pieces and hoisted piece by piece
to the platform at the foot of the tower,—a task
similar to that performed by the soldiers in charge of
the heavy artillery at the passage of Mont Saint-
Bernard.   They put the wagon together again and
took such care to efface all signs of their work, that
it seemed as if it must have been carried thither by
the devil. or by a fairy's magic wand.   After this
mighty exploit the knights, being hungry and
thirsty, betook themselves in a body to La Cognette's and were soon sitting about the table in
the little low room, where they laughed heartily
in anticipation of the wry face Fario would make
when he went to look for his wagon, about ten
o'clock.

Naturally the knights did not indulge in their
antics every night.   The combined genius of all
the Sganarelles, Mascarillos and Scapins in the
world would not have sufficed to invent three hundred and sixty practical jokes a year.   In the first
place, circumstances were not always propitious;
the moon shone too brightly; the last trick had
annoyed virtuous people too deeply; and again one
or another would decline to lend a hand when one
of his own kindred was to be the victim.   But if
the rascals did not see one another every night at
La Cognette's, they were sure to meet during the

day and take part together in the legitimate pleasures of the chase or the wine-harvest in autumn,
and skating in winter. In this party of twenty
young men of the town, associated to protest against
its social somnolence, there were some who were
more intimately connected than others with Max,
and who made him their idol. Such a character as
his often arouses the fanatical adoration of youth.
Now, Madame Hochon's two grandsons, François
Hochon and Baruch Borniche, were Max's devoted
partisans. They looked upon him as being almost
their cousin, admitting the accuracy of provincial
opinion as to his left-handed relationship to Lousteau. Moreover, Max generously lent them the
money their grandfather Hochon denied them for
their amusements; he took them to the hunt, he
formed their characters; in short, he exerted much
greater than family influence over them. Being
both orphans, the young men, although of age, were
still under the guardianship of Monsieur Hochon,
their grandfather, because of certain circumstances
which will be explained when the illustrious Monsieur Hochon makes his appearance in this Scene.

At that moment, François and Baruch—we will
call them by their Christian names for greater
clearness—were seated, one at Max's right, the
other at his left, in the centre of the table, which
was dimly lighted by four smoky two-ounce candles.
The party had consumed twelve or fifteen bottles of
different kinds of wine—there were only eleven
knights present. Baruch, whose name is sufficient

13

indication that there was still a remnant of Cal-
vinism at Issoudun, said to Max, when the wine had
unloosed all their tongues:

"You will soon find yourself threatened in the
centre of your line—"

"What do you mean by that?" Max demanded.

"Why, my grandmother has received from Madame
Bridau, her goddaughter, a letter in which she an-
nounces her speedy arrival with her son. My
grandmother had two rooms put in order yesterday
for their reception."

"What has that to do with me?" said Max, taking up his glass, emptying it at a draught and re-
placing it on the table with a comical gesture.

Max was at this time thirty-four years old. One
of the candles beside him cast its light upon his
martial face, lighted up his forehead and caused his
white complexion, his flashing eyes, his slightly
curling, glossy, jet-black hair to show to excellent
advantage. His hair receded naturally from the
brow and temples, thus marking clearly the five
black tongues, which our ancestors called *the five
points*. Despite these sharp contrasts of white and
black, Max had a very attractive face which owed its
charm to a profile like that which Raphael gives to
his faces of the Virgin, to a well-modeled mouth, about
whose lips a gracious smile constantly played—
an expression which Max had permanently adopted.
The rich coloring that distinguishes the faces of the
natives of Berri added to his air of good-humor.
When he laughed outright, he showed thirty-two

teeth worthy to adorn the mouth of a *petite-maîtresse*. He was about five feet four inches tall and admirably well proportioned, neither stout nor thin. Although his hands were well-cared-for, white and rather pretty, his feet reminded one of the Faubourg de Rome and the foot-soldier of the Empire. He would certainly have made a magnificent general of division; his shoulders were adapted to carry the fortune of a marshal of France, and his breast broad enough for all the decorations of all the orders in Europe. His movements were guided by keen intelligence. In a word, he was born attractive, like almost all love children, and the noble blood of his real father manifested itself in him.

"Why, don't you know, Max, that Madame Hochon's goddaughter is Rouget's sister?" cried, from the end of the table, the son of a former surgeon-major named Goddet, the best physician in the town. "If she is coming here with her son the painter, it is for the purpose of securing the goodman's fortune of course, and so adieu to your harvest—"

Max frowned. Then, with a glance that ran from face to face around the table, he sought to discover the effect produced by this apostrophe upon the minds of his comrades, and answered again:

"What has that to do with me?"

"Why," said François, "it seems to me that, if old Rouget should revoke his will, in case he has made one in favor of La Rabouilleuse—"

At that point Max cut his votary short with these words:

"When, upon coming here, I heard you called *one of the five Hochons,* in accordance with the pun upon your name that has been current for thirty years past, I closed the mouth of the man that called you so, my dear François, and in such vigorous fashion that no one has ever repeated the idiotic remark since, in my presence at least! And this is how you repay me! you make use of an insulting *sobriquet* to designate a woman to whom I am known to be attached!"

Max had never before said so much concerning his relations with the person to whom François had just applied the name by which she was known at Issoudun. The quondam prisoner of the hulks had sufficient experience, the captain of the grenadiers of the Guard knew well enough what honor is, to guess the source of the disapproval of the town. And so he had never allowed any person whomsoever to say a word to him on the subject of Mademoiselle Flore Brazier, Jean-Jacques Rouget's servant-mistress, whom the respectable Madame Hochon so forcibly denominated a reptile. Moreover everyone was too well aware of Max's sensitiveness to speak to him on that subject unless he should begin the conversation, and he had never begun it. In fact, it was too dangerous to incur Max's wrath, or to stir him to anger, for his best friends to jest about La Rabouilleuse. When his *liaison* with that young woman was mentioned

before Commandant Potel and Captain Renard, the
two officers with whom he lived upon a footing of
equality, Potel replied:

"If he's Jean-Jacques Rouget's natural brother,
why shouldn't he live in his house?"

"And, after all," added Captain Renard, "the
girl is a morsel for a king; and, if he should fall in
love with her, where's the harm? Doesn't young
Goddet love Madame Fichet in order to have her
daughter as a reward for that labor?"

After this merited rebuke, François could not pick
up the thread of his ideas; and he was still more
confused when Max said to him gently:

"Go on."

"Faith, no!" cried François.

"You are wrong to lose your temper, Max," cried
Goddet. "Haven't we agreed that we can say anything to one another at La Cognette's? Should we
not all be mortal enemies of the man who remembered after leaving this place anything that was
said or thought or done here? The whole town
speaks of Flore Brazier as La Rabouilleuse; if that
name inadvertently escaped François, is that a
crime against the Order?"

"No," said Max, "but against our private friendship. I reflected and remembered that we were *in
idleness*, and I told him to go on."

Profound silence ensued. The pause was so irk-
some to the whole party that Max cried:

"I will go on for him"—*Sensation*—"for you
all"—*Amazement*—"and tell you what you are

thinking!"—*Profound sensation!*—"You are thinking that Flore, La Rabouilleuse, La Brazier, Père
Rouget's housekeeper—for they call him Père
Rouget, that old bachelor who will never have children!—you are thinking, I say, that that woman
has supplied all my needs since my return to
Issoudun. If I can throw three hundred francs a
month out of the window, feast you often as I am
doing to-night, and lend money to every one of you,
why I get the crowns to do it with from Mademoiselle Brazier's purse? Well, yes!"—*Profound sensation.*—"Damnation, yes! a thousand times yes!—
Yes, Mademoiselle Brazier has trained her guns on
the old man's inheritance—"

"She has earned it, between the father and the
son," said Goddet in his corner.

"You think," continued Max, after smiling at
Goddet's remark, "that I have formed the plan of
marrying Flore after Père Rouget's death, and that
in that case, this sister and her son, of whom I have
just heard for the first time in my life, will endan-
ger my future?"

"That's it!" cried François.

"That's what everyone about this table thinks,"
said Baruch.

"Well, you may set your minds at rest, my
friends," rejoined Max. 'A man warned is as
good as two.' Now I address my remarks to the
Knights of Idleness. If I require the services of the
order to send these Parisians away, will the order
lend me a hand?—Oh! within the bounds we have

imposed upon ourselves for our little jests," he added hastily, noticing a general movement. "Do you suppose I propose to kill them, to poison them? —I'm not an idiot, thank God! And after all, if the Bridaus should succeed and Flore should have no more than she has now, I should be content, do you hear? I love her enough to prefer her to Mademoiselle Fichet, even if Mademoiselle Fichet would have me!—"

Mademoiselle Fichet was the richest heiress in Issoudun, and the daughter's hand counted for much in the younger Goddet's passion for the mother. Frankness is so highly esteemed that the eleven knights rose as one man.

"You're a fine fellow, Max!"

"That's the way to talk, Max; we will be Knights of Deliverance."

"A fig for the Bridaus!"

"We'll bridle your Bridaus!"

"After all, kings have been known to marry shepherdesses!"

"What the devil! Père Lousteau was very fond of Madame Rouget; isn't there less harm in being fond of a housekeeper who is entirely free and unfettered?"

"And if the late Rouget was Max's father, as they say, why it's all in the family."

"Opinions are free!"

"Vive Max!"

"Down with the hypocrites!"

"Here's a health to the fair Flore!"

Such were the eleven replies, words of encouragement or toasts pronounced by the Knights of Idleness, justified, let us say at once, by their exceedingly loose morals. We see how great an interest Max had in becoming the grand master of the order. By inventing practical jokes, by accommodating the scions of the principal families, Max proposed to provide himself with supporters for the day of his rehabilitation. He rose gracefully and waved his glass, filled with Bordeaux wine, while his companions awaited his reply.

"I wish you no better luck than to have one and all, such a woman as the fair Flore! So far as the invasion of relations is concerned, I have no sort of fear for the present; as to the future, we will see when it comes!"

"Let's not forget Fario's wagon!"—

"Oh! that's in a safe place," said Goddet.

"I'll undertake to carry through that affair," cried Max. "Be at the market early and come and let me know when the goodman begins to look for his barrow."

The clock struck half-past three and the knights silently left the tavern to return to their homes, gliding along by the walls without the slightest sound, for they all wore felt shoes. Max walked slowly to Place Saint-Jean in the higher portion of the town, between Porte Saint-Jean and Porte Vilatte, the quarter of the wealthy bourgeois. Commandant Gilet had concealed his apprehensions, but the news he had heard touched him to the quick.

Since his stay upon, or under, the hulks, he had acquired a power of dissimulation equal in extent to his corruption. First and foremost, the forty thousand francs a year in landed estates which Père Rouget possessed, were the foundation of Gilet's passion for Flore Brazier, be sure of that! From the way in which he conducted himself, it is easy to see how great a feeling of security La Rabouilleuse had inspired in him concerning her future financial prospects, which she owed to the old bachelor's affection for her. Nevertheless, the news of the arrival of the lawful heirs was calculated to shake Max's faith in Flore's power. The savings of seventeen years were still invested in Rouget's name. Now, if the will that Flore said had been made long before in her favor should be revoked, those savings at least might be rescued by causing them to be transferred to the name of Mademoiselle Brazier.

"That fool of a girl has never mentioned the sister and nephews to me, in seven years!" exclaimed Max to himself, as he turned from Rue Marmouse into Rue de l'Avenier. "Seven hundred and fifty thousand francs scattered through ten or twelve different notaries' offices in Bourges, Vierzon and Châteauroux, can't be turned into cash or invested in government securities in a week, or without people finding it out in a gossiping province like this! First of all we must get rid of the relations; but when they are once out of the way, we will make haste and get hold of that money. Meanwhile, I will think it over—"

Max was tired out. With the assistance of his pass-key, he entered Père Rouget's house and went to bed without any noise, saying to himself:

"To-morrow my brain will be clear."

It will not be amiss to state whence the sultana of Place Saint-Jean acquired the sobriquet of La Rabouilleuse, and how she had become mistress of the Rouget household.

As he advanced in years, the old physician, father of Jean-Jacques Rouget and Madame Bridau, realized his son's absolute nullity; he thereupon held a very heavy hand upon him, in order to force him into a daily routine which might take the place of wisdom; but in that way he unwittingly fashioned him to undergo the yoke of the first tyrant who should succeed in throwing a halter about his neck. One day, as he was returning from his round of visits, the malicious, evil-minded old man spied a little girl of bewitching beauty in the Avenue de Tivoli on the edge of the meadows. At the sound of the horse's hoofs the child rose from the bed of one of the streams which, as seen from the high land of Issoudun, resemble silver ribbons on a green dress. Like a water-sprite, the little one suddenly exhibited to the doctor one of the loveliest heads of the Virgin that ever painter dreamed of. Old Rouget, who knew the whole province, did not know that miracle of loveliness. The child was almost naked; she wore a short skirt, torn and ragged, of coarse woolen stuff with alternate brown and white stripes. A sheet of coarse paper, tied

with a sprig of willow, was her only head gear.
Beneath the paper, which was covered with figures
and O's that justified its name of scholars' paper,
the loveliest fair hair that a daughter of Eve could
desire was twisted together and held in place by a
comb such as is used to comb out horses' tails.
Her pretty sun-burned neck, her breast, scarcely
covered by a ragged kerchief, which was once a
madras, showed white in spots beneath the tan.
The skirt, passed between her legs, partly raised
and fastened by a large pin, produced the effect of
a pair of bathing drawers. The feet and legs, which
could be seen through the limpid water, were remarkable for a delicacy of shape worthy of the
sculpture of the Middle Ages. The exquisite body,
exposed to the bright sunlight, had a reddish tinge
that did not lack charm. The neck and throat
deserved to be enveloped in cashmere and silk.
Lastly, the nymph had blue eyes with long lashes,
a glance from which would have brought a painter
or a poet to his knees. The physician, who was
enough of an anatomist to know a beautiful figure
when he saw one, realized all that art would lose if
that lovely model should be left to destroy her fine
proportions by working in the fields.

"Where did you come from, my dear? I never
saw you before," said the old doctor, at that time
seventy years of age.

The incident occurred in the month of September,
1799.

"From Vatan," was the reply.

A man of unpromising mien, who was some two
hundred feet away higher up the stream, raised his
head when he heard the voice of a bourgeois.

"Well, well, Flore, what are you doing?" he
cried. "If you don't stop talking and *rabouiller*,
the crabs will go away!"

"And what do you come here for, from Vatan?"
the doctor asked, not heeding the interruption.

"I *rabouille* for my Uncle Brazier there."

Rabouiller is a Berri word which describes admirably the operation to which it is applied: the
process of stirring up the water of a stream and
lashing it by means of a thick branch with the
twigs arranged in the form of a racket. The crabs,
frightened by this operation, which they cannot understand, rush headlong up stream, and in their confusion plunge into the midst of the snares the
fisherman has set at a suitable distance. Flore
Brazier held her *rabouilloir* in her hand with the
grace natural to innocence.

"But has your uncle permission to fish for crabs?"

"Why, aren't we living under the Republic, one
and indivisible?" cried Uncle Brazier from his place.

"We are living under the Directory," the doctor
replied, "and I know of no law that allows a man
from Vatan to fish on the territory of the commune
of Issoudun," replied the doctor. "Have you a
mother, my dear?"

"No, monsieur, and my father's at the asylum at
Bourges; he went mad on account of a sunstroke he
got in the fields, on his head—"

FLORE

———

Rabouiller *is a Berri word which describes admirably the operation to which it is applied: the process of stirring up the water of a stream and lashing it by means of a thick branch with the twigs arranged in the form of a racket. The crabs, frightened by this operation, which they cannot understand, rushed headlong up stream, and in their confusion plunge into the midst of the snares the fisherman has set at a suitable distance. Flore Brazier held her* rabouilloir *in her hand.*

"What do you earn?"

"Five sous a day in the season for *rabouillage*; I *rabouille* as far as La Braisne. In harvest time, I glean; in winter, I spin."

"You're about twelve years old?"

"Yes, monsieur."

"Would you like to come with me? You shall be well fed and well dressed, you shall have pretty shoes—"

"No, no, my niece must stay with me, I am responsible for her in the sight of God and men," said Uncle Brazier, who had approached his niece and the doctor. "I am her guardian, d'ye see!"

The doctor repressed his inclination to smile and maintained his serious expression, which any other man would certainly have abandoned at the aspect of Uncle Brazier. The guardian had upon his head a peasant's hat disfigured by the rain and the sun, pinked like a cabbage-leaf on which a number of caterpillars have lived, and patched with white cotton. Beneath the hat was a swarthy, wrinkled face, in which the mouth, nose and eyes formed four black points. His dilapidated jacket resembled a piece of tapestry and his trousers were of coarse toweling.

"I am Doctor Rouget," said the physician; "and as you are the child's guardian, bring her to my house on Place Saint-Jean; it won't be a bad day's work for you, nor for her."

And without awaiting a reply, the old man hurried back to Issoudun, feeling sure that Uncle

Brazier and the pretty *rabouilleuse* would respond to his invitation. And in fact, just as he was taking his seat at the table, his cook announced Citizen and Citizeness Brazier.

"Sit down," said the doctor.

Flore and her guardian, still barefooted, looked around the doctor's living-room with bewildered eyes. This is why.

The house Rouget had inherited from the Descoings stands in the centre of Place Saint-Jean, which is a long and narrow square embellished with a few sickly lindens. The houses in that neighborhood are more substantially built than elsewhere in the town, and the Descoings house is one of the best. It stands directly opposite Monsieur Hochon's. It has three windows on the front on the first floor, and on the ground floor a *porte cochère* giving entrance to a courtyard, beyond which is a garden. Under the arch of the *porte cochère* is the door of a huge room lighted by two windows on the street. The kitchen is behind this living-room, but separated from it by a staircase leading to the first floor and to the attic rooms above. At right angles to the kitchen are a wood-house, a shed in which they used to make lye, a stable for two horses and a carriage house, above which there are small lofts for oats, hay and straw; and there the doctor's man-servant slept at the time of which we are speaking.

The living-room, which was such a source of wonder to the little peasant girl and her uncle, had for decoration a wooden wainscoting, carved as such

things were carved under Louis XV., and painted
gray, a beautiful marble chimney-piece and above it
a large mirror with a carved and gilded.frame and
without piers, in which Flore gazed wonderingly at
her own reflection. Here and there against the
wainscoting were some few pictures, booty from
the abbeys of Déols, Issoudun, Saint-Gildas, La
Prée, Chézal-Benoît and Saint-Sulpice, and the con-
vents of Bourges and Issoudun, which the liberality
of our kings and of faithful worshipers had enriched with priceless gifts and the most beautiful
works of the Renaissance. Among the pictures
preserved by the Descoings and transmitted to the
Rougets, were a *Holy Family* by Albani, a *Saint
Jérôme* by Domenichino, a head of *Christ* by Gio-
vanni Bellini, a *Virgin* by Leonardo da Vinci, a *Christ
Bearing the Cross* by Titian, which came from the
Marquis de Belabre who maintained a siege and
was beheaded under Louis XIII. ; a *Lazarus* by Paul
Veronese, a *Marriage of the Virgin* by the Genoese
priest, two church pictures by Rubens, and a copy
of a Perugino, made by Perugino himself or by
Raphael; lastly, two Correggios and an Andrea del
Sarto. The Descoings had selected these from
among three hundred church pictures, guided solely
by their state of preservation and with no idea of
their value. Not only were several of them in
magnificent frames, but some were under glass. It
was because of the beauty of the frames and the
value that the *panes of glass* seemed to indicate that
the Descoings kept the canvases. The furnishings

of the room did not lack that luxuriousness which is so highly prized in our day, but of which nothing was thought at Issoudun in those days. The clock on the mantelpiece, between two superb silver candelabra with six branches, was of a conventual magnificence that pointed to Boulle. The carved oaken armchairs, all upholstered in tapestry due to the devout piety of ladies of high rank, would have commanded a high price to-day, for they were all surmounted by coronets and coats of arms.

Between the two windows was a rich console from some château, and on its marble top stood a huge Chinese jar in which the doctor kept his snuff.

Neither the doctor, nor his son, nor the cook, nor the manservant paid any heed to these beautiful objects. They expectorated on a hearth of exquisite beauty, the gilded mouldings of which were all spotted with verdigris. A pretty chandelier, half crystal and half porcelain flowers, was covered, like the ceiling from which it hung, with black spots which bore witness to the perfect liberty of action accorded to the flies. The Descoings had hung at the windows brocade curtains torn from the bed of some abbé *in commendam*. At the left of the door stood a chest worth some thousands of francs, which did service as a sideboard.

"Two glasses, Fanchette," said the doctor to his cook, "and give us some of the old wine."

Fanchette, a stout Berrichon woman, who was esteemed the best cook in Issoudun before the advent of La Cognette, hurried away with a rapidity that betrayed the doctor's despotism as well as some curiosity on her own part.

"What's an acre of vineyard worth in your part of the country?" said Rouget, filling a glass for the elder Brazier.

"A hundred crowns in silver—"

"Very good, leave your niece with me as a servant and she shall have a hundred crowns for her wages; as her guardian you will receive the hundred crowns—"

"Every year?—" exclaimed Brazier, opening his eyes until they became as large as saucers.

"I leave the matter with your conscience," the doctor replied. "She is an orphan; until she is eighteen Flore has no right to see the receipts."

"She's nearly twelve, that would make six acres of vineyard," said the uncle. "Oh! she's a very good child, gentle as a lamb, well made and very active and very obedient. The poor creature, she was the light of my poor brother's eyes!"

"I will pay one year in advance," said the doctor.

"Faith," rejoined the uncle, "make it two years and I'll let you have her, for she'll be better off with you than with us; my wife beats her, she can't bear her.—I'm the only one that protects her, the blessed creature, as innocent as a child that's just born."

The doctor struck by the word *innocent* in the last sentence, made a sign to Uncle Brazier and went out with him into the courtyard and thence into the

14

garden, leaving the *rabouilleuse* at the table with Fanchette and Jean-Jacques, who questioned her, and to whom she artlessly described her meeting with the doctor.

"Well, my dear little girl, adieu!" said Uncle Brazier, returning to the room and bestowing a kiss upon Flore's forehead. "You can well say that I have done the best thing for you by leaving you with this excellent and worthy father of the poor; you must obey him as you would me. But be very good and very polite and do whatever you're told—"

"You will prepare the room over mine," said the doctor to Fanchette. "This little Flore, who is well named surely, will sleep there from to-night. To-morrow we will send for the shoemaker and dress-maker. Put on another plate at once; she will dine with us."

The only subject of conversation in all Issoudun that evening, was the installation of a little *rabouilleuse* at Doctor Rouget's. That name clung to Mademoiselle Brazier, in that land of mockery, before, during, and after her prosperity.

*

It was the doctor's intention, doubtless, to do for
Flore Brazier on a small scale what Louis XV. did
on a great scale for Mademoiselle de Romans; but
he set about it too late in life: Louis XV. was still
young while the doctor was in the flower of old age.
From her twelfth to her fourteenth year, the lovely
Rabouilleuse enjoyed unalloyed happiness. Well-
dressed and much better provided with linen than
the wealthiest girl in Issoudun, she wore a gold
watch and jewels which the doctor gave her to encourage her in her studies, for she had a master who
was instructed to teach her to read, write and
cipher. But the almost animal life of the peasantry
had inspired in Flore such invincible repugnance
to the bitter draught of knowledge, that the doctor
went no farther with her education. His intentions
with regard to the child, whom he brushed up and
taught and moulded with painstaking care that was
the more touching because he was deemed incapable
of affection, were diversely interpreted by the gossiping bourgeoisie of the town, whose chatter gave
currency to unfortunate errors, as in the case of the
birth of Max and Agathe. It is no easy matter for
the public in small towns to disentangle the truth
from a mass of conjectures, contradictory comments,
and all the suppositions to which the most trivial
occurrence gives rise. The provinces—and the same

was true formerly of the politicians of Little Pro-
vence at the Tuileries—insist upon an explanation of
everything, and end by finding out everything.
But everyone leans to the construction of the event
which he favors; he finds the truth there, demon-
strates it and maintains that his version is the only
reliable one. Thus the truth, despite the out-of-
door life and the constant espionage of small towns,
is often obscured, and requires, in order to be established, either such a lapse of time that no one
then cares to know the truth, or the impartiality
assumed by the historian and the man of superior
mind, who view affairs from a lofty standpoint.

"What do you suppose that old ape means to do
with a girl of fifteen,—a man of his age?" someone
would say, two years after the advent of La Rabouilleuse.

"You are right," would be the reply, "his *fête-
days have long gone by.*"

"My dear fellow, the doctor is disgusted with his
son's stupidity, and he persists in his hatred for his
daughter Agathe; in that dilemma, perhaps he has
been living so quietly these two years past with the
idea of marrying the girl, if he can have by her a
fine, active well-built boy, as full of life as Max,"
some shrewd head would remark.

"Oh! don't talk nonsense! Can a man have
children at seventy-two, after leading the life
Lousteau and Rouget led from 1770 to 1787? Look
you, the old rascal has read the Old Testament, if
only as a doctor, and he has learned there how King

David warmed up his old age.—That's the whole of it, bourgeois!"

"They say that Brazier, when he's drunk, boasts at Vatan of having fooled him!" would cry one of those people who are always prone to believe in evil.

"Good God, neighbor, what don't they say at Issoudun?"

During the five years from 1800 to 1805, the doctor had all the pleasure of educating Flore without the annoyance which the ambitious pretensions of Mademoiselle de Romans are said to have caused Louis the Well-Beloved. The little Rabouilleuse was so well pleased upon comparing her situation with the doctor to the life she had led with her uncle Brazier that she complied, in all likelihood, with her master's demands as an Eastern slave would have done. With due respect to the philanthropists and idyl-makers, country people have few ideas touching certain virtues; and such scruples as they do entertain proceed from self-interest and not from any fondness for the good or the beautiful; brought up in sight of poverty, of constant labor, of want, the prospect leads them to consider any possible means of extricating themselves from the hell of hunger and everlasting toil as permissible, especially if the law does not forbid it. If there are exceptions, they are rare. Virtue, socially speaking, is the companion of well-being, and begins with education. Thus La Rabouilleuse was an object of envy to all the girls within a radius of ten

leagues, although her conduct was exceedingly rep-
rehensible from a religious standpoint.

Born in 1787, Flore grew up amid the saturnalia
of 1793 and 1798, whose reflections illuminated the
country districts, destitute of priests, of altars, of
religious services, of religion itself, where cohabita-
tion was a lawful marriage, and where the revolutionary maxims left a profound impression,
especially at Issoudun, a part of the country where
the tendency to rebel is traditional. In 1802, the
Catholic form of worship was hardly re-established.
It was a difficult task for the Emperor to find priests.
Even in 1806 many parishes were still unprovided,
the reassembling of a body of clergy decimated by
the scaffold was so slow a process after such a violent dispersion. In 1802, therefore, no one was
likely to blame Flore, except her own conscience.
Was not conscience likely to be weaker than the
promptings of self-interest in the ward of Uncle
Brazier? If, as everything leads us to suppose,
the cynical doctor was compelled by his years to
respect a child of fifteen, La Rabouilleuse was none
the less considered a very sophisticated young
woman. Nevertheless, some persons chose to discover a certificate of her innocence in the cessa-
tion of the doctor's care and attentions, for he was
more than cold to her during the last two years of
his life.

Old Rouget had killed people enough to know
when his own end was at hand; and when his
notary, finding him upon his death-bed wrapped in

the cloak of encyclopædist philosophy, urged him to make some provision in the girl's favor, he said:

"Very well, let us emancipate her."

That remark was characteristic of the old man, who never failed to draw upon the profession of the person he was talking with for his sarcastic allusions. By covering his evil deeds with a mantle of wit, people were easily induced to forgive them in a country where wit is always in the right, especially when it is based upon a well-understood personal interest. The notary saw in the words the cry of the intense hate of a man in whom nature had foiled the schemes of lust, the determination to be revenged upon the innocent object of an impotent passion. This opinion was in some sort confirmed by the doctor's obstinacy, for he left nothing to La Rabouilleuse, saying with a bitter smile: "She is quite rich enough in her beauty!" when the notary pressed him further upon the subject.

Jean-Jacques Rouget did not weep for his father, but Flore wept for him. The old doctor had made his son very unhappy, especially after he attained his majority, which was in 1791; while he had given the little peasant girl the material happiness, which, to country people, is ideal happiness. When Fanchette said to Flore after the funeral: "Well, what is to become of you now that monsieur is no more?" Jean-Jacques's eyes shone, and for the first time his lifeless face became animated, seemed to be illumined by a gleam of thought, and expressed a sentiment.

"Leave us," he said to Fanchette, who was clearing away the table.

At seventeen, Flore still preserved the graceful figure and refined features, the distinguished beauty which charmed the doctor, and which women of the world have the art of preserving, but which fade and die among peasant women as swiftly as the flowers of the field. But the tendency to corpulence which assails all lovely country girls when they do not lead a life of toil and privation in the fields and the blazing sun, was already beginning to be noticeable in her. Her bust had developed. Her plump, white shoulders were well rounded and gracefully joined to her neck, in which there were already some creases; but the outline of her face was still pure and the chin was still delicate.

"Flore," said Jean-Jacques, his voice trembling with emotion, "you are used to this house?"

"Yes, Monsieur Jean."

As he was on the point of making his declaration, the heir found that his tongue was tied by the memory of the dead man so recently buried, and he asked himself how far his father's benevolence had extended. Flore, who was gazing at her new master, incapable of suspecting his simplemindedness, waited some time for him to speak again; but she left him at last, not knowing what to think of his obstinate silence. However thorough the education La Rabouilleuse had received from the doctor, more than one day was likely to pass before she understood the character of Jean-Jacques, whose story may be told in a few words.

At his father's death, Jean-Jacques, being then thirty-seven years old, was as timid and as submissive to the paternal discipline as any child of twelve.

This timidity should tell the story of his childhood, his youth, his whole past life, to those who would not admit the possibility of such a character or of the facts of this narrative, which, alas! are of common occurrence everywhere, even among princes, for Sophie Dawes was taken by the last of the Condés from a plight much worse than that of La Rabouilleuse.

There are two kinds of timidity: timidity of mind and timidity of the nerves; a moral and a physical timidity. One is independent of the other. The body may be afraid and tremble, while the mind remains calm and courageous, and *vice versa*. This fact affords a key to many moral singularities. When the two forms of timidity are united in one man, he will amount to nothing throughout his life. Such complete timidity is the characteristic of those people of whom we say: "He is an idiot." Noble qualities often lie hidden in the idiot. It may be that we are indebted to this twofold infirmity for the existence of some monks who have passed their lives in a trance. This unfortunate physical and moral condition is produced by the perfection of the organs and the mind as well as by defects still undetected. Jean-Jacques's timidity proceeded from a certain numbness of his faculties, which a skilful teacher or

surgeon like Desplein would have awakened.   In
him as in persons afflicted with cretinism, the sense
of love had inherited the strength and activity that
the intellect lacked, although he still retained
sufficient intelligence to take care of himself.   The
violence of his passion, stripped of the ideality in
which it revels in all young people, increased his
timidity.   He never could make up his mind to pay
court to a young woman at Issoudun.   Now, neither
young women nor bourgeois matrons could make
advances to a young man of medium height, of
shamefaced, ungracious demeanor, and with a commonplace face which two great, protruding eyes of
a pale green hue would have made unspeakably
ugly, even if the flattened features and sallow complexion had not made it prematurely old.   The
society of a woman actually blotted out the poor
fellow, who felt impelled by his passion as violently
as he was restrained by the paucity of ideas due to
his lack of education.   Motionless between two
equal forces, he did not know what to say and
shuddered at the idea of being questioned, he was
so in dread of being obliged to reply!   Desire, which
usually loosens the tongue so promptly, seemed to
freeze his.   Thus Jean-Jacques remained alone and
sought solitude, being in no wise oppressed thereby.
The doctor perceived, too late to remedy the evil,
the ravages caused by such a temperament and
such a character.   He would have liked to marry his
son; but as it was a question of subjecting him to
another person's domination, which might become

absolute, he hesitated.   Was it not simply abandoning the management of his fortune to a stranger,
a woman of whom he knew nothing?   Now, he
knew how difficult it is to form an accurate esti-
mate of the character of the woman by studying
the girl.   And so, while he was looking about for a
person whose education or opinions offered such
guarantees as he required, he tried to turn his son
into the path of miserliness.   He hoped thus to
endow the idiot with a sort of instinct in default of
intellect.   He accustomed him in the first place to a
life of routine, and bequeathed to him certain fixed
ideas concerning the investment of his income;
then he spared him the principal difficulties to be
encountered in the management of landed estates by
leaving all the property in good condition and let
on long leases.

But the one fact that was destined to dominate
the poor creature's whole life escaped the shrewd
old man's perspicacity.   Timidity resembles dissimulation; it has all its profundity.   Jean-Jacques
loved La Rabouilleuse madly.   Nor could anything
be more natural.   Flore was the only woman with
whom he came in contact, the only one he could
watch at his leisure, gazing at her on the sly,
studying her every hour of the day; Flore illumined
his father's house for him, she afforded him, unwittingly, the only pleasures that brightened his
youth.   Far from being jealous of his father, he
was delighted with the education he gave Flore: did
he not require a wife who would be easy of access,

and to whom he would not have to pay court? Passion, which—remember this—carries its own mind with it, may endow fools, zanies and idiots with a species of intelligence, especially in their youth. In the most brutish man we always find the animal instinct, which, in its persistence, bears some resemblance to a thought.

The next day Flore, whom her master's silence had caused to reflect upon her situation, expected some important communication; but, although he hovered about her, and looked askance at her with a lustful expression, Jean-Jacques could find no words to say to her. At last, when the dessert was on the table, the master resumed the scene of the previous evening.

"You are comfortable here?" he said.

"Yes, Monsieur Jean."

"Very well, stay here."

"Thank you, Monsieur Jean."

This strange state of affairs lasted three weeks. One night, when the silence in the house was un-broken, Flore, happening to awake, heard the regular breathing of some person at her door, and was terrified to find Jean-Jacques lying on the landing like a dog, having evidently made a hole at the bottom of the door in order to look into the room.

"He loves me," she thought; "but he will contract rheumatism at that business."

The next day Flore looked at her master with a significant expression. This dumb and almost instinctive passion had touched her; the poor fool no longer seemed so ugly to her, although his temples and forehead were covered with lumps like ulcers, the ghastly wreath that is the attribute of vitiated blood.

"You wouldn't like to go back to the fields, would you?" said Jean-Jacques when they were alone.

"Why do you ask me that?" she said, looking him in the eye.

"To find out," Rouget answered, turning as red as a boiled lobster.

"Do you intend to send me back?" she asked.

"No, mademoiselle."

"Well, then, why do you want to know? You have some reason."

"Yes, I would like to know—"

"What?"

"You wouldn't tell me!" said Rouget.

"Yes, on the word of a virtuous girl."

"Ah! that's the point," rejoined Rouget in dismay. "You are a virtuous girl—"

"*Pardè*, yes!"

"Is that true?"

"Why, when I tell you—"

"Come, are you the same as you were when you stood there, barefooted, the day your uncle brought you here?"

"A pretty question, on my word!" replied Flore, blushing.

The heir, abashed, hung his head and did not raise it again. Flore, amazed to find a reply so flattering to a man, received with such consternation, left the room.   Three days later, at the same moment, for they seemed mutually to select the dessert as the battlefield, Flore began the conversation by saying to her master:

"Have you anything against me?"

"No, mademoiselle," he replied; "no—" *A pause.*—"Quite the contrary."

"You seemed annoyed the other day to know that I was a virtuous girl—"

"No, I only wanted to know—" *Another pause.*— "But you wouldn't tell me—"

"On my word," said she, "I will tell you the whole truth—"

"The whole truth about—my father?" he asked in a choking voice.

"Your father," she said, looking straight into her master's eyes, "was a fine man—He liked to laugh, I tell you!—a figure—But, poor dear man!—it wasn't the will that he lacked—However, on account of some grudge or other against you he had intentions—oh! wicked intentions.   He often made me laugh, though!—Well?"

"Well, Flore," said the heir, taking La Rabouil-leuse's hand, "as my father was nothing to you—"

"And what did you suppose he was to me?"—she cried, in the tone of a maiden offended at an insulting supposition.

"Well, listen—"

"He was my benefactor, that's all.   Ah! he would have liked me to be his wife,—but—"

"But," said Rouget, resuming possession of the

hand Flore had withdrawn from his, "as he was nothing to you, you can stay here with me, can't you?"

"If you wish," she said, lowering her eyes.

"No, no, if you wish," exclaimed Rouget. "Yes, you shall be—mistress here. Everything in the house shall be for you, you shall take care of my fortune, it shall be the same as your own—for I love you and I have always loved you, since the moment you came into this room, barefooted."

Flore did not reply. When the silence became oppressive, Jean-Jacques invented this brilliant argument:

"Say, isn't that better than going back to the fields?" he asked with visible ardor.

"Goodness, Monsieur Jean, as you choose!" she replied.

However, despite that *as you choose!* poor Rouget found that he had made no progress. Men of his character require to be certain of a thing. The effort they make in avowing their love is so great and costs them so dearly that they know that they are in no condition to renew it. Thence arises their attachment to the first woman who accepts them. Events can be judged only by their results. Ten months after his father's death, Jean-Jacques had changed completely: his pale, lead-colored face, disfigured, as we have said, by excrescences on the temples and forehead, had grown brighter and clearer, and his cheeks were almost ruddy. In a word, his face exhaled happiness. Flore required

her master to take the utmost care of his person; she
appealed to his self-esteem to induce him to dress
decently; she stood on the doorstep when he went
out to walk, and watched him until he was out of
sight. The whole town noticed these changes,
which made a different man of Jean-Jacques.

"Have you heard the news?" people said in
Issoudun.

"What do you mean?"

"Jean-Jacques has inherited everything from his
father, even La Rabouilleuse."

"Don't you think the deceased doctor was malicious enough to leave his son a housekeeper?"

"She's a perfect treasure to Rouget at all
events," was the general verdict.

"She's a sly one! but she's very beautiful and
she'll make him marry her."

"What a chance that girl has had!"

"It's the kind of a chance that only pretty girls
have."

"Nonsense! do you believe that? Why, there's
my uncle Borniche-Héreau; you've heard of Mademoiselle Ganivet, she was as ugly as the seven
deadly sins, and yet she got a thousand crowns a
year out of him—"

"Pshaw! that was in 1778!"

"Rouget's doing wrong all the same; his father
left him a good forty thousand a year, and he might
have married Mademoiselle Héreau."

"The doctor tried, but she wouldn't have him;
Rouget's too big a fool—"

"Too big a fool! women are very happy with men of that stamp."

"Is your wife happy?"

Such was the general tone of the current gossip in Issoudun. If they began, according to the manners and customs of the province, by laughing at this quasi-marriage, they ended by praising Flore for devoting herself to the poor fellow. Thus did Flore Brazier succeed to the government of the Rouget household, from father to son, as young Goddet expressed it. And now it will be well to sketch the story of her government, for the instruction of old bachelors.

*

Old Fanchette was the only person in Issoudun to disapprove of Flore Brazier's becoming queen in Jean-Jacques Rouget's house; she protested against the immorality of the arrangement and took the part of outraged morals. To be sure, she was deeply humiliated to have for her mistress, at her age, a *rabouilleuse*, a small girl who came to the house barefooted. Fanchette possessed three hundred francs a year in the Funds, for the doctor had made her invest her savings in that way; her late master left her an annuity of a hundred crowns, so that she could live comfortably, and she left the house nine months after the doctor's funeral, on April 15, 1806. Will not this date indicate to perspicacious folk the period at which Flore ceased to be a virtuous girl?

La Rabouilleuse, who was shrewd enough to foresee Fanchette's defection—for there is nothing like the exercise of power to teach you the secrets of politics—had made up her mind to do without a servant. For six months, and without seeming to be so engaged, she studied the culinary processes which made Fanchette a first-rate cook worthy to serve a doctor. In the matter of high living, doctors may be placed on the same plane as bishops. The doctor had perfected Fanchette. In the provinces, the lack of occupation and the monotony of the life lead the mind to expend its surplus energy upon the kitchen. People do not dine so luxuriously in the provinces as in Paris, but they dine better; the dishes are carefully considered and studied. In the heart of the provinces there are Carêmes in short petticoats, unknown geniuses, who can make a simple dish of *haricots verts* worthy of the nod of the head with which Rossini greets anything that is perfectly successful. When he took his degrees at Paris, the doctor followed the chemical courses of Rouelle, and he had retained certain ideas which proved of advantage in the matter of culinary chemistry. He is renowned at Issoudun for several improvements in the art of cooking, little known outside of Berri. He discovered that an omelette is more delicate when the whites and yolks of the eggs are not beaten together with the brutality that cooks usually put into that operation. According to him, the white should be beaten until it resembles foam and the yolk introduced a little at a time, and you should not use a frying-pan, but a *cagnard* made of porcelain or earthenware. The *cagnard* is a sort of thick plate with four feet, so that, when it is put on the stove, the air circulates underneath and prevents the heat from cracking it. In Touraine the *cagnard* is called a *coquemar*. Rabelais, I think, speaks of a *cauquemarre* for cooking *coquesigrues*, which goes to prove the great antiquity of the utensil. The doctor had also found a way to kill the acrid taste of *sumach*; but that secret, which unluckily he confined to his kitchen, has been lost.

Flore, being a born frier and roaster, two accomplishments which can be acquired neither by observation nor by hard work, surpassed Fanchette in a short time.   In preparing herself to be a first-rate cook, she was thinking of Jean-Jacques's welfare; but she was herself, let us say, reasonably fond of good cheer.   As she was, like all uneducated people, incapable of occupying her mind with brainwork, she expended her energy upon the duties of housekeeping.   She polished the furniture and restored its lustre, and kept everything about the house so clean and neat that a Dutchwoman would not have been ashamed of it.   She directed the avalanches of soiled linen and the deluges of boiling water called lye, which, according to provincial custom, is made only three times a year.   She watched the linen with a housekeeper's eagle eye, and mended it.   Impelled by a jealous desire to become familiar with the secret of the management of money, she gradually assimilated what little Rouget knew about business matters, and added to her store of knowledge by conversation with the late doctor's notary, Monsieur Héron.   She also gave her little Jean-Jacques excellent advice.   Sure of being always the mistress, she was as saving and avaricious in his interest as if her own interests were at stake.   She no longer had to fear her uncle's demands; two months before the doctor's death, Brazier died from the effects of a fall received as he was leaving the wine-shop in which he passed all his time after fortune came upon him. Flore had also lost her father. And so she served her master with all the affection to be looked for on the part of an orphan, overjoyed to create new family ties and to find an interest in life.

During this period, earth was a paradise to poor Jean-Jacques, who adopted the peaceful habits of existence of a domestic animal, embellished by a sort of monastic regularity. He slept late. Flore, who went to market and put the house in order early in the morning, awakened her master so that he found his breakfast awaiting him when he had finished dressing. After breakfast, about eleven o'clock, Jean-Jacques went out to walk, chatted with the people he met, and returned about three to read the newspapers—the one published in the department and one published in Paris, which he received three days after their publication, greasy from the thirty hands through which they had passed, soiled with the grains of snuff that had dropped on them and covered with dirt from all the tables over which they had been dragged. Thus the bachelor passed his time until dinner, and he made that repast last as long as possible. Flore told him all the gossip of the town, the idle stories that were in circulation and that she had collected. About eight o'clock the lights were put out. To retire early, is a method of economizing fuel and light much resorted to in the provinces, but it tends to make people stupid by abuse of the blessing of sleep. Too much sleep deadens and thickens the intelligence.

Such was the life of these two people for nine years, a life at once empty and full, in which the great events were an occasional journey to Bourges, Vierzon, Châteauroux, or even farther, when neither Monsieur Héron nor the notaries of those towns had any mortgage investments. Rouget lent his money on first mortgages at five per cent, with release of the wife's rights when the borrower was married. He never lent more than a third of the real value of the property, and he exacted notes to his order representing a supplementary interest of two-and-a-half per cent, distributed over the time that the loan was to run. Such were the rules his father had urged him always to observe. Usury, that insurmountable obstacle to the ambition of the peasantry, is devouring the country districts. Thus seven-and-a-half per cent seemed so reasonable a rate that Jean-Jacques had his choice of loans; for the notaries who extorted handsome commissions from the people for whom they procured money on such favorable terms, always gave the old bachelor notice.

During those nine years, Flore, insensibly and involuntarily, acquired absolute dominion over her master. In the first place, she treated him very familiarly; and, without failing in due respect, she so overawed him by her superior intelligence and strength of will, that he became his servant's servant. The great child himself invited this domination by allowing himself to be so coddled and petted that Flore with him was like a mother with her son.

And so Jean-Jacques eventually came to have for her the feeling that makes its mother's protection necessary to a child. But there were also ties of a very different kind between them! In the first place, Flore did all the business and managed the house. Jean-Jacques depended upon her so implicitly in every matter of consequence, that without her, life would have seemed to him not difficult simply, but impossible. The girl had become a necessity of his existence; she humored all his whims, and she knew them so well! He loved to look at that bright face which always smiled upon him, the only one that had ever smiled upon him, the only one that would ever wear a smile for him! Her purely material happiness, expressed in the commonplace phrases which form the bulk of conversation in Berri households, and eloquently depicted upon those magnificent features, was in some sort the reflection of his own happiness. Jean-Jacques's pitiful condition when Flore's face was clouded by something that annoyed or displeased her, disclosed to her the extent of her power over him, and, in order to make sure of it, she determined to use it. With such women, to use always means to abuse. La Rabouilleuse undoubtedly made her master enact some of those scenes buried among the mysteries of private life, of which Otway has given us the model in the midst of his tragedy of *Venice Preserved*, in the scene between the Senator and Aquilina—a scene which realizes the magnificence of the horrible! Flore thereupon felt so certain of her empire that it did not occur to her, unfortunately for her and for him, to induce him to marry her.

Toward the close of the year 1815, Flore, at twenty-seven years, had attained the full development of her beauty. Plump and fresh, fair as a farmer's wife of Le Bessin, she was the ideal type of what our ancestors used to call *une belle commère*. Her beauty, which was not unlike that of a superb barmaid, filled out and well-fed, made her resemble, aside from the imperial nobility of bearing, Mademoiselle Georges in her prime. Flore had the same lovely, rounded arms, the same full figure, the same satiny flesh, the same charming profile, but less severe than the actress's. Flore's expression was one of tenderness and sweetness. Her glance did not command respect as did that of the loveliest Agrippina who has trod the boards of the Théâtre-Français since the days of Racine; it invited to sensual delights.

In 1816, La Rabouilleuse saw Maxence Gilet and fell in love with him at first sight. She received full in the heart the mythological arrow, the vivid expression of a natural effect, which the Greeks represented thus, having no conception of the chivalrous, ideal, melancholy passion to which Christianity gave birth. Flore was then too lovely for Max to disdain the conquest. Thus La Rabouilleuse, at twenty-eight, fell a victim to genuine love, an idolatrous, infinite love, the love which includes all methods of loving, Gulnare's as well as Medora's.

As soon as the penniless officer became acquainted
with the situation of Jean-Jacques Rouget and
Flore, with respect to each other, he saw a prospect
of something better than an ordinary love affair in
a liaison with La Rabouilleuse. In order to assure
his future, he could ask nothing better than to become an inmate of Rouget's house, for he soon
fathomed the old bachelor's feeble character. Flore's
passion necessarily had an influence upon Rouget's
life and domestic tranquillity. For a whole month,
the master of the house, who had become immeas-
urably alarmed, saw an ominous, gloomy, sullen
expression upon Flore's face which was wont to be
so bright and smiling. He was compelled to undergo
outbursts of premeditated ill-humor, exactly like a
married man whose wife is contemplating an act of
infidelity. When, in the midst of a succession of
cruel rebuffs, the poor fellow made bold to ask the
reason of this change, her eyes fairly blazed with
hatred, and there was an aggressive, contemptuous
tone in her voice that poor Jean-Jacques had never
heard before.

"*Parbleu!*" said she, "you have no heart or
soul. Here for sixteen years I've worn out my
youth in this house, and I never discovered that you
had a stone there!" she exclaimed, striking herself
on the heart. "For the last two months you've
seen the commandant coming here, a victim of the
Bourbons, who was cut out to be a general, and who
is without a sou, and dropped down in this God-
forsaken province where a man can't earn enough

to buy shoes. He has to sit on a chair all day at the mayor's office, to earn—how much?—six hundred miserable francs—a fine thing! And you with your six hundred and fifty-nine thousand francs out at interest, and your sixty thousand francs a year, and your expenses, thanks to me, less than a thousand crowns a year, everything included, even my petticoats and everything else,—you don't think of offering him a lodging here, when the whole second floor is empty. You'd rather the rats and mice should have the place to dance in than put a human being there, even a man that your father always believed was his son! Do you want to know what you are? I'll tell you: you're a fratricide! But I know why! You saw that I took an interest in him and you don't like it. Although you look like a fool, you are shrewder than the shrewdest,—because you're—Well, yes, I do take an interest in him and a deep interest too—"

"But, Flore—"

"Oh! don't *but Flore* me! You can go out and get another Flore—if you can find one!—for I hope this glass of wine will poison me if I don't leave your old barrack of a house. Thank God, I haven't cost you anything in the twelve years I've been here, and you've had your pleasure cheap. Anywhere else I could have earned a handsome living, doing everything as I do here: scrubbing, cleaning, watching the lye, going to market, cooking, looking after your interests in everything, and wearing myself out from morning till night—And this is my reward!"

"But, Flore—"

"Oh! yes, Flore—You will find plenty of Flores, with your fifty-one years and your poor health and frightful stoop,—I know that well enough! And when you think that you're not amusing—"

"But, Flore—"

"Let me alone!"

She left the room, slamming the door so violently that the house rang with the noise and seemed to totter on its foundations. Jean-Jacques opened the door softly, and walked even more softly to the kitchen, where he found Flore, still grumbling.

"But, Flore," said the imbecile, "this is the first I have heard of your wish; how do you know whether I want him or don't want him?"

"In the first place," she replied, "we need a man in the house. People know that you have ten, fifteen, twenty thousand francs; and if anybody should take it into his head to come and rob you, he'd murder us. For my part, I'm not at all anxious to wake up some fine morning cut in four pieces, as they did to the poor servant-girl who was fool enough to defend her master! But, if it's known that we have a man in the house who's as brave as Cæsar, and who is up to snuff—Max would swallow three robbers in the time it takes to say it —I should sleep easier. Perhaps people will tell you foolish stories—that I love him here, that I adore him there!—Do you know what answer you'll make to them? why, you'll say that you know it, but your father recommended poor Max to you on

his deathbed. Everybody will hold his tongue
then, for the pavements of Issoudun will tell you
that he paid his board at school, *na!* In the nine
years I've been eating your bread—"

"Flore—Flore—"

"There's more than one in this town who has
tried to make up to me, *da!* They offered me gold
chains here and watches there. 'My dear little
Flore, if you'll leave that old fool of a Père Rouget'
—for that's the way they talked to me about you.—
'What, leave him? Oh! yes, of course, an innocent child like that! what would become of him?'
I always answered. 'No, no, where the goat is
tied, she must browse.' "

"That is true, Flore, I haven't anybody but you
in the whole world, and I am too happy. If it will
please you, my child, why, we will have Maxence
Gilet here; he can eat with us—"

"*Parbleu!* I should think so."

"There, there, don't be angry—"

"Where there's enough for one, there's enough
for two," she replied with a laugh. "But, if you
are really good, do you know what you'll do, my
boy?—You'll go and take a walk in the neighborhood of the mayor's office about four o'clock, and
you'll fix it so as to meet Monsieur le Commandant
Gilet and invite him to dinner. If he makes any
objection, just tell him it will please me, and he's
too polite to refuse. And then, between the fruit
and the cheese, if he talks to you about his misfortunes, and about the hulks—you ought to be smart

enough to start him on the subject—you must offer
to take him in here.   If he doesn't seem to like the
idea, don't you be alarmed, for I will find a way to
convince him."

As he walked slowly along Boulevard Baron, the
old bachelor reflected, as far as he was capable of
reflection, upon this incident.   If he parted from
Flore—the bare thought of such a thing bewildered
him—what other woman could he find?—Should he
marry?—At his age, he would be married for his
money and would be deceived even more heartlessly
by his wife than by Flore.   Moreover, the thought
of being deprived of her affection, illusory though
it were, caused him horrible anguish.   And so he
was as agreeable as he possibly could be to Commandant Gilet.   As Flore desired, the invitation
was delivered before witnesses, in order to spare
Max's honor.

Flore and her master were reconciled; but, from
that day, Jean-Jacques detected various little indications of a complete change in the state of La
Rabouilleuse's affections.   For a fortnight she complained, in the shops she patronized, at the market
and to the women with whom she was accustomed
to gossip, of the tyranny of Monsieur Rouget, who
proposed to take his *soi-disant* natural brother into
his house.   But no one was deceived by this
comedy, and Flore was looked upon as an exceedingly artful and shrewd young woman.   Père Rouget
deemed himself very fortunate to have Max installed
in his house, for he found him always ready to

confer little attentions upon him, but entirely without servility. Gilet talked and argued and sometimes walked with him.

As soon as the officer had taken up his quarters in the house, Flore was unwilling to act longer as cook. Cooking spoiled her hands, she said. At the request of the grand master of the order, La Cognette recommended one of her relations, an old maidservant, whose master, a curé, had recently died without leaving her anything and an excellent cook withal, who would be devoted to Max and Flore in life and death. La Cognette promised her kinswoman in the name of those two powers a pension of three hundred francs after ten years of loyal, faithful, discreet and honest service. La Védie, a woman of about sixty, was remarkable by reason of a face disfigured with small-pox and a corresponding ugliness of features. After she entered upon her functions, La Rabouilleuse became Madame Brazier. She wore corsets, she had dresses of silk, of fine woolen and of cotton, according to the season. She had collarettes, very expensive neckerchiefs, embroidered caps, lace tuckers, wore laced boots, and dressed with a richness and elegance that made her seem younger than she was. She was like a rough diamond, cut and mounted by the jeweler so as to display its full value. She wanted to do honor to Max. At the end of the first year, in 1817, she sent to Bourges for a horse, supposed to be of English blood, for the poor commandant, who was tired of walking. Max had discovered in the neighborhood

a former lancer in the Garde Impériale, a Pole
named Kouski, who had fallen upon evil days,
and who asked nothing better than to become one
of Monsieur Rouget's family in the capacity of manservant to the commandant. Max was Kouski's
idol, especially after the duel with the three royalists. Thus, after 1817, Père Rouget's household
was composed of five persons, three of whom were
masters, and the household expenses increased to
about eight thousand francs a year.

At the moment when Madame Bridau returned to
Issoudun, for the purpose, as Master Desroches expressed it, of rescuing an inheritance so seriously
compromised, Père Rouget had arrived by degrees
at a sort of vegetative existence. In the first place,
immediately upon Max's accession to power, Mademoiselle Brazier placed the table upon an episco-
pal footing. Rouget, being thus led into the way of
high living, ate more and more, seduced by the
toothsome dishes prepared by La Védie. But, despite the large quantities of nourishing food that he
consumed, he gained but little flesh. From day to
day he failed visibly, like a man who was completely tired out,—by the labor of digestion perhaps,
—and there were deep black rings about his eyes.
But if he was questioned concerning his health
when he was out walking, he would always reply
that he had never been better in his life. As he
had always been looked upon as somewhat wanting
in intelligence, the constant failure of his faculties
was not noticed. His love for Flore was the only

thing that kept him alive, he had no existence except in her; his weakness where she was concerned
had no limits; he would obey a mere glance of her
eyes, he watched the creature's movements as a dog
watches his master's slightest gestures. In fact, as
Madame Hochon expressed it, Père Rouget at fifty-
seven seemed older than Monsieur Hochon, who was
then eighty.

The reader will imagine, and rightly, that Max's
apartment was worthy of that fascinating youth.
Indeed, in the six years that he had occupied it,
the commandant had made his quarters perfect in
point of comfort, even to the most trivial details, as
much for his own comfort as for Flore's. But it
was only Issoudun comfort; a floor of colored tiles,
elaborate wall-papers, mahogany furniture, mirrors
in gilt frames, muslin curtains with red borders, a
bed with a canopy and with curtains arranged as
provincial upholsterers arrange them for a wealthy
bride, and at that time considered the height of
magnificence; the sort of thing that we see in
ordinary fashion-plates, and so common that Paris
shopkeepers will have none of them for their nuptial
apartments. There were—and a shocking thing it
was, which made much talk in Issoudun—rush
mattings on the stairs, to deaden the sound of footsteps, of course; thus Max could return home at
daybreak without awakening anyone; and Rouget
never suspected his guest's complicity in the nocturnal exploits of the Knights of Idleness.

*

About eight o'clock, Flore, clad in a pretty calico dressing-gown with innumerable little pink stripes, with a lace cap on her head and her feet in fur-lined slippers, softly opened the door of Max's bedroom; but as she saw that he was asleep, she stood silently beside the bed.

"He came in so late," she said; "it was half-past three! He must have a tremendous constitution to stand such amusements. How strong he is, the love of a man!—What were they doing last night?"

"Hallo! there you are, my little Flore," said Max, awaking suddenly, after the manner of soldiers, who are accustomed by the exigencies of warfare to awake in complete possession of their faculties and their self-possession, however suddenly they may be aroused.

"You're asleep, I will go."

"No, stay, there are some serious matters—"

"You did some crazy thing last night, I suppose?"

"Oh! nonsense!—It's a matter that concerns ourselves and yonder old fool. Look here! you never mentioned his family to me.—And now the family are coming down here, to turn us out, of course."

"Ah! I'll give him a good shaking for that," said Flore.

(243)

"Mademoiselle Brazier," said Max gravely, "the interests involved are too serious to go at the matter blindly. Send me my coffee; I'll take it in bed and think over the line of conduct we must adopt. Come back at nine o'clock and we will talk. Meanwhile, act as if you knew nothing at all."

Thunderstruck by the news, Flore left Max and went to prepare his coffee; but, fifteen minutes later, Baruch rushed into the room and said to the grand master:

"Fario is looking for his barrow!"

In five minutes Max was dressed and in the street, and he walked slowly, as if he were out for a stroll, to the foot of the tower, where he saw a crowd of considerable size.

"What's the matter?" said Max, forcing his way into the crowd until he reached the Spaniard's side.

Fario was a little, wizened old man, as ugly as the typical Spanish grandee. A pair of small eyes blazing in holes that might have been bored by a gimlet and were very close to the nose, would have caused him to be taken for a fortune-teller at Naples. The little man seemed mild and gentle, because he was grave and calm and moderate in his movements, and he was called Goodman Fario; but his gingerbread-colored complexion and his apparent mildness concealed from the ignorant and betrayed to the observing mind the half-Moorish character of a Granada peasant whom nothing had yet aroused from his phlegmatic indolence.

"Are you sure you brought your wagon here?"

said Max, after he had listened to the lamentations of the dealer in grain, "for there are no thieves in Issoudun, thank God!"

"It was there—"

"If you left the horse harnessed to the wagon, may he not have carried it off?"

"There's my horse," said Fario, pointing to the creature, which was tethered some thirty feet away.

Max walked gravely to the spot where the horse was standing, so that he could, by raising his eyes, see the foot of the tower, for the crowd was below. Everybody followed him, and that was just what the rascal desired.

"Has anyone in a moment of absent-mindedness happened to put a wagon in his pocket?" cried François.

"Come, search yourselves!" said Baruch.

Shouts of laughter arose on all sides. Fario swore. On the lips of a Spaniard, oaths indicate the last degree of wrath.

"Is your wagon light?" inquired Max.

"Light!" Fario retorted. "If these fellows who are laughing at me had it on their feet, their corns wouldn't trouble them any more."

"It must be devilish light," said Max, pointing to the tower, "for it has flown up to the platform."

At his words, all eyes were raised and for an instant there was something like an *émeute* on the market-place. Everyone pointed to the magic vehicle and everybody's tongue was in motion.

"The devil protects the innkeepers, who sell

their souls to him," said Goddet to the stupefied tradesman: "he wanted to teach you not to leave wagons lying around in the streets instead of putting them under the shed at the inn."

At that apostrophe the crowd hooted, for Fario was commonly reputed to be a miser.

"Come, my good man," said Max, "you mustn't lose courage. We will go up to the tower and find out how your wagon got there. God bless my soul, we'll lend you a hand.—Are you coming, Baruch? —And do you," he said in François's ear, "keep the crowd back so that there's nobody under the platform when you see us there."

Fario, Max, Baruch and three other knights climbed to the tower. During the perilous ascent, Max pointed out to Fario that there were no marks or tracks of any sort to indicate the passage of the wagon. So that Fario believed that there was some witchcraft in the business and he lost his head completely. When they had all reached the summit and examined the surroundings, the thing seemed absolutely impossible.

"How am I going to get it down?" said the Spaniard, whose little black eyes expressed fear for the first time, and his yellow, wrinkled face, which looked as if it could not change color, actually turned pale.

"How?" said Max. "Why, that doesn't seem to me a very difficult matter."

And, taking advantage of the grain-dealer's stupefaction, he moved the wagon by the shafts, with his strong hands, in such a way as to push it off the platform; and, just as it was about to fall, he cried in a voice of thunder:

"Stand from under!"

But there was no danger of accident; the crowd, warned by Baruch and agape with curiosity, had withdrawn to a sufficient distance to see what took place on the platform. The wagon broke in an infinite number of pieces in the most picturesque manner imaginable.

"Now it's down," said Baruch.

"Ah! brigands! ah! *canaille!*" cried Fario, "perhaps it was you who brought it up here."

Max, Baruch and their three companions began to laugh at the Spaniard's insults.

"We tried to do you a service," said Max coldly; "I came near being carried down with your infernal wagon, while I was moving it for you, and that's how you thank us, is it?—What country do you come from, pray?"

"I come from a country where they never forgive," retorted Fario, trembling with rage. "My wagon will be your cabriolet to ride to the devil on!—unless," he added, becoming as mild as a lamb, "you will give me a new one in place of it."

"We will talk about that," said Max, going down.

When they were at the foot of the tower among the first groups of laughing on-lookers, Max took Fario by a button of his jacket and said to him:

"Yes, my good Père Fario, I will make you a present of a magnificent wagon, if you choose to give me two hundred and fifty francs; but I can't promise that it will be made to climb towers, like this one."

This last jest found Fario as cool as if he were concluding a bargain.

"Well! well!" he retorted, "if you should give me enough to replace my poor wagon, it would be a better use than you ever made of Père Rouget's money!"

Max turned pale, and raised his redoubtable fist upon Fario; but Baruch, who knew that the blow would not fall upon Fario alone, picked the Spaniard up like a feather, and said to Max in an undertone:

"Don't make a fool of yourself!"

The commandant, thus called to order, began to laugh and said to Fario:

"If I did accidentally smash your wagon, you have tried to insult me, so we're quits."

"Not yet!" muttered Fario. "But I'm very glad to find out what my wagon was worth."

"Ah! Max, you'll find out whom you're talking to!" said a witness of this scene, who did not belong to the Order of Idleness.

"Adieu, Monsieur Gilet, I don't thank you yet for your surprise," said the grain-dealer, mounting his horse and riding away amid a general shout.

"We will keep the tires for you," cried a wheelwright, who had come to the spot to see the effects of the fall.

One of the shafts had stuck in the ground and stood as straight as a tree. Max was pale and thoughtful,

touched to the quick by the Spaniard's remark.
For five days, Fario's wagon was the principal subject of conversation in Issoudun. It was destined
to travel, as young Goddet said, for it made the
tour of Berri, and the jests of Max and Baruch were
repeated throughout the province. Thus, and this
was what the Spaniard felt most keenly, he
was still the byword of three departments a week
after the event, and the principal subject of gossip.
Max and La Rabouilleuse were also the subject of
innumerable remarks, in connection with the vindictive Spaniard's crushing retort—remarks that
were only whispered at Issoudun, but spoken aloud
at Bourges, Vatan, Vierzon and Châteauroux.
Maxence Gilet was sufficiently acquainted with the
province to know how venomous these remarks
were likely to be.

"One can't prevent people from talking," he
thought. "Ah! I made a bad stroke there."

"Well, Max," said François, taking him by the
arm, "they arrive this evening."

"Who?"

"The Bridaus! My grandmother has just had a
letter from her goddaughter."

"Look you, my boy," said Max in his ear, "I
have reflected deeply on this matter. Neither Flore
nor I must seem to bear the Bridaus any ill-will.
If the heirs leave Issoudun, it must be your people,
the Hochons, who send them away. Examine these
Parisians carefully; and when I have had a look at
them, we will see to-morrow, at La Cognette's,

what we can do to them, and how we can set your
grandfather against them."

"The Spaniard has found the weak spot in Max's
armor," said Baruch to his cousin François as they
returned to Monsieur Hochon's, looking after their
friend as he entered Rouget's house.

While Max was accomplishing this feat, Flore,
notwithstanding her companion's advice, could not
restrain her wrath; and, without knowing whether
she should assist or derange his plans, she burst out
against the poor old bachelor.   When Jean-Jacques
incurred his maid-servant's anger, he was deprived
at one fell swoop of the attentions and vulgar bland-
ishments which were his only enjoyment.   In a
word, Flore made her master do penance.   No more
of the little affectionate phrases with which she
embellished her conversation, in different tones, and
with glances more or less tender: "My little dear,
—my darling—my baby—my ducky—my pet," etc.
A cold, abrupt *you*, ironically respectful, entered
the wretched creature's heart at such times like the
blade of a knife.   That *you* served as a declaration
of war.   Then, instead of assisting the goodman to
arise, chatting with him, anticipating his wishes,
gazing at him with that sort of admiration which all
women have the art of expressing and which charms
the more, the more outspoken it is, and saying to
him: "You're as fresh as a rose!—How well you
look!—How handsome you are, old Jean!"— in
short, instead of regaling him while he dressed with
the drolleries and flattery that entertained him,

Flore left him to dress all alone. If he called her, she answered from the foot of the stairs:

"Well, well, I can't do everything at once, look after your breakfast and wait on you in your room. Aren't you old enough to dress yourself without help?"

"*Mon Dieu!* what have I done to her?" said the old man to himself, receiving one of these sharp retorts when he asked for hot water with which to shave.

"Védie, carry monsieur some hot water," cried Flore.

"Védie?—" muttered the goodman, bewildered by the dread of her anger which was weighing upon him.—"What in the world's the matter with madame this morning, Védie?"

Flore Brazier insisted upon being spoken of as *Madame* by her master, Védie, Kouski and Max.

"She's learned something about you that she don't like, it seems," replied Védie, assuming a profoundly important manner. "You are wrong, monsieur. Look you, I am only a poor servant, and you may tell me that I have no right to poke my nose into your business; but if you should search among all the women on this earth, like the king in Holy Scripture, you wouldn't find madame's equal. You ought to kiss the ground she walks on. Bless me, if you make her unhappy, you are stabbing yourself to the heart! She had tears in her eyes."

Védie left the poor man completely crushed; he

dropped into a chair, gazed into space like a melancholy lunatic, and forgot to shave. These alternations of affection and coldness produced upon this feeble creature, who lived only through the amorous fibres, the abnormal effects produced upon the body by a sudden transition from tropical heat to arctic cold. They were attacks of moral pleurisy, which exhausted him like attacks of physical disease. Flore was the only person in the world who could produce this effect upon him; for to her alone he was as kind as he was foolish.

"Well, you haven't shaved, eh?" she said, appearing at the door.

Her appearance caused a violent shock to Père Rouget, whose pale, thin face flushed for a moment; but he dared not complain of the assault.

"Your breakfast is waiting! But you can come down in your dressing-gown and slippers, for you'll breakfast alone."

Without awaiting a reply, she disappeared. To be compelled to breakfast alone was that one of his penances which caused the goodman the most distress: he liked to talk as he ate. When he reached the foot of the staircase, Rouget was attacked with a violent fit of coughing, for the excitement had revived his catarrh.

"Cough! cough!" said Flore in the kitchen, indifferent as to whether her master heard her or not. —"*Pardè!* the old villain is strong enough to stand it without our worrying ourselves about him. If he ever coughs up his soul, it won't be till after we—"

Such were the amenities which La Rabouilleuse addressed to Rouget in her angry moments. The poor man sat down at a corner of the table in the middle of the room, in a state of profound depression, and gazed at his old furniture and his old pictures with a desolate air.

"You might have put on a cravat," said Flore, entering the room. "Do you think a neck like yours, redder and more wrinkled than a turkey's, is a pleasant thing to look at?"

"Why, what have I done to you, Flore?" he asked, raising to her face his great pale green eyes, filled with tears, and venturing to meet her cold glance.

"What have you done?" she retorted. "Don't you know what you've done? There's a hypocrite! —Your sister Agathe, who's as much of a sister to you as I am to the tower of Issoudun, according to your own father, and who is nothing at all to you, is coming from Paris with her son, that wretched two-sou painter; they're coming to see you—"

"My sister and my nephews coming to Issoudun?" he said in blank amazement.

"Oh! pretend to be surprised so as to make me think you didn't write to them to come! How innocent, to be sure! Never fear, we won't trouble your Parisians, for before they put their feet in this house, ours won't make any more dust here. Max and I will have gone, never to return. As to your will, I'll tear it in four pieces under your nose, do you hear? You can leave your money to your

family as long as we're not your family. Then
you'll see if people who haven't seen you for thirty
years, who never saw you, will love you for your
own sake! Your sister ain't the one to take my
place! A thirty-six carat pious fraud!"

"Is that all it is, my little Flore?" said the old
man. "I won't receive my sister or my nephews.
I swear to you that this is the first I have heard of
their coming, and it's a scheme planned by Madame
Hochon, the old devotee—"

Max, who heard Père Rouget's reply at the door,
suddenly entered the room, saying in the tone of a
master:

"What's the matter?"

"My dear Max," rejoined the old man, happy to
purchase the protection of the soldier, who, by an
understanding with Flore, always took Rouget's
part, "I swear by all that is most holy that I have
just heard the news. I never wrote to my sister;
my father made me promise not to leave her any of
my property, but rather to give it to the church.—
At all events, I won't receive my sister Agathe or
her sons."

"Your father was wrong, my dear Jean-Jacques,
and madame is much more wrong," said Max.
"Your father had his reasons; he is dead and his
hatred should die with him.—Your sister is your
sister, your nephews are your nephews. You owe
it to yourself to receive them kindly, and to us as
well. What would people say in Issoudun?—
Heavens and earth! I have enough on my back

now; all I lack is to hear it said that we keep you
hidden, that you are not free, that we have embittered you against your lawful heirs, that we are
using undue influence to secure your inheritance.—
Deuce take me if I don't break camp at the next
insult! One is quite enough! Let's have breakfast."

Flore, once more as soft as an ermine, assisted
Védie to lay the table. Père Rouget, overflowing
with admiration for Max, took him by the hand,
led him into the embrasure of one of the windows,
and said to him in an undertone:

"Ah! Max, if I had a son, I should not love him
as I love you. Flore was right: you two are my
family.—You are a man of honor, Max, and everything you have just said was very fine."

"You ought to entertain your sister and your
nephew, but make no change in the disposition of
your property," said Max, cutting him short. "In
that way, you will satisfy your father and the
world."

"Well, my dear little loves," cried Flore gayly,
"the salmi will get cold.—Here, my old pet, here's
a wing," she said, smiling upon Jean-Jacques
Rouget.

With that the goodman's horselike face lost its
cadaverous hue, and there was the smile of a *Thé-
riaki* upon his drooping lips, but he was attacked
by another fit of coughing, for the joy of being restored to favor excited him as violently as the grief
of being made to do penance. Flore rose, took from

her shoulders a little cashmere shawl and put it
about the old man's neck like a cravat, saying:

"You're a silly goose to make yourself sick like
that for nothing at all. There, you old idiot! that
will make you feel better, it was against my
heart—"

"What a sweet creature!" said Rouget to Max,
while Flore went to fetch a black velvet cap to
cover his almost bald head.

"As sweet as she is lovely," Max replied; "but
she is quick-tempered like all those who carry their
heart in their hand."

Perhaps we shall be reproved for the crudity of
this picture and told that the outbreaks of La Rabouilleuse's temper are depicted with those realistic
features which the painter should leave in the
shadow. But this scene, repeated a hundred times
with ghastly variations, is, in its vulgar details
and in its horrible truthfulness, the type of the
scenes that all women play, on whatever rung of
the social ladder they may stand, when any selfish
interest has turned them aside from the path of
obedience and they have seized upon the supreme
power. In their eyes, as in the eyes of great politicians, the end justifies the means. Between Flore
Brazier and the duchess, between the duchess and
the wealthiest bourgeoise, between the bourgeoise
and the most superb of kept women, there are no
differences save those due to the education they
have received and the surroundings amid which
they live. The sulky moods of the great lady take

the place of La Rabouilleuse's violent outbreaks. On every floor of the social structure, bitter jests, clever sarcasm, cold disdain, hypocritical complaints, premeditated quarrels obtain the same success as the vulgar sallies of this Madame Everard of Issoudun.

Max described the Fario episode in such amusing fashion that he made the goodman laugh. Védie and Kouski, who had come to the door to hear the story, roared in the corridor. As for Flore, she laughed like a madwoman. After breakfast, while Jean-Jacques was reading the newspapers,—for they subscribed to *Le Constitutionnel* and *La Pandore*,—Max took Flore up to his room.

"Are you sure that he has made no other will since he made you his heir?"

"He hasn't anything to write with," she replied.

"But he may have dictated one to some notary," said Max. "If he hasn't done it, we must take care that he doesn't. We will welcome the Bridaus with open arms, but let us try to turn into cash, as soon as possible, all the mortgage investments. Our notaries will ask nothing better than to change loans: it's meat and drink to them. The Funds are going up every day; we are going to conquer Spain and rescue Ferdinand VII. from his Cortes: so they may go above par next year. Therefore it will be an excellent scheme to invest the goodman's seven hundred and fifty thousand francs in consols at eighty-nine!—But try to have them put in your name. That will be just so much saved!"

"A famous idea," said Flore.

"And as eight hundred and ninety thousand francs would yield fifty thousand a year, you must induce him to borrow a hundred and forty thousand for two years, to be paid half at a time. In two years, we shall get a hundred thousand francs at Paris, and ninety here, so we risk nothing."

"What would become of us without you, my dear Max?" said she.

"To-morrow night at La Cognette's, after we have seen the Parisians, I'll find some way to have them sent back to Paris by the Hochons themselves."

"What a mind you have, my angel! You're a love of a man."

*

Place Saint-Jean is situated in the centre of a
street called Grande-Narette in its upper portion
and Petite-Narette in the lower.   In Berri, the word
narette is used to describe the same conformation of
the land as the Genoese word *salita*, that is to say,
a street on a very steep slope.   The *Narette* is very
steep from Place Saint-Jean down to the Porte
Vilatte.   Old Monsieur Hochon's house is opposite
that in which Jean-Jacques Rouget lived.   Often
one could see, from the window at which Madame
Hochon sat, what was going on at Père Rouget's,
and vice versa, when the curtains were drawn aside
or the doors left open.   Monsieur Hochon's house
resembles Rouget's so closely, that the two must
have been built by the same architect.   Hochon,
formerly collector of taxes at Selles in Berri,
although born at Issoudun, had returned thither to
marry the sister of the subdelegate, the gallant
Lousteau, exchanging his post at Selles for that of
collector at Issoudun.   Having retired from business
as early as 1786, he evaded the storms of the Revolution, giving his full support to its principles, like
all the *honest men* who shout with the victors.
Monsieur Hochon did not steal his reputation as an
inveterate miser.   But should we not run the risk
of repeating ourselves by undertaking to describe
him?   One of the miserly exploits that made him

famous will suffice to give you a perfect conception of Monsieur Hochon.

At the time of the marriage of his daughter, since dead, to a Borniche, it was necessary to give the Borniche family a dinner. The bridegroom-elect, who was presumptive heir to a large fortune, died of chagrin caused by ill-success in business, and above all, by the refusal of his father and mother to assist him. The old Borniches were still alive, overjoyed that Monsieur Hochon took upon himself the management of the business, because of his daughter's marriage-portion, which he made a mighty effort to save. On the day the marriage contract was signed, the grandparents of both families were assembled in the living-room, the Hochons on one side, the Borniches on the other, all in their Sunday clothes. In the midst of the reading of the contract, which was performed with due solemnity by the young notary Héron, the cook entered and asked Monsieur Hochon for some string to tie up the turkey, an essential part of the repast. The ex-tax-collector produced from the depths of his coat pocket a bit of cord, which had evidently been used before to tie some package, and handed it to her; but before she reached the door he called after her: "You must give it back to me, Gritte!" Gritte is the ordinary abbreviation of Marguerite in Berri. You will understand now Monsieur Hochon's character, as well as the jest current in the town concerning this family, which consisted of the father, mother and three children: *the five Hochons*.

From year to year, old Hochon had grown more finical and fussy, and he was at this time eighty-five years old! He was one of the men who stop in the middle of the street and interrupt an animated conversation, to stoop and pick up a pin, saying: "That's good luck!" and stick it into the cuff of their sleeve. He complained bitterly of the modern way of making cloth, remarking that his frock coat had lasted him only ten years. Tall, thin and wrinkled, with a yellow skin, a man of few words who read little, never tired himself and was as punctilious as an Oriental in the observance of formalities, he maintained a very strict regimen in his household, measuring out the food and drink for his family, which was quite numerous, consisting of his wife, born Lousteau, his grandchildren Baruch and Adolphine, heirs of old Borniche, and his other grandson, François Hochon.

Hochon, his oldest son, drafted in 1813 by the requisition of young men of good family who had escaped the conscription and were called *guards of honor*, was killed at the battle of Hanau. He had married, very early in life, a rich wife, in order not to be caught by any sort of conscription; but he ran through all her fortune, foreseeing his end. His wife, who followed the French army at a distance, died at Strasbourg in 1814, leaving debts which old Hochon did not pay, confronting the creditors with this axiom of ancient jurisprudence: *Women are minors.*

Thus people could still speak of the five Hochons,

as the family was composed of the three grandchildren and two grandparents. And the jest still lived on, for a jest never grows old in the provinces. Gritte, at this time sixty years old, was the only servant.

The house, although very large, contained but little furniture. Nevertheless, they could accommodate Joseph and Madame Bridau very comfortably in two rooms on the second floor. Old Hochon always regretted having kept two beds, each accompanied by an old armchair in the natural wood, upholstered, a walnut table on which was a water-pitcher of the so-called watering-pot pattern in its blue-bordered basin. The old man kept his crop of winter pears and apples, medlars and quinces on the straw in those two rooms, in which the rats and mice played at will; so that they exhaled an odor of fruit and mice. Madame Hochon had everything thoroughly cleaned; the paper which had peeled off in spots was secured by wafers; she embellished the windows with little curtains cut from her old muslin dresses. Then, upon her husband's refusal to buy some small list mats, she gave her own bed-rug to her little Agathe, speaking of that mother of forty-seven as: "Poor little girl!" She borrowed two night-tables from the Borniches, and boldly hired two old commodes with copper handles at a second-hand establishment near La Cognette's. She possessed two pairs of precious wooden candlesticks, turned by her own father, who had a mania for turning. From 1770 to 1780 it was the fashion among the men of wealth to learn a trade, and Monsieur Lousteau senior, formerly chief clerk of excise, was a turner, as Louis XVI. was a locksmith. The decorations of the candlesticks consisted of circles made from the root of the rose, the peach and the apricot. Madame Hochon devoted her precious relics to her goddaughter's use! These preparations and this sacrifice redoubled the gravity of Monsieur Hochon, who did not yet believe in the arrival of the Bridaus.

On the morning of the day made memorable by the trick played upon Fario, Madame Hochon said to her husband, after breakfast:

"I hope, Hochon, that you will be civil to Madame Bridau, my goddaughter."

And having made sure that her grandchildren were not within hearing, she added:

"I control my own property; don't compel me to make up to Agathe in my will for a rude welcome here."

"Do you imagine, madame," replied Hochon mildly, "that, at my age, I don't know what ordinary, decent civility is?"

"You know what I mean, you old fox. Be agreeable to our guests, and remember how fond I am of Agathe."

"You were fond of Maxence Gilet too, who is about to devour a fortune that should go to your dear Agathe!—Ah! you warmed a serpent in your bosom that time; but, after all, the Rouget money is bound to go to some Lousteau or other."

After this allusion to the supposed parentage of
Agathe and Max, Hochon started to go out; but old
Madame Hochon, still erect and active, with a round
cap with bows on her powdered hair, a skirt of
changeable silk, tight sleeves and her feet in slippers, placed her snuff-box on her little table, and
said:

"Upon my word, I don't see how an intelligent
man like you, Monsieur Hochon, can repeat those absurd tales, which, unfortunately, cost my poor, dear
friend her happiness and my poor goddaughter her
father's fortune. Max Gilet is not my brother's son,
and I advised my brother strongly to save the crowns
he spent on him. And as to Madame Rouget, you
know as well as I that she was virtue itself—"

"And the daughter is worthy of the mother, for
she seems to me to be a great fool. After losing her
whole fortune, she has brought up her children so
well that one of them is in prison to be tried before
the Court of Peers on a criminal charge of conspiracy à la Berton. As for the other he's in a still
worse plight, he's a painter!—If your protégés stay
here until they have freed that donkey Rouget from
the claws of La Rabouilleuse and Gilet, we shall eat
more than a peck of salt with them."

"Enough, Monsieur Hochon; let us hope they
will save something out of it."

Monsieur Hochon took his hat and ivory-headed
cane, and left the house, astounded by this last remark, for he did not suppose that his wife possessed
so much resolution. Madame Hochon took up her

prayer-book to read the service of the mass, for her great age forbade her going to church every day; she found it difficult to go on Sundays and holidays. Since she had received Agathe's letter, she added to her ordinary prayers a petition to God to remove the scales from Jean-Jacques Rouget's eyes, to bless Agathe and to grant success to the enterprise she had urged her to undertake. Concealing her actions from her two grandsons, whom she accused of being *heretics*, she requested the curé to say masses for Agathe's success during a nine-days' devotion performed by her granddaughter Adolphine Borniche, who acted as her proxy in offering up prayers at the church.

Adolphine, at this time eighteen years old, who had worked for seven years beside her grandmother in that dull household of methodical and monotonous habits, performed her nine-days' devotion the more readily because she longed to inspire some sentiment in Joseph Bridau, that artist whom Monsieur Hochon failed to appreciate, and in whom she took the liveliest interest because of the monstrosities attributed to him by her grandfather.

The old man, the virtuous people, the leaders of society, the fathers of families, approved Madame Hochon's conduct; and their good wishes for her goddaughter and her sons harmonized with the secret contempt that Maxence Gilet's conduct had long since inspired in them. Thus the news of the arrival of Père Rouget's sister and nephew produced two parties in Issoudun: the party of the old,

wealthy bourgeoisie, who had to content themselves
with good wishes and with watching the progress
of affairs without taking part; and that of the
Knights of Idleness and the partisans of Max, who
unfortunately were capable of doing much mischief
to the Parisians and their cause.

On the day in question, about three o'clock,
Agathe and Joseph alighted at the Messageries office
on Place Misère. Although fatigued, Madame
Bridau felt rejuvenated at the sight of her native
province, where at every step something reminded
her of her youthful days. In the existing condition
of affairs at Issoudun, the arrival of the Parisians
was known throughout the town in less than ten
minutes. Madame Hochon went out on her doorstep to welcome her godchild and embraced her as
if she had been her own daughter. After seventy-
two years of an empty, monotonous life, in which,
if she looked back, she saw the coffins of her three
children, all dead and all unfortunate, she had
created for herself a sort of factitious maternity for
a young woman whom she had had in her pocket,
to use her own expression, for sixteen years. In
the gloom of the province she had cherished the old
friendship, the childhood and its memories, as if
Agathe were present; and she was a passionate
advocate of the Bridau interest. Agathe was led
in triumph to the living-room, where the worthy
Monsieur Hochon sat, cold as a stone.

"There's Monsieur Hochon, how do you think he
looks?" said the godmother.

"Why, just the same as he did when I saw him last," said the Parisian.

"Ah! it's easy to see that you are from Paris, you are complimentary," said the old man.

The introductions took place; young Baruch Borniche, a tall youth of twenty-two; young François Hochon, aged twenty-four; and little Adolphine, who blushed and did not know what to do with her hands and still more so with her eyes, for she did not want to seem to be looking at Joseph Bridau, who was the object of the curious scrutiny of old Hochon, and the two young men, but from different standpoints.

The miser was saying to himself:

"He's just out of the hospital, he probably has a convalescent's appetite!"

The two young men were saying to themselves:

"What a brigand! what a head! we shall find our work cut out for us with him."

"This is my son the painter, my good Joseph!" said Agathe at last, pointing to her son.

In the tone in which the word *good* was uttered, there was an effort in which Agathe's whole heart was revealed; she was thinking of the Luxembourg prison.

"He has a sickly look," cried Madame Hochon, "he doesn't look like you."

"No, madame," said Joseph with the brutal frankness of the artist, "I resemble my father, and in his ugliness too!"

Madame Hochon pressed Agathe's hand, which

she held in hers, and glanced at her. The pressure and the glance plainly said: "Ah! my child, I can understand your preferring that scamp of a Philippe to him."

"I never saw your father, my dear boy," said Madame Hochon aloud; "but it's enough for you to be the son of your mother for me to love you. You have plenty of talent too, according to what the late Madame Descoings wrote me, for she was the only one of the family from whom I had any tidings of you of late years."

"Talent!" rejoined the artist, "not yet; but with time and patience, I may win both fortune and renown."

"By painting?"—said Monsieur Hochon with profound irony.

"Come, Adolphine," said Madame Hochon, "go and see to the dinner."

"Mother," said Joseph, "I will go and look after our trunks, which are just coming in."

"Hochon, show Monsieur Bridau the rooms," said the grandmother to François.

As the dinner hour was four o'clock and it was now only half-past three, Baruch went into the town to talk about the Bridau family, to describe Agathe's toilet and especially Joseph, whose worn, unhealthy, strongly marked face resembled the portrait of an ideal brigand. Joseph was the topic of conversation in every Issoudun household that day.

"It seems as if Père Rouget's sister must have

caught a glance from a gorilla during her pregnancy," said one; "her son looks like one."—"He
has the face of a brigand and the eyes of a basi-
lisk."—"They say he's a strange sight, enough to
frighten one."—"All the artists in Paris are like
that."—"They're as wicked as red donkeys and
as mischievous as monkeys."—"It's the same with
their profession."—"I have just seen Monsieur
Beaussier, who says he wouldn't care to meet him in
the woods at night; he saw him in the diligence."—
"He has hollows above his eyes like a horse's, and
he gesticulates like a madman."—"The fellow looks
as if he were capable of anything; perhaps he was
the cause of his brother, a tall, handsome man, turning out ill."—"Poor Madame Bridau doesn't seem
to be happy with him."—"Suppose we take advantage of his being here to have our portraits *drawn* ?"

Such remarks as these, spread through the town
as if by the wind, resulted in arousing inordinate
curiosity. All those who were on visiting terms
with the Hochons determined to call that very
evening in order to examine the Parisians. The
arrival of these two personages in a stagnant town
like Issoudun produced the effect of a piece of tim-
ber falling among a crowd of frogs.

Having deposited his mother's effects and his
own in the two attic rooms and taken note of their
contents, Joseph directed his attention to the great
silent house, where the walls, the staircase and the
wainscoting were without ornament of any sort and
seemed to distil the cold, and where nothing was to

be found save what was strictly necessary. He was impressed by the abrupt transition from poetic Paris to the dull, silent province. But when he went downstairs and found Monsieur Hochon cutting slices of bread for the whole family, he understood Molière's Harpagon for the first time in his life.

"We should have done better to go to the inn," he said to himself.

A glance at the dinner confirmed his apprehensions. After a soup, whose thinness indicated that more attention was paid to quantity than quality, a piece of boiled beef was served, triumphantly surrounded with parsley. The vegetables, on a separate dish at one side of the table, formed an important item in the economy of the repast. The beef was planted in the centre of the table, accompanied by three other dishes: hard-boiled eggs on sorrel opposite the vegetables; a salad all mixed with nut-oil opposite some small jars of cream in which the vanilla was replaced by burned oats, which no more resembled vanilla than coffee made of chicory resembles genuine mocha. Butter and radishes in two plates at the ends of the table, horse-radish and pickles completed this course, which met with Madame Hochon's approbation. The good old soul nodded her head as if overjoyed to see that her husband, for the first day at least, had done things well. The old man answered with a glance and a shrug of the shoulders easy to translate: "See what mad extravagance you make me commit!"

Immediately after it had been carved by Monsieur Hochon in slices resembling the soles of dancing pumps, the boiled beef was replaced by three pigeons. The wine was a native production, of the vintage of 1811. At her grandmother's suggestion, Adolphine had placed a bunch of flowers at each end of the table.

"We must take things as they come!" thought the artist as he looked at the table.

And he fell to like a man who had breakfasted at Vierzon at six o'clock in the morning, on an execrable cup of coffee. When he had eaten his bread and asked for more, Monsieur Hochon rose, felt slowly for a key in the depths of his coat pocket, opened a cupboard behind him, took up a fragment of a twelve pound loaf, ceremoniously cut off another slice, broke it in two pieces, placed them on a plate and passed the plate across the table to the young painter, with the silent self-possession of an old soldier who says to himself at the beginning of a battle: "I may be killed to-day." Joseph took half of the slice and understood that he must not ask again to be helped twice to bread. No member of the family expressed any surprise at this episode, monstrous as it seemed to Joseph. The conversation went on without interruption. Agathe learned that the house in which she was born, her father's house before he inherited the Descoings's, had been purchased by the Borniches, and she expressed a desire to see it once more.

"The Borniches will undoubtedly come here this

evening," said her godmother, "for we shall have the whole town; everybody wants to see you," she said to Joseph, "and they will invite you to call on them."

The servant brought on for dessert some of the famous soft cheese of Touraine and Berri, made of goat's-milk and which reproduces so perfectly the designs of the vine-leaves on which it is served, that it would seem as if engraving should have been invented in Touraine. On each side of the little cheeses, Gritte ceremoniously placed nuts and the indispensable biscuits.

"Come, Gritte, the fruit!" said Madame Hochon.

"But, madame, there isn't any more rotten," replied Gritte.

Joseph roared with laughter as if he were in his studio with his friends, for he understood at once that the precaution of beginning with unsound fruit had degenerated into a habit.

"Pshaw! we'll eat them all the same," he said, with the gayety of a man who has determined to make the best of everything.

"Pray go and fetch some, Monsieur Hochon!" cried the old lady.

Monsieur Hochon, deeply shocked by the artist's remark, brought peaches and pears and Sainte-Catherine plums.

"Adolphine, go and pick some grapes," said Madame Hochon to her granddaughter.

Joseph looked at the two young men with an expression that said: "Do you owe your well-fed appearance to such a diet as this?" Baruch understood the meaning glance and began to smile, for he and his cousin Hochon had never complained. The character of the food served at home was a matter of indifference to young men who supped three times a week at La Cognette's. Moreover, before dinner, Baruch had received notice that the grand master desired all the members at midnight, to be sumptuously entertained by him, and to receive his request for assistance. This repast of welcome offered to his guests by old Hochon will serve to show how necessary the nocturnal feasts at La Cognette's were to the proper nourishment of two tall fellows supplied with their full complement of teeth.

"We will take the liqueur in the salon," said Madame Hochon, rising and motioning to Joseph to ask for his arm.

As they left the room first, she had an opportunity to say to the painter:

"Well, my poor boy, that dinner won't give you indigestion, but I had much difficulty in procuring even that for you. You will have to fast here, you will get enough to eat to keep you alive and that's all. But submit to the table with patience."

The good-humored frankness of the excellent old lady, as she thus alleged charges against herself, pleased the artist.

"I shall soon have lived fifty years with that man without ever hearing twenty crowns jingle in

18

my purse! Oh! if it had not been a question of saving a fortune for you, I would never have invited you and your mother to my prison."

"But how do you stand it?" said the artist innocently, with the gayety that never deserts French artists.

"Ah!" she replied, "I pray."

Joseph shuddered slightly as he heard these words, which so ennobled the old woman in his mind, that he stepped back to look at her face; he found it radiant, wearing such a touchingly serene expression, that he said:

"I will paint your portrait!"

"No, no," said she, "I am too weary of the world to want to remain here on canvas!"

As she uttered those melancholy words in a cheerful tone, she took from a cupboard a flask containing black currant wine, a home-made liqueur of her own manufacture; she had procured the receipt from the renowned nuns to whom we owe Issoudun cake, one of the greatest creations of the French confectioner's art, and one which no cook, pastry-cook or confectioner has ever succeeded in imitating. Monsieur de Rivière, ambassador at Constantinople, used to order enormous quantities of it every year for Mahmoud's seraglio. Adolphine held a lacquered plate filled with the old-fashioned *petits verres* with engraved sides and gilt rims; and as her grandmother filled one, she offered it to some one of the company.

"Pass them round, my father will have one!"

cried Agathe gayly, reminded of her youth by that time-honored ceremony.

"Hochon will go out to his club directly to read the newspapers, and we shall have a moment to ourselves," said the old lady in a low tone.

Ten minutes later, the three women and Joseph were left alone in the salon, the floor of which was never scrubbed, but simply swept, and the hangings in their carved oaken frames with gilt mouldings and all the simple, almost sombre furniture seemed to Madame Bridau to be just as she had last seen it. The Monarchy, the Revolution, the Empire, the Restoration, which respected few things, had respected that salon; their splendors and their disasters had not left the slightest trace.

"Ah! my dear godmother, my life has been a cruelly unhappy one compared to yours," cried Madame Bridau, amazed to find everything as before, even to a stuffed canary, which she had known in its lifetime, and which stood on the mantelpiece between the old clock, the old copper sconces and two silver candlesticks.

"My child," the old woman replied, "storms rage in the heart. The more struggles we have had with ourselves, the more necessary and the greater the resignation. Let us talk of your affairs, not of me. You are exactly opposite the enemy," she added, pointing to the windows of the Rouget house.

"They're just sitting down at the table," said Adolphine.

This young girl, who was a sort of recluse, was

constantly looking out of the window, hoping to gain some light touching the enormities imputed to Maxence Gilet, La Rabouilleuse and Jean-Jacques, concerning whom a few words had reached her ears, when she was sent away in order that they might talk freely about them. The old lady bade her leave her alone with Madame Bridau and her son until some caller should arrive.

"For I know my Issoudun by heart," she said, looking at the two Parisians, "and we shall have ten or twelve swarms of inquisitive acquaintances to-night."

Madame Hochon had hardly had time to tell her guests the various incidents and details relative to the astounding empire that La Rabouilleuse and Maxence Gilet had acquired over Jean-Jacques Rouget, not by the synthetic method in which they have been presented to the reader, but by adding to them the innumerable comments, descriptions and hypotheses with which they were embellished by the kind and unkind gossips of the town—she had hardly time to finish her story when Adolphine announced the arrival of the Borniches, the Beaussiers, the Lousteau-Prangins, the Fichets and the Goddet-Héreaus, in all fourteen persons, whose figures could be seen in the distance.

"You see, my dear," the old lady concluded, "it's no simple matter to take that fortune out of the wolf's jaws—"

"It seems to me so difficult, with such a miserable fellow as you make him out, and a gossiping creature like that lively woman, that I fear it is impossible," said Joseph. "We must remain at Issoudun at least a year to combat their influence and overthrow their domination of my uncle. The fortune isn't worth all that bother, to say nothing of having to degrade one's self by stooping to all sorts of baseness. My mother has only a fortnight's leave of absence, her place is sure and she must not run the risk of losing it. I myself have some important orders to execute in October for a peer of France—orders that Schinner procured for me. And you see, madame, my fortune is in my brushes!"

This harangue was greeted with profound amazement. Madame Hochon, although superior in intelligence to her surroundings, did not believe in painting. She looked at her goddaughter and pressed her hand again.

"This Maxence is a second edition of Philippe," Joseph whispered to his mother; "but more politic and more careful of himself than Philippe.—Well, madame," he exclaimed aloud, "we won't annoy Monsieur Hochon long by our stay here!"

"Ah! you are young and you don't know the world!" said the old lady. "In a fortnight, with a little tact, you can accomplish something; listen to my advice and be guided by me."

"Oh! very gladly," Joseph replied, "for I feel that I am absurdly incapable in matters of domestic policy; I don't know, upon my word, what Desroches himself would tell us to do if my uncle refuses to see us to-morrow."

Mesdames Borniche, Goddet-Héreau, Beaussier, Lousteau-Prangin and Fichet entered the room with their husbands in attendance. After the usual greetings, when the visitors were seated, Madame Hochon had no choice but to present her goddaughter Agathe and Joseph to them. Joseph remained in his easy-chair, occupied in stealthily studying the sixty faces, which, as he told his mother, posed for him *gratis* between half-past five and nine o'clock. His attitude throughout the evening, in presence of the patricians of Issoudun, did not tend to change public opinion concerning him in the little town: one and all took their leave deeply impressed by his mocking glances, disturbed by his smiles, or terrified by his face, which wore a sinister expression to people who did not recognize the oddity of genius.

At ten o'clock, when everybody had gone to bed, the godmother took her godchild to her bedroom and kept her there till midnight. Sure of being undisturbed, the two women confided to each other the disappointments of their life and exchanged their sorrowful experiences. As she realized the vastness of the desert in which a beautiful, unappreciated soul had wasted its strength, as she listened to the last echoes of that mind which had missed its destiny, as she learned of the sufferings of that essentially generous and charitable heart, whose generosity and charity had never had an opportunity to make themselves manifest, Agathe no longer deemed herself the more unfortunate, when she reflected how many distractions and small pleasures life in Paris had afforded her, to allay the bitter afflictions sent by God.

"Do you, my godmother, who are devout and pious, explain my faults to me, and tell me what God punishes in me."

"He prepares us, my child," the old lady replied as the clock struck twelve.

*

At midnight the Knights of Idleness stole along one by one like ghosts under the trees of Boulevard Baron, and walked back and forth there, talking in undertones.

"What are we going to do?" was the first question asked by each one as he approached.

"I think," said François, "that Max proposes to treat us."

"No, affairs have a very serious look for La Rabouilleuse and for him. He has probably thought out some trick to play on the Parisians—"

"It would be a very good thing to send them away."

"My grandfather," said Baruch, "is so dismayed at having two more mouths in the house to feed, that he would be glad of any pretext—"

"Well, knights!" said Max softly, as he joined his companions, "what are you staring at the stars for? They won't drip kirsch for us. Come! to La Cognette's! to La Cognette's!"

"To La Cognette's!"

This cry, uttered in unison, produced a horrible uproar which passed over the town like the shout of troops rushing to the assault; then the most profound silence reigned. The next day, more than one man said to his neighbor:

"Did you hear a frightful yell last night about

one o'clock? I thought there must be a fire some-where."

A supper worthy of La Cognette delighted the eyes of the twenty-two guests, for every member of the order was present. At two o'clock, just as they were beginning to *siroter*,—a word taken from the dictionary of the order, which well expresses the act of sipping wine to taste it,—Max began as follows:

"My dear knights, this morning, in connection with our memorable exploit with Fario's wagon, your grand master was so sorely wounded in his honor by that vile dealer in grain, a Spaniard of Spaniards—oh! the hulks!—that I resolved that I would let the villain feel the weight of my ven-geance, while confining myself strictly to the pre-scribed conditions of our amusements. After reflecting upon the subject throughout the day, I have thought out a method of playing a most ex-cellent practical joke upon him, a joke that may well drive him mad. While avenging the order, which has been insulted in my person, we shall contribute to the support of certain animals held in veneration by the Egyptians, little beasts, which are God's creatures after all, and which men un-justly persecute. Good is the child of evil, and evil is the child of good; such is the supreme law! I there-fore command you all, under pain of displeasing your very humble grand master, to procure as secretly as possible twenty rats each, or, if God so wills, twenty she-rats big with young. Get your contin-gents together within three days. If you can

secure a greater number, the surplus will be grate-
fully received. Keep the interesting rodents without food, for it is essential that the dear little
creatures should be consumingly hungry. Take note
that I will accept mice or field-mice as rats. If we
multiply twenty-two by twenty, we shall have four
hundred and more accomplices, who, if they are let
loose in the old Capuchin church where Fario has
stored all the grain he has purchased, will be likely
to consume a considerable quantity. But we must
be up and doing! Fario is to deliver a large amount
of grain within a week; now, I propose that my
Spaniard, who travels about the neighborhood on
his business, shall find a terrible shrinkage. Gentlemen, I am not entitled to the credit of this invention," he said, observing indications of general
approbation. "Let us render unto Cæsar the things
that are Cæsar's, and unto God the things that are
God's. This is an imitation of Samson's foxes in
the Bible. But Samson was an incendiary and consequently not much of a philanthropist; whereas we,
like the Brahmins, are the protectors of persecuted
races. Mademoiselle Flore Brazier has already set
all her mousetraps, and Kouski, my right arm, is on
the hunt for field-mice. I have said."

"I know where to find an animal," said Goddet,
"that is worth forty rats."

"What is it?"

"A squirrel."

"And I tender a little monkey that will get tipsy
on wheat," said a novice.

"It won't do," said Max. "He would find out where those animals came from."

"We can take there during the night," said young Beaussier, "a pigeon from each of the pigeon-cotes at the farms hereabout, and put them through a hole in the roof, and there will soon be several thousand pigeons there."

"For the next week, then, Fario's storehouse is the order of the night," cried Gilet, smiling at big Beaussier. "You know that they rise early at Saint-Paterne. Let no one go there without turning the soles of his list shoes wrong-side out. Chevalier Beaussier, originator of the pigeons, has charge of the affair. For my own part, I will take good care to sign my name in the piles of wheat. You are to be the quartermasters of Messieurs the rats. If the warehouse boy sleeps at the Capuchins, some of us will have to get him very tipsy and do it very skilfully, in order to entice him far away from the scene of the orgy to which the rodents are to be invited."

"You don't mention the Parisians?" said Goddet.

"Oh!" said Max, "we must study them. Nevertheless I offer my beautiful fowling-piece, which came from the Emperor, a masterpiece of the Versailles factory, worth two thousand francs, to anyone who will invent some way of playing a trick upon the Parisians that will put them in such bad odor with Monsieur and Madame Hochon that they will be turned out of doors by the old people, or

AT LA COGNETTE'S

At two o'clock, just as they were beginning to siroter,—*a word taken from the dictionary of the order, which well expresses the act of sipping wine to taste it,*—Max *began as follows:*

"My dear knights,—"

go of their own accord; it being understood, of course, that the ancestors of my friends Baruch and François are not to be put to too much inconvenience."

"That suits me! I'll think it over," said Goddet, who was passionately fond of hunting.

"If the author of the trick doesn't care for my gun, he shall have my horse," said Max.

After the banquet, twenty brains tortured themselves to concoct a plot against Agathe and her son, conformably to the programme laid before them. But only the devil, or chance, could succeed, the conditions imposed made it such a difficult matter to accomplish.

The next morning Agathe and Joseph went downstairs a moment before the second breakfast, which was served at ten o'clock. The name of first breakfast was bestowed upon a glass of milk accompanied by a slice of bread and butter, of which the members of the family partook in bed or immediately after rising. While awaiting Madame Hochon, who, notwithstanding her advanced age, conscientiously observed all the formalities with which the duchesses of the time of Louis XV. surrounded their toilet, Joseph spied Jean-Jacques Rouget standing in the doorway of the opposite house; he naturally pointed him out to his mother, who did not recognize her brother, he was so utterly changed from what he was when she had last seen him.

"There's your brother," said Adolphine, as she

entered the room with her grandmother leaning on her arm.

"What an idiot!" cried Joseph.

Agathe clasped her hands and looked up at the sky.

"My God, what have they brought him to? Can that be a man of only fifty-seven?"

She examined her brother attentively and saw behind him Flore Brazier, bareheaded, disclosing beneath a gauze neckerchief trimmed with lace, a back like snow and a breast of dazzling whiteness, arrayed as sumptuously as a rich courtesan, in a grenadine dress,—a silk material then in vogue, —with so-called leg-of-mutton sleeves, ending at the wrist in a pair of superb bracelets. A gold chain rustled over La Rabouilleuse's corsage, as she brought Jean-Jacques his black silk cap so that he might not take cold, evidently a premeditated scene.

"That's a beautiful woman," cried Joseph, "and it's a rare sight!—She was made to be painted, as they say! What a color! Oh! what superb tones! what flat surfaces, what rounded outlines, what shoulders! She's a magnificent caryatid! She would be a famous model for a Titian Venus!"

Adolphine and Madame Hochon fancied that he was talking Greek; but Agathe, standing behind her son, made them a sign indicating that she was accustomed to the idiom.

"You consider a woman beautiful who is stealing a fortune from you?" said Madame Hochon.

"That doesn't interfere with her being a fine model! just stout enough, without spoiling the hips and the outlines—"

"You're not in your studio, my dear," said Agathe, "and Adolphine is here."

"True, I am wrong; but as I have seen nothing but she-monkeys all along the road, from Paris here, I—"

"But how am I to see my brother, my dear godmother?" said Agathe, "for if he is with that creature—"

"Pshaw! I will go and see him," said Joseph. "He doesn't seem such a shocking object to me since I have found out that he has wit enough to rejoice his eyes with a Titian Venus."

"If he weren't an idiot," said Monsieur Hochon, who made his appearance at that moment, "he would quietly have got married and had children, and you wouldn't have any chance of obtaining his money. It's an ill wind that blows nobody good."

"Your son's idea is a good one," said Madame Hochon, "let him go first to call upon him; he can make him understand that, if you are to come, he must be alone."

"And in that way, you will offend Mademoiselle Brazier," said Monsieur Hochon. "No, no, madame, swallow the bitter draught. If you can't secure the whole fortune, try at least to get a small legacy."

The Hochons were not strong enough to contend with Maxence Gilet. Before breakfast was done, the Pole brought a letter to Madame Bridau from his master, Monsieur Rouget. Here is the letter, which Madame Hochon asked her husband to read aloud:

"My Dear Sister,

"I learn from strangers of your arrival at Issoudun. I can imagine the motive that has led you to prefer Monsieur and Madame Hochon's house to mine; but, if you come to see me, you will be received as you should be. I should have come first to call upon you, if the state of my health did not compel me to remain at home just at this time. I offer you my affectionate regrets. I shall be charmed to see my nephew, whom I invite to dine with me to-day: for young men are less sensitive than women as to the company they keep. I shall be very glad if Messieurs Baruch Borniche and François Hochon will come with him.

                    "Your affectionate brother,

                              "J.-J. ROUGET."

"Say that we are at breakfast, that Madame Bridau will reply very soon and that the invitations are accepted," said Monsieur Hochon to his servant.

And the old man put his finger to his lips to impose silence on everybody. When the street door had closed, Monsieur Hochon, who had no reason to suspect the intimacy between his two grandsons and Maxence, bestowed one of his most cunning glances upon his wife and Agathe.

"He no more wrote that than I am able to give away twenty-five louis.—It's the soldier with whom we are in correspondence."

"What does that mean?" asked Madame Hochon.

"Never mind, we will reply. As for you, monsieur," she said, glancing at the artist, "you must
go and dine there; but if—"

The old lady checked herself at a glance from her
husband. As he realized the warmth of his wife's
affection for Agathe, old Hochon was afraid that she
would leave a legacy to her goddaughter in case she
should receive nothing at all from Rouget. Although
he was fifteen years older than his wife, the miser
hoped to outlive her, and to find himself some day
in control of the whole of their joint property.
That hope was his fixed idea. Therefore Madame
Hochon had shrewdly divined the surest method of
obtaining some concessions from her husband, by
threatening to make a will. The result was that
Monsieur Hochon sided with his guests. Moreover, an enormous inheritance was involved; and
he desired, in a spirit of social justice, to see it go
to the natural heirs instead of being looted by
strangers who were unworthy of esteem. Lastly,
the sooner the question was settled, the sooner his
guests would depart. As soon as the combat between those who sought to steal the inheritance
and the heirs-at-law, which hitherto had existed
only as a project in his wife's mind, became an
actual fact, Monsieur Hochon's mind, benumbed by
the dull life of the province, awoke to full activity.
Madame Hochon was agreeably surprised when she
discovered that same morning, by virtue of an
affectionate word or two let fall by old Hochon concerning her goddaughter, that the Bridaus had

19

acquired an auxiliary who was so competent and so cunning.

About noon the combined intellects of Monsieur and Madame Hochon, Agathe and Joseph—the two last-named were amazed to see how scrupulous the old people were in their choice of words—gave birth to the following reply, intended solely for Flore and Maxence:

" MY DEAR BROTHER,

" If I have allowed thirty years to pass without returning to Issoudun, without maintaining my former relations with anybody, not even with you, my conduct is to be attributed not only to the strange and unwarranted prejudice my father conceived against me, but also to the misfortunes, and the good fortunes too, of my life in Paris; for, although God made the wife happy, he has sorely smitten the mother. You are probably aware that my son, your nephew Philippe, is in prison, charged with a capital offence, because of his devotion to the Emperor. So you will not be surprised to learn that a widow, who is obliged to accept a humble position in a lottery office, in order to live, has come to seek comfort and assistance from those who saw her born. The profession embraced by the son who accompanies me is one of those that require the greatest amount of study, of sacrifice and of talent before showing any results. Renown comes before fortune in that profession. That is to say that, if Joseph does honor to our family, he will still be poor. Your sister, my dear Jean-Jacques, would have endured in silence the effects of paternal injustice; but forgive the mother for reminding you that you have two nephews, one who carried the Emperor's despatches at the battle of Montereau, who served in the Garde Impériale at Waterloo, and who is now in prison; the other who, when he was thirteen years old, was drawn by a genuine vocation, into a difficult but glorious career. And so

I thank you for your letter, brother, with my whole heart, both on my own account and for Joseph, who will certainly accept your invitation. Your illness excuses everything, my dear Jean-Jacques, and I will come and see you. A sister is always at home in her brother's house, whatever manner of life he may have adopted. I embrace you affectionately.

"AGATHE ROUGET."

"Now the battle is on. When you go and see him, you can talk plainly to him about his nephews," said Monsieur Hochon.

The letter was delivered by Gritte, who returned in ten minutes to tell her masters all that she had seen or heard, according to provincial custom.

"Madame," said she, "since last night they have cleaned the whole house, which madame left—"

"Who is madame?" asked old Hochon.

"Why that's what everybody in the house calls La Rabouilleuse," replied Gritte. "She had let the living-room and everything that concerned Monsieur Rouget get into a shocking state; but, since yesterday, the house is what it was before Maxence went there to live. You can see yourself in all the furniture. La Védie told me that Kouski went away on horseback at five o'clock this morning and returned about nine, with provisions. She says they're going to have the finest dinner, such a dinner as if it was for the Archbishop of Bourges. They're putting the small pots in the big ones and everything is turned topsy-turvy in the kitchen. 'I mean to give my nephew a feast,' the goodman said, and he inquired about everything. It seems

that *the Rougets* were much flattered by the letter.
Madame came to tell me so.—Oh! she has dressed
herself up, I tell you!—such a fine rig! I never
saw anything finer. Madame has two diamonds in
her ears, diamonds worth a thousand crowns each,
so La Védie says, and lace! and rings on her fingers, and bracelets that you'd say came from a real
shrine, and a silk dress as beautiful as an altar-
front!—She says to me: 'Monsieur is delighted
to know his sister is such a good soul, and I hope
she will allow us to make as much of her as she
deserves. We count on the good opinion she'll
have of us after the way we receive her son.—Monsieur is anxious to see his nephew.'—Madame had
on little black satin shoes, and stockings—oh! they
were wonders! There's flowers in the silk and
little holes like lace so that you can see her pink
flesh through them. Oh! she knows what she's
about, I tell you, with a pretty little apron in front
of her that La Védie says is worth our wages for
two years.''

"Oho! we must look out for ourselves," said the
artist, smiling.

"Well, Monsieur Hochon, what are you thinking
about?" said the old lady when Gritte had left the
room.

Madame Hochon called Agathe's attention to her
husband, who sat with his head in his hands and
his elbows on the arms of his chair, plunged in reflection.

"You have to do with a veritable Master Gonin!"

said the old man. "With such ideas as yours, young man," he added, looking at Joseph, "you are not fitted to contend against a tempered blade like Maxence. Whatever I may say to you, you will make some foolish mistake; but at all events, tell me to-night everything that you have seen, heard and done. Now go!—God be with you! Try to have an interview with your uncle alone. If, in spite of all your endeavors, you don't succeed, that very fact will throw some light on their plans but if you are alone with him for an instant, where you can't be overheard, why you must pump him concerning his own situation, which isn't a happy one, and plead your mother's cause."

At four o'clock, Joseph crossed the strait that separated the Hochon mansion from the Rouget mansion—the sort of avenue of sickly lindens, about two hundred feet long, and as wide as Grande-Narette. When the nephew presented himself at the door, Kouski, in polished boots, black trousers, white waistcoat and black coat, preceded him to announce him. The table was already laid in the living-room, and Joseph, who readily distinguished his uncle, walked straight to him, kissed him and bowed to Flore and Maxence.

"We have never seen each other since I was born," said the painter affably; "but better late than never."

"You are welcome, my boy," said the old man, looking stupidly at his nephew.

"Madame," said Joseph to Flore, with the true

artist's impulsiveness, "this morning I envied my uncle his good fortune in being permitted to admire you every day!"

"Isn't she beautiful?" said the old man, his lustreless eyes becoming almost brilliant.

"Beautiful enough to serve as a painter's model."

"Nephew," said Père Rouget as Flore nudged him with her elbow, "this is Monsieur Maxence Gilet, a gentleman who served the Emperor in the Impériale Garde as your brother did."

Joseph rose and bowed.

"Monsieur your brother was in the dragoons, I believe, and I was in the infantry," said Maxence.

"Horse or foot," said Flore, "one risks one's skin just the same!"

Joseph scrutinized Max as closely as Max scrutinized Joseph. Max was dressed as fashionable young men dressed in those days, for he had his clothes made in Paris. Sky-blue trousers, with very ample folds, set off his feet to advantage as they showed only the ends of his spurred boots. His waist was encased in a white waistcoat with buttons of burnished gold, and laced tightly behind so that it could be used as a belt. The waistcoat, being buttoned to the neck, set off his broad chest, and his black satin stock compelled him to hold his head erect, in military fashion. He wore a short black coat, very well made. A pretty gold chain hung from his waistcoat pocket, in which the edge of a flat watch could be seen. He was playing

with a key of the style known as *à criquet,* which
Bréguet had recently invented.

"He's a very good-looking fellow," said Joseph to
himself, admiring as an artist the animated features,
the air of strength and the clever gray eyes which
Max inherited from his father the gentleman. "My
uncle must be exceedingly stupid; this lovely girl
has sought compensation, and the three keep
house together. Such things have been known
before!"

At that moment, Baruch and François arrived.

"You haven't been to see the tower of Issoudun,
have you?" Flore asked Joseph. "If you would
like to take a little walk before dinner, which won't
be served for an hour, we could show you the great
curiosity of the town."

"Gladly," said the artist, unable to discover the
slightest objection to the proposed plan.

While Flore had gone to put on her hat and gloves
and her cashmere shawl, Joseph suddenly sprang to
his feet at the sight of pictures, as if a magician
had touched him with his wand.

"Ah! you have pictures, uncle!" he said, examining the one that had caught his eye.

"Yes," the goodman replied, "they came to us
from the Descoings, who purchased the spoils of all
the religious houses and churches in Berri during
the Revolution."

Joseph was not listening, but was gazing in admiration at one picture after another.

"Magnificent!" he cried. "Oh! what a picture!

They didn't spoil them! Well! well! better and better, just as it is at Nicolet's—"

"There are seven or eight very large ones in the garret, which they kept on account of the frames," said Gilet.

"Let's go and see them!" said the artist, and Maxence led the way to the garret.

Joseph returned to the living-room very enthusiastic over what he had seen. Max whispered a moment to La Rabouilleuse, who led Goodman Rouget into the window recess; and Joseph overheard these words, spoken in an undertone, but so that they should not be lost upon him:

"Your nephew is a painter; you will never do anything with those pictures, so be generous and give them to him."

"It seems," said the goodman, walking with Flore's support to the spot where his nephew stood in ecstasy before an Albani, "it seems that you're a painter—"

"I am only a *rapin* as yet," said Joseph.

"What's that?" queried Flore.

"A beginner," he replied.

"Very well," said Jean-Jacques, "if these pictures will be of any service to you in your profession, I will give them to you—but without the frames. Oh! no, the frames are gilded, and then they're curious things; I'll put in them—"

"*Parbleu!* uncle," cried Joseph delighted beyond measure, "you will put in them the copies I will send you, which will be of the same dimensions—"

"But that will take time, and you will need canvas and colors," said Flore. "You will have to spend money.—Come, Père Rouget, offer your nephew a hundred francs a picture; you have twenty-seven of them.—There are eleven in the garret, I believe; they are all enormous ones and you ought to pay double for them—say four thousand francs in all.—Yes, your uncle can well afford to pay you four thousand francs for the copies, as he keeps the frames! However, you will have to have frames, and they say the frames are worth more than the pictures; there's gold in them!—Say, monsieur," added Flore, shaking the goodman's arm. "It isn't very dear, is it? your nephew will make you pay four thousand francs for new pictures in place of your old ones.—It's a kind way," she whispered in his ear, "of giving him four thousand francs, he doesn't seem to me very well supplied with money."

"Well, nephew, I will pay you four thousand francs for the copies."

"No, no," said honest Joseph, "four thousand francs and the pictures is too much; for, you see, the pictures are valuable—"

"Accept, idiot!" said Flore, "as he's your uncle."

"Very well, I accept," said Joseph, bewildered at the turn affairs had taken, for he recognized a Perugino.

So it was that the artist's face wore a very cheerful expression when he left the house with La Rabouilleuse on his arm, and Max's plans were admirably served thereby. Neither Flore, nor Rouget, nor Max, nor anyone in Issoudun could form any idea of the value of the pictures, and the crafty Max thought that he had purchased Flore's triumph for a mere bagatelle. She held her head very high as she walked along on the arm of her master's nephew, on the best of terms with him in the face of the whole gaping town. People stood at their doors to watch the triumph of La Rabouilleuse over the family. This astounding incident made the profound sensation upon which Max counted. And so, when the uncle and the nephew returned to the house about five o'clock, nothing was talked about from one end of the town to the other but the perfect understanding between Max and Flore and Père Rouget's nephew. The story of the gift of the pictures and the four thousand francs was already in circulation. The dinner, at which Lousteau, one of the judges of the local court and mayor of Issoudun, was present, was a splendid affair. It was one of those provincial dinners which last five hours. The most exquisite wines enlivened the conversation. At dessert, about nine o'clock, the painter, sitting between Flore and Max and opposite his uncle, had become quite intimate with the officer, whom he considered one of the best fellows on earth.

Joseph retired at eleven o'clock, almost tipsy. As for Goodman Rouget, Kouski carried him to bed, helplessly intoxicated; he had eaten like a foreign actor and drunk like the sands of the desert.

"Well," said Max, when he and Flore were left alone at midnight, "isn't this better than making wry faces at them? The Bridaus will be well received, they will take their little gifts and, being overwhelmed with favors, they can but sing our praises; they will go their way in peace and leave us in peace. To-morrow morning we two and Kouski will take down all the pictures and send them to the painter so that he will have them when he wakes up; then we'll put the frames in the garret, and repaper the living-room with one of those varnished papers, covered with scenes from Télémaque, such as I have seen at Monsieur Mouilleron's."

"Oh! yes, that will be much prettier," cried Flore.

*

The next day Joseph did not wake until noon. From his bed he saw the canvases piled one upon another; they had been brought into his room without his hearing a sound. While he was examining the pictures anew, selecting the *chefs-d'œuvre*, studying the style of the different painters and looking for their signatures, his mother had gone to see her brother and thank him, being urged to do so by old Hochon, who, knowing of the foolish conduct of the painter the night before, was beginning to despair of the Bridaus' cause.

"You have some very sly creatures for adversaries," he said; "in all my life I have never seen a man carry himself as that soldier does: war seems to shape young men. Joseph allowed himself to be taken in! He went to walk with La Rabouilleuse on his arm! I have no doubt that they closed his mouth with wine and wretched daubs and four thousand francs. Your artist let Maxence off very cheap."

The far-sighted old man had marked out a line of conduct for his wife's goddaughter to pursue, bidding her enter into Maxence's ideas and cajole Flore, in order to attain a certain measure of intimacy with her, as a means of procuring a few moments alone with Jean-Jacques. Madame Bridau was greeted most affably by her brother, who had learned his lesson from Flore. The old man was in bed, ill from his excessive indulgence of the preceding night. As Agathe could hardly touch upon serious subjects in the first few moments, Max deemed it magnanimous and advisable to leave the brother and sister alone. It showed excellent judgment on his part. Poor Agathe found her brother so ill that she could not deprive him of Madame Brazier's care.

"Besides," she said, "I am anxious to make the acquaintance of one to whom I am indebted for my brother's happiness."

These words afforded evident pleasure to the goodman, who rang for Madame Brazier. Flore was not far away, as may well be imagined. The two female antagonists bowed to each other. La Rabouilleuse waited upon the old man with the most humble and affectionate solicitude; she thought that monsieur's head was too low, she changed the position of the pillows, she was like a bride of yesterday. As a result of her attentions, the old fellow's emotions overflowed.

"We owe you much gratitude, mademoiselle," said Agathe, "for the proofs of attachment you have given my brother for so many years, and for the way in which you devote yourself to his happiness."

"It is true, my dear Agathe," said the goodman, "she has shown me what happiness is, and she is a woman of many excellent qualities, too."

"Indeed, my brother, you could not have rewarded

mademoiselle too handsomely, and you should have made her your wife. Yes, I am too much of a Christian not to wish to see you obey the precepts of religion. You would both be happier by not placing yourself at odds with law and morality. I came, brother, to ask your assistance at a time of great affliction; but do not think that we propose to make the slightest suggestion as to the way in which you are to dispose of your fortune."

"Madame," said Flore, "we know that monsieur your father was unjust to you. Monsieur your brother can tell you," she said, gazing fixedly at her victim, "that the only quarrels we have ever had have been about you. I insist upon it that monsieur owes you the share of the fortune of which my poor benefactor deprived you, for your father was my benefactor,"—she assumed a tearful tone,—"I shall never forget him—But your brother, madame, has listened to reason—"

"Yes," said Goodman Rouget, "when I make my will, you shall not be forgotten."

"Let us not talk about that, brother; you know nothing about me as yet."

From this beginning, the reader will readily imagine how the visit passed off. Rouget invited his sister to dinner two days later.

During those three days the Knights of Idleness captured an enormous number of rats, mice and field-mice, which were set at liberty, one fine night, in the midst of the grain, to the number of four hundred and thirty-six, many of them mothers big

with young, and all famished. Not content with
having procured these boarders for Fario, the
knights made holes in the roof of the Capuchin
church, and introduced a half-score of pigeons taken
from ten different farms, who could bill and coo
there at their leisure, because Fario's warehouseman was enticed away by a rascal, with whom he
drank from morning till night and paid no heed to
his master's grain.

Madame Bridau, contrary to old Hochon's opinion, believed that her brother had not yet made his
will; she proposed to ask him what his intentions
were with regard to Mademoiselle Brazier on the
very first occasion that she was left alone with him,
for Flore and Maxence were luring her on with the
hope which was destined always to be disappointed.

Although the knights were all trying to devise a
method of putting the Parisians to flight, they could
think of nothing but wild impossibilities.

After a week had elapsed—the first half of the
time the Parisians were to remain at Issoudun—they
were no farther advanced than on the first day.

"Your solicitor doesn't know the provinces," said
old Hochon to Madame Bridau. "The thing that
you came here to do can't be done in fourteen days
or in fourteen months; you ought not to leave your
brother, and then you might inspire religious ideas
in his mind. You can't undermine the fortifications
Flore and Maxence have constructed unless you
have priests for sappers. That's my opinion, and
it is time to adopt it."

"You have strange ideas of the clergy," said Madame Hochon to her husband.

"Oh! yes," cried the old man, "there spoke the devotee!"

"God would not bless an undertaking that rested on an act of sacrilege," said Madame Bridau. "To turn religion to such ends—Oh! we should be more criminal than Flore."

This conversation took place during breakfast, and François and Baruch were listening with all their ears.

"Sacrilege!" cried old Hochon. "Why if some honest abbé, clever as I have known some of them to be, knew what a dilemma you are in, he would see no sacrilege in bringing back to God your brother's straying soul, inspiring in him genuine repentance for his sins and making him send away the woman who causes the scandal, while assuring her a proper competence; in demonstrating to him that his conscience would be at peace if he should give a few thousand francs a year to the archbishop's little seminary and leave his fortune to his natural heirs."

The habit of passive obedience the old man had exacted from his children and after them from his grandchildren,—who were also under his guardianship and for whom he was amassing a handsome fortune, acting for them, he said, as if he were acting for himself,—made it impossible for Baruch and François to offer the slightest sign of astonishment or disapprobation; but they exchanged a significant

20

glance, by which they told each other how preju-
dicial and fatal to Max's interests the plan seemed
to be.

"It is a fact, madame," said Baruch, "that, if you
wish to obtain your brother's fortune, the only true
way is to remain at Issoudun whatever time is
necessary to—"

"You will do well, mother," said Joseph, "to
write to Desroches concerning the whole matter.
For my own part, I desire nothing more from my
uncle than what he has given me."

After satisfying himself of the great value of the
thirty-nine pictures, Joseph had carefully taken
out the tacks and pasted paper over them, using
ordinary paste; he had then placed them one
upon another in an immense box and had sent it by
carrier to Desroches, to whom he proposed to write
a letter of advice. The precious freight had started
on its journey the night before.

"You are easily satisfied," said Monsieur Hochon.

"Why, I shall have no trouble in getting a hundred and fifty thousand francs for the pictures."

"A painter's idea!" said Hochon with a disdain-
ful glance at Joseph.

"Listen, mother," said Joseph; "I will write to
Desroches, explaining the condition of affairs here.
If Desroches advises you to remain, you will remain. We can always find another place as good
as yours."

"I don't know what your uncle's pictures are, my
dear," said Madame Hochon to Joseph as they left

the table, "but they ought to be good ones, judging from the places they came from. If they are worth no more than forty thousand francs, a thousand francs each, don't mention it to anybody. Although my grandchildren are well brought up and close-mouthed, they might, without intending any mischief, speak of this alleged find of yours; then all Issoudun would know it, and our adversaries must not suspect it. You act like a child!"

In fact, before noon many people in Issoudun, and notably Maxence Gilet, were informed of Joseph's opinion of the value of the pictures, and the result was that everybody hunted up old pictures they had forgotten, and some execrable daubs were brought to light. Max repented having urged the old man to give away the pictures, and his rage against the heirs, when he heard of old Hochon's plan, was augmented by what he called his own stupidity. Religious influence was the only thing to be feared with such a feeble creature. Thus the information he received from his two friends confirmed Maxence Gilet in his resolution to turn all Rouget's mortgages into cash and to borrow upon his real estate, in order to effect an investment in consols as speedily as possible; but he considered it still more urgent to drive the Parisians away. Now, the genius of all the Mascarillos and Scapins that ever lived would not have solved that problem.

Flore, prompted by Max, declared that it tired monsieur too much to take his usual walk, and that he ought, at his age, to take the air in a carriage.

This pretext was invented to cover the necessary expeditions to Bourges, Vierzon, Châteauroux, Vatan and all the other places which the plan of turning the goodman's investments into cash required Rouget and Max and Flore to visit, without the knowledge of their neighbors. At the end of that week, therefore, all Issoudun was amazed to learn that Goodman Rouget had gone to Bourges to buy a carriage, a step which was explained by the Knights of Idleness in a manner favorable to La Rabouilleuse. Flore and Rouget purchased a dilapidated berlin, with cracked windows and torn leather curtains, that was twenty-two years old and had seen nine campaigns; being part of the goods and chattels of a deceased colonel and friend of Grand Maréchal Bertrand, who, during the absence of that faithful friend of the Emperor, had been entrusted with the care of his property in Berri. It was painted a dark green and was not unlike a calèche, but the pole had been changed so that it could be used with a single horse. It belonged to that class of vehicles which the general shrinkage of fortunes has made so fashionable, and which were then frankly called *demi-fortunes*, although they were originally known as *seringues*. The lining of this *demi-fortune*, sold for a calèche, was worm-eaten, its decorations resembled a veteran's stripes, it rattled like old iron; but it cost only four hundred and fifty francs. Max purchased from the regiment then in garrison at Bourges a fat, honest, half-pay mare to draw it. He had the carriage repainted a

deep brown, purchased a decent second-hand harness, and the whole town of Issoudun was stirred
from centre to circumference while awaiting a sight
of Père Rouget's equipage.

The first time that the goodman used his calèche,
the clatter brought every family to its doorstep, and
there was not a window that had not its quota of
interested spectators.   The second time, the old
bachelor drove as far as Bourges, where, to spare
himself the trouble of the operation advised, or if
you please, ordained by Flore Brazier, he visited
a notary and executed a power of attorney to Maxence Gilet, empowering him to collect and discharge
all the mortgages named in the power.   Flore reserved to herself the duty of assisting monsieur to
transfer his investments in Issoudun and the neighboring cantons.   Rouget called upon the principal
notary at Bourges, and requested him to negotiate
a loan of a hundred and forty thousand francs upon
his real estate.   Nothing was known at Issoudun of
these transactions, they were accomplished so
quietly and so skilfully.   Maxence, being an excellent horseman, could go to Bourges and return on
his horse between five in the morning and five at
night, and Flore never left the old bachelor.   Père
Rouget had consented without remonstrance to the
plan Flore submitted to him; but he insisted that
the certificate for fifty thousand francs a year in the
Funds should be taken out in the name of Mademoiselle Brazier as beneficiary, and in his own name
as legal owner.   The tenacity displayed by the old

man in the domestic contention that this affair
aroused caused Max some uneasiness, for he thought
that he could detect therein some reflections inspired
by the presence of his natural heirs.

In the excitement of these important transactions,
which Maxence desired to conceal from the eyes of
the town, he forgot the dealer in grain. Fario prepared to carry out his contracts for delivery, after
divers journeys and manipulations whose object
was to raise the price of cereals. On the day following his return, he noticed that the roof of the
Capuchins church was black with pigeons—he lived
just opposite. He cursed himself for neglecting to
have the roof examined, and went at once to his
storehouse, where he found that half of his grain
had been devoured. Countless traces of the presence of mice and rats and field-mice revealed another
cause of disaster. The church was a veritable
Noah's ark. But rage made the Spaniard as white
as a sheet when, upon endeavoring to ascertain the
extent of the damage and of his loss, he noticed
that all the grain below had sprouted, as it were,
under the action of a large quantity of water which
it had occurred to Max to introduce into the heart of
the heaps of wheat by means of a tin pipe. The
presence of the pigeons and rats could be explained
by the animal instinct; but the hand of man stood
revealed in this last malicious stroke.

Fario sat on the altar steps, in a chapel, and
buried his face in his hands. After half an hour
of truly Spanish meditation, he saw the squirrel

that Goddet had insisted upon giving him for a
boarder playing with his tail on the cross beam that
supported the arch of the roof.   He rose coolly and
exhibited to his warehouseman a face as calm as an
Arab's.

Fario did not complain; he returned to his
house and went out to hire men to put the good
grain in bags and spread the damp wheat in the
sun, in order to save as much as possible; then he
turned his attention to his deliveries, after estimat-
ing his loss at three-fifths.   But, as his own manip-
ulation had raised prices, he lost still more in
purchasing the three-fifths that he lacked; thus his
total loss was more than one-half.   The Spaniard, who had no enemies, rightly attributed this
vindictive performance to Gilet.   It was proved to
his satisfaction that Max and some others, who were
the authors of all the nocturnal pranks, had hoisted
his wagon up to the platform of the tower, and had
amused themselves by ruining him: his actual loss
amounted to something like a thousand crowns,
almost the entire capital that he had laboriously accumulated since the peace.   Inspired by his thirst
for vengeance, the man displayed the persistence
and craft of a spy who has been promised a handsome reward.   Lying in ambush at night, in the
streets of Issoudun, he finally acquired proof of
the misbehavior of the Knights of Idleness: he
saw them, he counted them, he spied upon their
meetings and their banquets at La Cognette's;
then he concealed himself in order to be the

witness of one of their practical jokes and became thoroughly posted as to their way of employing their nights.

Despite his numerous journeys and his preoccupation, Maxence did not choose to neglect the nocturnal expeditions: in the first place, in order not to arouse any suspicion of the great scheme that was in process of execution with relation to Père Rouget's fortune, and secondly, in order to keep his friends occupied. Now, the knights had agreed to play one of those tricks which are talked about for years. They proposed, on a certain night, to give poisoned pellets to all the watch-dogs in the town and faubourgs. Fario heard them as they left La Cognette's tavern, congratulating themselves in advance upon the sensation the exploit would arouse, and the general mourning that would follow this new slaughter of the innocents. And then what apprehension the wholesale execution would cause, of sinister designs upon the houses thus deprived of their guardians.

"Perhaps it will make people forget Fario's wagon!" said Goddet.

Fario did not need the confirmation of his suspicions afforded by those words; he had already resolved upon his course.

After a stay of three weeks in Issoudun, Agathe recognized, as did Madame Hochon, the justness of the old miser's ideas: it would take several years to overcome the influence that La Rabouilleuse and Max had acquired over her brother. Agathe had made no progress in obtaining Jean-Jacques's confidence, for she had never succeeded in being alone with him. On the contrary, Mademoiselle Brazier publicly proclaimed her triumph over the heirs by taking them out to drive in the calèche, Agathe sitting by her side on the back seat, with Père Rouget and his nephew facing them. The mother and son awaited impatiently a reply to their confidential letter to Desroches. But, on the night preceding that on which the dogs were to be poisoned, Joseph, who was bored to death at Issoudun, received two letters, the first from Schinner, the great painter, whose age made possible a closer intimacy than with Gros, their master, and the second from Desroches.

The first, postmarked Beaumont-sur-Oise, was in these words:

"MY DEAR JOSEPH,

"I have finished the principal paintings at the Château de Presles for the Comte de Sérizy. I have left the panel-borders and the decorations; and I have recommended you so highly, both to the count and to Grindot the architect, that you have only to take your brushes and come. The price is fixed at a figure that will be satisfactory to you. I am going to Italy with my wife, so you can take Mistigris, who will be of assistance to you. The young rascal has talent, and I have placed him at your service. He is fidgeting about already like a jack-in-the-box at the idea of amusing himself at the Château de Presles. Adieu, my dear Joseph; if I am absent, if I do not exhibit at the next Exposition, you can take my place! Yes, dear Jojo, your picture is a masterpiece, I am certain of that; but a masterpiece that will raise a shout of romanticism, and you are laying up for yourself such a life as the devil would lead in a holy-water sprinkler. After all, as that rascal Mistigris says, who twists and makes puns on all the proverbs, life is *un qu'on bat*.* What in the devil are you doing at Issoudun? Adieu.

" Your friend,

" SCHINNER."

Desroches's letter was as follows:

" MY DEAR JOSEPH,

" This Monsieur Hochon seems to me an old man of great sense, and you have given me a most exalted idea of his capacity: he is entirely right. As you ask my opinion, it is this: that your mother should stay at Issoudun with Madame Hochon, paying a reasonable sum, say four hundred francs a year, to indemnify her hosts for the cost of her board. In my opinion, Madame Bridau ought to follow Monsieur Hochon's advice. But your good mother will have countless scruples in dealing with people who have none at all, and whose conduct is a masterpiece of tact. This Maxence is a dangerous fellow and you are quite right: he seems to me to be a much cleverer man than Philippe. The scamp makes his vices serve the ends of his fortune, and doesn't amuse himself *gratis*, like your brother, whose follies had nothing to redeem them. All that you tell me frightens me, but I could not accomplish much by coming to Issoudun. Monsieur Hochon, hidden behind your mother, will be of more use to you than I could be. As for yourself, you may as well return to Paris, for you are of no earthly use in a matter that requires constant attention, minute observations, servile attentions, discretion in speech and dissimulation in action, all of which are antipathetic to artists. If they have told you that no will has been made, depend upon it that one was made long ago. But wills are revocable, and so long as your imbecile of an uncle is alive, he is certainly susceptible to the influence of remorse and religion. Your fortune will be the result of a

---

* The play is on the similar pronunciation of *un qu'on bat*—a man that one beats—and *un combat*—a combat—and cannot be reproduced in a translation.

conflict between La Rabouilleuse and the Church. There will certainly come a time when that woman will lose her power over the goodman and when religion will be omnipotent. So long as your uncle has made no gift *inter vivos* or changed the nature of his investments, everything will be possible when religion has taken the upper hand. Therefore you must request Monsieur Hochon to keep an eye on your uncle's property, so far as he can do so. It is important to know if the real estate is mortgaged, and how and in whose name his money is invested. It is so easy to arouse fears for his life in an old man, in case he is stripping himself of his property in favor of strangers, that an heir-at-law, however little craft he may command, might put a stop to such a spoliation at the outset. But is your mother, with her ignorance of the world, her unselfishness, her religious principles, capable of running such a machine?—However, I can do nothing more than open your eyes. Everything you have done thus far has been calculated to give your antagonists the alarm, and perhaps they are putting themselves in shape for the battle!"

"That's what I call a consultation that amounts to something," cried Monsieur Hochon, proud to have earned the appreciation of a Paris solicitor.

"Oh! Desroches is a fine fellow," said Joseph.

"It might be well to read that letter to the two women," suggested the old miser.

"Here it is," said Joseph, handing him the letter. "For my own part, I propose to leave to-morrow, and I will go and pay my respects to my uncle."

"Ah!" said Monsieur Hochon, "Monsieur Desroches, in a postscript, asks you to burn the letter."

"You can burn it after you have shown it to my mother," said the painter.

Joseph dressed, crossed the little square and made his appearance at his uncle's just as he was finishing his breakfast.   Max and Flore were at the table.

"Don't disturb yourself, my dear uncle, I came to bid you good-bye."

"Are you going away?" said Max, exchanging a glance with Flore.

"Yes, I have some work to do at Monsieur de Sérizy's château; I am especially anxious to go there, as the count's arms are long enough to be of service to my poor brother in the Chamber of Peers."

"Very well, work away," said Goodman Rouget with a stupid air; he seemed to Joseph extraordinarily changed.   "A man must work—I am sorry you are going."

"Oh! my mother will remain some little time longer," said Joseph.

Max made a movement with his lips, which the housekeeper noticed, and which signified: "They mean to follow the plan Baruch told me about."

"I am very glad I came," said Joseph, "for I have had the pleasure of making your acquaintance and you have enriched my studio—"

"Yes," said La Rabouilleuse, "instead of telling your uncle the value of his pictures, which are said to be worth more than a hundred thousand francs, you shipped them off to Paris in a hurry. Poor dear man, he's like a child!—We've been told at Bourges that there was a little Poulet,—what do you call him?—a Poussin that used to be in the choir of the cathedral before the Revolution, that is worth thirty thousand francs by itself."

"That wasn't well done of you, nephew," said the old man at a sign from Max which Joseph could not see.

"Come, honestly now," interposed the soldier with a laugh, "on your honor, what do you think your pictures are worth? *Parbleu!* you played a game on your uncle and you were within your right; an uncle is made to be pillaged! Nature denied me any uncles; but, *sacrebleu!* if I had had any, I would not have spared them."

"Did you know what *your* pictures were worth, monsieur?" said Flore to Rouget.—"How much did you say, Monsieur Joseph?"

"Why," said the painter, turning as red as a beet, "the pictures are worth something."

"They say you reckoned them at a hundred and fifty thousand francs at Monsieur Hochon's," said Flore. "Is that true?"

"Yes," said the painter, who was as straightforward as a child.

"And did you intend to give your nephew a hundred and fifty thousand francs?" Flore asked the goodman.

"Never, never!" replied Rouget, with Flore's eyes fixed upon his face.

"There's a way to arrange all this," said Joseph, "and that is to return them to you, uncle!"

"No, no, keep them," said the goodman.

"I will send them back to you, uncle," Joseph continued, wounded by the insulting silence of Maxence Gilet and Flore Brazier. "I have in my brush the means of making my fortune, without owing anything to anybody, even to my uncle.—I salute you, mademoiselle.—I wish you a very good day, monsieur."

And Joseph crossed the square in a state of irritation which all artists will understand. The whole Hochon family was in the salon. When they saw Joseph gesticulating and talking to himself, they asked him what the matter was. Thereupon the painter, open as the day, described the scene that had taken place, before Baruch and François, and, within two hours it became the principal topic of conversation throughout the town, where everyone embellished it with details, more or less amusing, of his own invention. Some maintained that the painter had been roughly handled by Max; others that he had shown a lack of respect for Mademoiselle Brazier, and that Max had turned him out of doors.

"What a child your child is!" said Hochon to Madame Bridau. "The booby has been taken in by a scene that they have been keeping in reserve for his last day. For the last fortnight, Max and La Rabouilleuse have known the value of the pictures, which he was foolish enough to mention here before my grandchildren, who couldn't make haste enough to chatter about it to the whole world. Your artist ought to have gone away unexpectedly."

"My son does right to return the pictures if they are so valuable," said Agathe.

"If they're worth, as he says, two hundred thousand francs, it's rank idiocy to have placed himself in a position where he must return them," said old Hochon; "for you would have at least that much of the property; whereas, in the way things are going now, you won't get anything!—Why, this is almost a sufficient reason for your brother to refuse to see you again."

*

Between midnight and one o'clock, the Knights of Idleness began their gratuitous distribution of comestibles to the dogs of the town. This memorable performance was not completed until three o'clock in the morning, at which hour the graceless rascals repaired to La Cognette's to sup. At half-past four, just at dawn, they returned home. As Max was turning from Rue de l'Avenier into Grand' Rue, Fario, who was lying in ambush in a recess, dealt him a blow with a knife, straight to the heart, withdrew the blade and fled to the ditches of Vilatte, where he wiped the knife on his handkerchief. He then washed his handkerchief in the Rivière-Forcée and calmly returned to Saint-Paterne, where he climbed up to a window that he had left open, and went to bed. He was awakened by his new warehouseman, who found him in a deep sleep.

As he fell, Max uttered a terrible cry, which nobody could misunderstand. Lousteau-Prangin, the son of a magistrate who was a distant relative of the former subdelegate's family, and Goddet, who lived at the foot of Grand' Rue, ran up the hill at full speed, saying to themselves:

"Someone has killed Max!" and shouting "Help!"

But no dog barked, and the people were so used

to the ruses of the disturbers of the night, that no one rose. When the two knights arrived, Max had fainted. It was necessary to go and arouse the senior Goddet. Max had recognized Fario; but when, at five o'clock in the morning, he recovered consciousness, when he saw that several people were gathered about him and felt sure that his wound was not mortal, it occurred to him that he might use the assault to good advantage, and he exclaimed in a feeble voice:

"I thought I saw the eyes and face of that infernal painter!"

Thereupon Lousteau-Prangin hurried to his father, the examining magistrate. Max was carried home by Père Cognet, the younger Goddet and two neighbors whom they aroused from their sleep. La Cognette and Goddet senior walked beside Max, who lay on a mattress borne upon two poles. Monsieur Goddet refused to do anything until Max was in bed. The wounded man's bearers naturally looked across at Monsieur Hochon's door while Kouski was dressing, and they saw the servant sweeping. In that house, as in most provincial houses, the doors were opened very early. The only words Max had uttered had aroused suspicion, and Monsieur Goddet the elder called out:

"Is Monsieur Joseph Bridau in bed, Gritte?"

"He went out about half-past four," she said; "he walked up and down his room all night; I don't know what was the matter with him."

This naïve reply was followed by murmurs of

horror and exclamations which led the woman to cross the square, curious to see whom they were bringing to Père Rouget's.

"Well, your painter's a fine fellow!" someone said to her.

And the procession entered the house, leaving the servant speechless: she had seen Max lying on the mattress, his shirt soaked with blood, and apparently dying.

An artist will divine what had kept Joseph awake and excited through the night: he imagined himself the byword of the bourgeois of Issoudun; they would take him for a cut-purse, for anything but the one thing he wished to be, an upright man, a loyal artist! Ah! he would have given his picture for the power to fly like a swallow to Paris and throw his uncle's pictures in Max's face. To be the despoiled and be considered the despoiler!—what a mockery! So it was that, early in the morning, he had rushed out to the avenue of poplars that leads to Tivoli, to give free rein to his agitation. While the innocent youth was promising himself, as a consolation, that he would never return to that province, Max was planning an outrage of the most shocking kind to a sensitive mind. When Monsieur Goddet had probed the wound and discovered that the knife struck a small wallet and, very luckily, was turned aside thereby, although inflicting a frightful wound, he did what all doctors, and especially provincial surgeons are wont to do—he gave himself an air of importance by saying that *he could not answer for Max's life as yet;* then, having dressed the vicious trooper's side, he left the house.

This decree of science was communicated by the surgeon to La Rabouilleuse, Jean-Jacques Rouget, Kouski and La Védie.   La Rabouilleuse returned to her dear Max, weeping bitterly, while Kouski and La Védie informed the people assembled at the door that the commandant's life was almost despaired of.   This news resulted in attracting about two hundred people, who stood in groups on Place Saint-Jean and the two Narettes.

"I shall not be more than a month in bed, and I know who struck me," said Max to La Rabouilleuse. "But we will take advantage of the opportunity to get rid of the Parisians.   I have already said that I thought I recognized the painter; so do you assume that I am going to die and try to have Joseph Bridau arrested; we'll let him eat prison fare for a day or two.   I think I know the mother well enough to be sure that she will hurry back to Paris with her painter.   Then we shall have no more reason to fear the priests that they intended to let loose on our old idiot."

When Flore went downstairs, she found the crowd quite ready to adopt such impressions as she chose to give it; she appeared with tears in her eyes, and observed, sobbing, that the painter, *who had a villainous face anyway,* had quarreled hotly with Max the night before concerning some pictures he had *prigged* from Père Rouget.

"The brigand—for you only have to look at him to be sure that's what he is—thinks that if Max were out of the way, his uncle would leave him his money; as if," said she, "a brother isn't a nearer relation to us than a nephew! Max is Doctor Rouget's son. *The old man told me so before he died—*"

"Ah! he intended to do the job just as he was going away, he arranged it very nicely," said one of the Knights of Idleness; "he's going to-day."

"Max hasn't a single enemy in Issoudun," said another.

"Besides, Max recognized the painter," said La Rabouilleuse.

"Where is the damned Parisian?—Let's find him!" someone cried.

"Find him?"—was the reply. "He left Monsieur Hochon's house at daybreak.

One of the knights hastened to Monsieur Mouilleron's office. The crowd increased from moment to moment and the sound of voices became threatening. Grande-Narette was filled with animated groups. Others were standing in front of the church of Saint-Jean. A party of men occupied the Porte Vilatte at which Petite-Narette ends. It was impossible to pass out of Place Saint-Jean above or below. You would have said that some long procession had halted there. Messieurs Lousteau-Prangin and Mouilleron, the commissioner of police, the lieutenant of the gendarmerie and his brigadier, accompanied by two gendarmes, had

some difficulty in forcing their way through the
crowd to Place Saint-Jean, which they entered between two solid lines of people, whose shouts and
exclamations might and did prejudice them against
the Parisian who was so unjustly accused, but to
whom circumstances seemed to point.

After a conference between Max and the magistrates, Monsieur Mouilleron detailed the commissioner of police with the brigadier and one gen-
darme, to inspect what, in the language of the
public prosecutor's office, is called *the theatre of
the crime*. Then Messieurs Mouilleron and Lousteau-Prangin, accompanied by the lieutenant of
gendarmes, went from Père Rouget's across the
square to Monsieur Hochon's house, where two gendarmes were on guard at the foot of the garden and
two others at the door. The crowd was still increasing. The whole town was assembled in
Grand' Rue, in a state of intense excitement.

Gritte had already rushed home in dismay and
said to her master:

"Monsieur, they're going to sack your house.—
The whole town is up in arms! Monsieur Maxence
Gilet has been assaulted and he's going to die—
and they say it was Monsieur Joseph that struck
him!"

Monsieur Hochon dressed himself hurriedly and
went downstairs; but finding himself confronted by
a furious mob he turned back abruptly and bolted
his door. By questioning Gritte, he learned that
his guest had left the house at daybreak after

having paced his room all night in great excitement, and that he had not returned. Greatly alarmed, he went to Madame Hochon's room and, finding that the noise had awakened her, he told her the shocking news, which, whether true or false, had brought all Issoudun in a frenzy to Place Saint-Jean.

"Of course he is innocent," said Madame Hochon.

"But before his innocence is established they may break in and pillage us," said Monsieur Hochon, who had become as pale as a ghost.—He had gold in his cellar.

"How is Agathe?"

"She is sleeping like a dormouse!"

"Ah! so much the better," said Madame Hochon, "I wish she could sleep until the affair is cleared up. Such a blow might kill the poor dear!"

But Agathe was awake, and had gone downstairs half-dressed, Gritte's reticence when she questioned her having sown confusion in her head and her heart. She found Madame Hochon, with pale face and eyes filled with tears, standing with her husband at one of the windows of the living-room.

"Courage, my dear! God sends us our afflictions," said the old woman. "Joseph is accused—"

"Of what?"

"Of an evil deed that he cannot have committed," Madame Hochon replied.

When she heard those words and saw the lieutenant of gendarmes with Messieurs Mouilleron and Lousteau-Prangin enter the room, Agathe fainted.

"Here," said Monsieur Hochon to his wife and

Gritte, "take Madame Bridau away; women are always in the way at such times as this. Both of you go to her room with her.—Be seated, messieurs," added the old man. "The mistake to which I am indebted for your visit will soon be cleared up, I trust."

"Even if there is a mistake," said Monsieur Mouilleron, "the crowd is in such a state of exasperation, and the excitement runs so high that I have fears for the safety of the accused. I should like to lock him up at the Palais de Justice and satisfy the people."

"Who would have suspected that Monsieur Maxence Gilet could inspire such affection?"—said Lousteau-Prangin.

"One of my men informs me that twelve hundred people are pouring into the square from the Faubourg de Rome at this moment, yelling for the culprit's death," observed the lieutenant of gendarmes.

"Where is your guest?" Monsieur Mouilleron asked Monsieur Hochon.

"He went out to walk in the country, I think—"

"Recall Gritte," said the examining magistrate gravely; "I was hoping that Monsieur Bridau had not left the house. You are aware, of course, that the crime was committed only a few steps from here, at daybreak?"

While Hochon went to fetch Gritte, the three functionaries exchanged significant glances.

"I never liked that painter's face," said the lieutenant to Monsieur Mouilleron.

"My girl," said the magistrate to Gritte as she entered the room, "you saw Monsieur Joseph Bridau leave the house this morning, they tell me?"

"Yes, monsieur," she replied, trembling like a leaf.

"At what time?"

"As soon as I got up; he walked up and down his room in the night and he was dressed when I came down."

"Was it light?"

"Just daybreak."

"He seemed excited?"

"Dear me, yes! it seemed to me as if something was the matter."

"Send one of your men for my clerk," said Lousteau-Prangin to the lieutenant, "and let him bring some warrants of—"

"*Mon Dieu!* don't be hasty," said Monsieur Hochon. "The young man's agitation is susceptible of a very different explanation from the premeditation of a crime: he was to start for Paris to-day, because of a matter in which Gilet and Mademoiselle Flore cast some suspicion on his probity."

"Yes, the affair of the pictures," said Monsieur Mouilleron. "It was the subject of a very warm dispute yesterday, and an artist is very hot-headed they say."

"Who in all Issoudun had any reason for killing Maxence?" asked Lousteau. "No one; no jealous

husband, or anyone else, for the boy never injured
a soul."

"But what was Monsieur Gilet doing in the
streets of Issoudun at half-past four o'clock?" demanded Monsieur Hochon.

"Stay, Monsieur Hochon, let us attend to our
business," retorted Mouilleron; "you don't know
all: Max recognized your painter."

At that moment a great uproar arose at the
farther end of the town, and became louder and
louder, rolling along Grande-Narette like a peal of
thunder.

"There he is! there he is! he's arrested!—"

These words could be distinguished above the
rumbling accompaniment of a horrible clamor. The
explanation was this: poor Joseph Bridau, as he
was quietly returning by the mill of Landrôle, in
order to be at home for breakfast, was recognized,
when he reached Place Misère, by all the groups at
once. Luckily for him, two gendarmes came running up and rescued him from the men from Faubourg de Rome, who had already seized him
unceremoniously by the arms while clamoring for
his death.

"Room! room!" cried the gendarmes, and they
called two of their comrades to take their stations,
one in front of Bridau and the other behind him.

"You see, monsieur," said one of the men who
held the painter, "our skins are in danger as well
as your own. Innocent or guilty, we must protect
you against the uprising caused by the assault on

Commandant Gilet; and these people don't trouble
themselves to accuse you of it, they believe you
are the murderer, they are easily influenced.   Monsieur Gilet is adored by these people, who—just
look at them!—act as if they proposed to do justice
on you themselves.   Ah! we saw them in 1830
beating the excise officers, who were in a very uncomfortable plight."

Joseph Bridau became as pale as death, and had
to summon his strength in order to be able to walk.

"After all," he said, "I am innocent; let us go
on!"

The artist had his cross to bear!   He was hooted
at, insulted, threatened with death, during that
ghastly journey from Place Misère to Place Saint-
Jean.   The gendarmes were obliged to draw their
sabres upon the furious crowd, who threw stones at
them.   They came near wounding the gendarmes,
and some of the projectiles struck Joseph's legs and
shoulders and hat.

"Here we are!" said one of the gendarmes, as
the party entered Monsieur Hochon's living-room,
"and it's been no easy work, lieutenant."

"The next thing to do is to disperse this crowd,
and I can see only one way to do it, messieurs," the
officer said to the magistrates.   "That is to put
Monsieur Bridau between you two and take him to
the Palais de Justice; I and all my gendarmes will
surround you.   It's impossible to answer for consequences when you have to do with six thousand
madmen—"

"You are right," said Monsieur Hochon, still trembling for his gold.

"If that is the best you can do in the way of protecting an innocent man at Issoudun," said Joseph, "I congratulate you. I have already come near being stoned to death—"

"Do you want to see your host's house taken by assault and pillaged?" said the lieutenant. "Can we keep back with our swords a whole mob pressed on from behind by a street full of angry men, who don't know the forms of law?"

"Very well! let us be off, messieurs; we will have an explanation later," said Joseph, recovering all his self-possession.

"Make room, my friends!" said the lieutenant; "*he* is under arrest and we are taking him to the palace."

"Respect the law, my friends!" said Monsieur Mouilleron.

"Wouldn't you rather see him guillotined?" said one of the gendarmes to a threatening group.

"Yes, yes," said one fierce fellow, "he will be guillotined."

"They're going to guillotine him," echoed the women.

At the end of Grande-Narette, the people said to one another:

"They're taking him off to guillotine him, they have found the knife on him!—Oh! the cur!—There's your Parisian!—The fellow has crime written on his face!"

Although all Joseph's blood had rushed to his head, he was wonderfully calm and cool during the journey from Place Saint-Jean to the Palais de Justice. Nevertheless, he was very glad when he was safely seated in Monsieur Lousteau-Prangin's office.

"It is unnecessary, messieurs, I am sure, for me to tell you that I am innocent," he said, addressing Monsieur Mouilleron, Monsieur Lousteau-Prangin and the clerk; "I can only request you to assist me to establish my innocence. I know nothing of the affair."

When the magistrate had pointed out to Joseph all the facts that seemed to raise a presumption of his guilt, concluding with Max's declaration, Joseph was dumfounded.

"Why, it was after five o'clock when I left the house," he said. "I went down Grand' Rue, and at half-past five I was looking at the façade of your church of Saint-Cyr. I talked with the bell-ringer, who had just rung the *Angelus*, and asked him various questions about the building, which has a curious unfinished appearance to me. Then I walked through the Vegetable Market, where there were already some few women. From there I walked through Place Misère and across Pont aux Anes, to the mill of Landrôle, where I stood and watched the ducks for five or six minutes; the mill hands must have noticed me. I saw some women going to the stream to wash, and they must be there still; they began to laugh at me and remarked that

I was not handsome. I answered that there were jewels in ugly faces. From there, I walked along the broad avenue as far as Tivoli, where I talked with the gardener.—Send and verify these statements, and do not put me under arrest; for I give you my word that I will remain in your office until you are convinced of my innocence."

This straightforward speech, delivered without hesitation, and with the unconstrained manner of a man who nad no fear for the outcome, made some impression upon the magistrates.

"Very good; we must find all these people and summon them here," said Mouilleron, "but it's not an affair of a single day. Make up your mind, therefore, in your own interest, to remain in custody here."

"If I may write to my mother and console her, poor woman.—Oh! you shall read the letter."

This request was too reasonable not to be granted, and Joseph wrote these few words:

" Have no uneasiness, my dear mother; the error of which I am the victim will soon be corrected; I have already furnished the means of correcting it. To-morrow, or perhaps this evening, I shall be free. I embrace you and beg you to tell Monsieur and Madame Hochon how deeply I regret this trouble, for which I am in no way to blame, for it is the result of an accident which I do not yet understand."

When the letter arrived, Madame Bridau was suffering from a very severe nervous attack, and the potions that Monsieur Goddet was trying to force her to swallow had no effect. But the letter was like a soothing balm. After another paroxysm or two, she fell into the state of prostration that follows such attacks. When Monsieur Goddet next called upon his patient, he found her regretting that she had left Paris.

"God has punished me," she said with tears in her eyes. "Was it not my duty to trust to Him and depend upon His loving-kindness to make me my brother's heir?"

"Madame, if your son is innocent, Maxence is an infernal villain," Monsieur Hochon whispered to her, "and we shall not come out ahead in this business; so return to Paris.".

"Well, how is Monsieur Gilet?" Madame Hochon asked Goddet.

"The wound, although serious, is not mortal. He will be all right after a month's nursing. I left him writing to Monsieur Mouilleron to request your son's release, madame," he said to his patient. "Ah! Max is a fine fellow. I told him what condition you were in, and he then recalled a detail of his assassin's costume which satisfied him that it could not have been your son: the murderer wore felt shoes, and it is very certain that your son wore boots when he left the house—"

"Ah! may God forgive him the wrong he has done me!"

At nightfall a man had brought Gilet a letter, in printed characters, thus conceived:

" Captain Gilet should not leave an innocent man in the hands of the law. The man who dealt the blow promises not to repeat it, if Monsieur Gilet causes Monsieur Joseph Bridau's release without denouncing the real culprit."

Having read this letter and burned it, Max wrote a letter to Monsieur Mouilleron embodying the circumstance reported by Monsieur Goddet, and begging him to release Joseph and to call upon him, so that he might explain the matter. At the moment that this letter reached Monsieur Mouilleron, Lousteau-Prangin had just completed the examination of the bell-ringer, one of the vegetable women, the laundresses, the mill hands at Landrôle and the gardener at Frapesle, and had satisfied himself of the truth of Joseph's statements. Max's letter completed the exculpation of the accused man, whom Monsieur Mouilleron in person escorted to Monsieur Hochon's. Joseph was welcomed by his mother with such an outburst of genuine maternal affection, that the poor misunderstood youth gave thanks to chance, as the husband in La Fontaine's fable gave thanks to the robber, for the annoyance which brought forth such demonstrations of affection.

"Oh!" said Monsieur Mouilleron, with a very knowing air, "I saw at once, from the way you looked at the angry mob, that you were innocent; but, notwithstanding my conviction, I know Issoudun so well that I was sure the best way to protect you was to take you into custody, as we did. Ah! you did carry yourself wonderfully!"

"I was thinking of something else," the artist

replied simply. "An officer told me once that he was arrested in Dalmatia, under circumstances almost identical with these, by an excited mob as he was returning from a walk. The similarity of our experiences was in my mind, and I was looking at all those faces with the idea of painting an *émeute* in 1793.—In fact I was saying to myself: 'You idiot! you have got just what you deserve for coming down here in quest of an inheritance, instead of painting in your studio.'"

"If you will allow me to offer you a little advice," said the king's attorney, "you will hire a carriage from the master of the post and start at eleven o'clock to-night for Bourges and take the Paris diligence there."

"That is my advice also," said Monsieur Hochon, who was burning with the desire to say farewell to his guest.

"And I desire nothing so much as to leave Issoudun, although I leave my only friend behind me," said Agathe, taking Madame Hochon's hand and kissing it. "When shall I see you again?"

"Ah! my love, we shall not meet again till we meet in Heaven!—We have suffered enough here on earth for God to take pity on us," she added in a whisper.

A few moments later, after Monsieur Mouilleron had talked with Max, Gritte surprised Monsieur and Madame Hochon, Agathe, Joseph and Adolphine beyond measure, by announcing Monsieur Rouget. He came to say good-bye to his sister and to offer his calèche for the drive to Bourges.

22

"Ah! your pictures have done a deal of harm!"
Agathe said to him.

"Keep them, sister," replied the goodman, who
did not even yet believe in the value of the daubs.

"Neighbor," said Monsieur Hochon, "our kinsfolk
are our best friends, our surest protectors, especially
when they resemble your sister Agathe and your
nephew Joseph!"

"It may be so!" replied the feeble-minded old
man.

"We all ought to think of ending our days like
Christians," said Madame Hochon.

"Oh! Jean-Jacques, what a day!" said Agathe.

"Will you use my carriage?" Rouget inquired.

"No, brother," was the reply; "I thank you and
wish you the best of health!"

Rouget allowed his sister and his nephew to kiss
him, and then took his leave, after bidding them
adieu without any sign of affection. At a word
from his grandfather, Baruch had hurried away to
La Poste. At eleven o'clock at night, the two
Parisians, ensconced in a wicker cabriolet, drawn
by one horse and driven by a postilion, turned their
backs upon Issoudun. Adolphine and Madame
Hochon had tears in their eyes. They were the
only persons that regretted the departure of Agathe
and Joseph.

"They have gone," said François Hochon, entering Max's room with La Rabouilleuse.

"Good; the trick is done," Max replied, pros-
trated as he was by the fever.

"But what did you say to Père Mouilleron?" queried François.

"I told him that I had almost given my assassin the right to lie in wait for me at a street corner, and that he was the kind of man to kill me like a dog before he was arrested, if the affair was prosecuted. Consequently I urged Mouilleron and Prangin to pretend to make a most diligent search for my assassin, but to let him alone unless they wanted to see me a dead man."

"I hope, Max," said Flore, "that you're going to keep quiet at night for a while."

"At all events, we're well rid of the Parisians!" cried Max. "The man who stabbed me hardly expected to do us so great a service."

The next day, with the exception of those excessively peaceable and reserved persons who shared the opinions of Monsieur and Madame Hochon, the departure of the Parisians, although due to a deplorable mistake, was celebrated throughout the town as a victory of the provinces over Paris. Some friends of Max expressed themselves in unmeasured terms concerning the Bridaus.

"Those Parisians imagined that we are all idiots and that they only had to hold out their hats and it would rain inheritances!"

"They came after wool, but they went back fleeced, for the nephew didn't suit his uncle's taste."

"And they were acting on the advice of a Paris solicitor, if you please."

"Oh! they had a scheme all arranged, had they?"

"Why, yes, a scheme to get control of Père Rouget; but the Parisians found they weren't strong enough, and the solicitor won't laugh at us Berrichons."

"Do you know, it's an outrage?"

"That's the kind of people they are in Paris!"

"La Rabouilleuse saw that she was attacked and she defended herself."

"And she did just right."

In the eyes of the whole town the Bridaus were Parisians, foreigners; they preferred Max and Flore to them.

*

The satisfaction with which Agathe and Joseph returned to their humble apartments on Rue Mazarine after this fruitless campaign, can readily be imagined. During the homeward journey, the artist had recovered his cheerful humor, interrupted by his arrest and by twenty hours of close confinement; but he could not divert his mother's mind. The fact that the court was about to begin the trial of the military conspiracy made it the more difficult for her to forget her grief. Philippe's conduct, despite the skill of his counsel, who was advised by Desroches, aroused suspicions that were by no means favorable to his character. And so, as soon as he had informed Desroches of all that had taken place at Issoudun, Joseph at once started off with Mistigris for the Comte de Sérizy's château, in order to hear nothing of the trial, which lasted twenty days.

It is useless to repeat here facts that are a part of contemporaneous history. Whether because he had played some part agreed upon beforehand, or because he was one of the informers, Philippe was sentenced to be kept under surveillance by the police for a term of five years, and was obliged to leave Paris, on the very day of his release, for Autun, the town which the director-general of the

police of the kingdom assigned as his place of residence during the five years. This form of punish-
ment is very similar to the detention imposed upon
prisoners on parole who have been given a town for
their prison. Upon being informed that the Comte
de Sérizy, one of the peers selected by the Chamber
to try the conspirators, was employing Joseph upon
the decorations of his château at Presles, Desroches
requested an audience of that Minister of State and
found him extremely well disposed toward Joseph,
with whom he had accidentally become acquainted.
Desroches explained the financial position of the
two brothers, recalling the services rendered by
their father and the way in which the government
of the Restoration had disregarded them.

"Such injustice, monseigneur," said the solicitor, "is a permanent source of irritation and
discontent! You knew the father; the least you
can do is to put the children in a way to make
their fortunes."

He thereupon set forth succinctly the condition of
the family affairs at Issoudun, and urged the all-
powerful Vice-President of the Council of State to
use his influence with the director-general of police
to have Philippe's place of residence changed from
Autun to Issoudun. Lastly he spoke of Philippe's
horrible destitution, requesting an allowance of sixty
francs a month, which, he said, the War Department ought, from very shame, to grant a former
lieutenant-colonel.

"I will obtain all that you suggest," said the

minister, "for it seems to me no more than just at every point."

Three days later, Desroches, armed with the necessary documents, went to the prison of the Court of Peers, and secured the release of Philippe, whom he took with him to his house on Rue de Béthisy. There the young solicitor preached at the truculent trooper one of those unanswerable sermons in which solicitors call things by their right names, making use of unvarnished terms to describe the conduct and to analyze and reduce to their simplest expression the sentiments of clients in whom they are sufficiently interested to sermonize them. Having humbled the conceit of the Emperor's ex-orderly by reproaching him with his inexcusable dissoluteness, his mother's misfortunes and the death of old Madame Descoings, he described to him the condition of affairs at Issoudun, interpreting them according to his own views and laying bare in their entirety the characters of Maxence Gilet and La Rabouilleuse and the plan they had formed. Being endowed with very keen perception in such matters, the convicted conspirator listened much more attentively to this part of Desroches' sermon than to the first part.

"Affairs being in this position," said the solicitor, "you can repair whatever is reparable in the wrong you have done your excellent family, for you cannot restore to life the poor woman to whom you gave the death-blow; but you only can—"

"What am I to do?" asked Philippe.

"I have obtained your transfer from Autun to Issoudun."

Philippe's wasted face, which had become almost sinister under the influence of sickness, suffering and privation, was instantly lighted up by a gleam of joy.

"You only, I say, can rescue your uncle's fortune, which is already, it may be, half-way down the throat of that wolf called Gilet," continued Desroches. "You know all the details, and now it is for you to act accordingly. I mark out no plan for you, I have no ideas on the subject; indeed, everything depends upon how the land lies. You have to do with no contemptible adversaries; the rascal is as shrewd as possible, and the way in which he tried to recover the pictures your uncle gave Joseph, and the audacity with which he loaded a crime on your brother's back, indicate an adversary who is capable of anything. Therefore be prudent, and try to be wise by premeditation if you can't be wise by temperament. Without saying anything to Joseph, whose artist's pride would have rebelled, I have sent the pictures back to Monsieur Hochon, and have written him to deliver them to no one but you. This Maxence Gilet is a brave fellow."

"So much the better," said Philippe, "I rely upon the rascal's courage for success, for a coward would leave Issoudun."

"Well, think of your mother, whose affection for you is beyond words; of your brother whom you have made your milch-cow."

"Aha! he told you about those trifles, did he?" cried Philippe.

"Why, am I not the friend of the family, and don't I know a deal more about you than they do?"

"What do you know?" demanded Philippe.

"You betrayed your comrades—"

"I!" cried Philippe; "I, one of the Emperor's orderlies? That won't do!—We hoodwinked the Chamber of Peers, the courts, the government and the whole cursed outfit. The king's people saw nothing but fire!—"

"That's all right, if it's true," rejoined the solicitor; "but you see the Bourbons can't be overthrown, they have Europe on their side, and you ought to think about making your peace with the Minister of War. Oh! you'll do it when you're a rich man. In order to enrich yourself and your brother, get possession of your uncle. If you choose to manage prudently an affair that demands so much adroitness, discretion and patience, you have plenty of work cut out for your five years."

"No, no," said Philippe, "I must go about it at once; this Gilet may change the form of my uncle's property, put it in this girl's name, and all will be lost."

"Monsieur Hochon is a judicious man, who takes an accurate view of things; consult him. You have your ticket, your place is engaged on the Orléans diligence at half-past seven, your trunks are packed; come to dinner!"

"I own nothing but what I have on my back,"

said Philippe, unbuttoning his threadbare blue coat; "but I lack three things, which I beg you will ask my friend Giroudeau, Finot's uncle, to send me: my sabre, my sword and my pistols!"

"You lack something else of a different nature," said the solicitor, shuddering as he looked at his client. "You will receive your allowance in advance for three months, in order to clothe yourself decently."

"Hallo! you here, Godeschal!" cried Philippe, recognizing Mariette's brother in Desroches's chief clerk.

"Yes, I have been with Monsieur Desroches two months."

"He will remain here, I hope," said Desroches, "until he purchases an office of his own."

"And how is Mariette?" asked Philippe, moved by his awakened memories.

"She is waiting for the opening of the new opera-house."

"It would cost her very little," said Philippe, "to secure the revocation of my sentence—However, as she chooses!"

After the meagre repast set before Philippe by Desroches, who boarded his chief clerk, the two lawyers put the political prisoner aboard the diligence and wished him good luck.

On the second of November, All Souls' Day, Philippe Bridau appeared before the commissioner of police at Issoudun to have the date of his arrival minuted upon his certificate; then he secured lodgings, in accordance with that functionary's advice, on Rue de l'Avenier.

The news that one of the officers compromised in the last conspiracy had been banished to Issoudun was soon circulated through the town, and created an even greater sensation than it might otherwise have done when it was known that the officer in question was the brother of the unjustly accused artist.

Maxence Gilet, who had entirely recovered from his wound, had completed the difficult operation of turning Père Rouget's mortgage investments into cash and reinvesting them in the public funds. The loan of a hundred and forty thousand francs negotiated by the old man upon his real estate caused a great sensation, for everyone knows everything in the provinces. In the interest of the Bridaus, Monsieur Hochon, intensely excited by this calamity, questioned old Monsieur Héron, Rouget's notary, as to the purpose of this change of investments.

"If Père Rouget changes his mind, Père Rouget's heirs-at-law will be greatly indebted to me!" cried Héron. "If it hadn't been for me, the goodman would have allowed the investment in the Funds to be made in the name of Maxence Gilet.—I told Mademoiselle Brazier that she ought to stick to the will, or run the risk of a prosecution for spoliation, in view of the numerous proofs of their schemes that would be afforded by the collections that were being made in all directions. To gain time, I advised Maxence and his mistress to let people forget this sudden change in the goodman's habits."

"Be the advocate and protector of the Bridaus, for they have nothing at all," said Monsieur Hochon, who could not forgive Gilet the agony caused by his dread of the pillaging of his house.

Maxence Gilet and Flore Brazier, feeling secure from attack, spoke jestingly of the arrival of Père Rouget's second nephew. The instant that Philippe should give them any cause for uneasiness, they could force Père Rouget to sign a power of attorney authorizing the transfer of the Funds to Maxence or to Flore, as they chose. If the will should be revoked, fifty thousand francs a year would be a very pretty plum with which to console themselves, especially after they had burdened the real estate with a mortgage of a hundred and forty thousand francs.

On the day following his arrival, Philippe called upon his uncle about ten o'clock. He had determined to appear in his shocking costume; and so, when the ex-patient at the Hôpital du Midi, when the prisoner of the Luxembourg entered the living-room, Flore Brazier shuddered instinctively at the repulsive sight. Gilet, too, felt the shock to his mental faculties and his sensibility, by which nature warns us of a latent hostility or an impending danger. If Philippe owed the indefinable sinister expression of his features to his latest misfortunes, his costume certainly intensified it. His pitiful blue redingote was buttoned to the neck, in military fashion, for deplorable reasons, but even so it showed far too much of what it attempted to conceal. The hem of his pantaloons, worn and frayed like a veteran's coat, indicated the depth of destitution. The boots left damp marks on the floor, ejecting muddy water through the half-open soles. The lining of the gray hat that the colonel carried in his hand was shockingly greasy. The bamboo cane, from which the varnish had disappeared, had evidently stood in the corner of every café in Paris and rested its twisted end in many vile dens. Over a velvet stock, which afforded glimpses in places of the pasteboard beneath, appeared a face whose expression was almost like Frédérick Lemaître's in the last act of *A Gambler's Life*,—a face in which the exhaustion of a still vigorous man betrays itself by a sort of coppery complexion, with an almost greenish tinge here and there. Such complexions are characteristic of dissolute men who have passed many nights over the gaming table; the eyes are surrounded by black rings, the eyelids are reddened rather than red; the forehead is threatening because of all the various forms of ruin it denotes. In Philippe's face,—for he had hardly recovered from his illness,—the cheeks were sunken and uneven. There was no hair upon his head save a few scattering locks that seemed to be dying about his ears. The pure blue of his once brilliant eyes had taken on the cold tints of steel.

"Good-morning, uncle," he said in a hoarse voice; "I am your nephew, Philippe Bridau. This is the way the Bourbons treat a lieutenant-colonel, a veteran of the Old Guard, one who carried the Emperor's despatches at the battle of Montereau. I should be ashamed if my coat were to fly open, because of mademoiselle.   After all, it's the law of play.   We undertook to begin the game again and we lost!   I have come to your town to live, by order of the police, with the handsome allowance of sixty francs a month.   So the good bourgeois need have no fear that I shall put up the price of food.   I see that you have the best of company."

"Ah! you're my nephew, are you?" said Jean-Jacques.

"Pray invite Monsieur le Colonel to breakfast," said Flore.

"Thanks, no, madame," Philippe replied, "I have breakfasted.   Besides, I would sooner cut off my hand than ask my uncle for a crust of bread or a centime, after what has taken place in this town with respect to my brother and my mother.   But it did not seem to me fitting to remain in Issoudun without paying my respects to him from time to time.—You can do whatever you please," he added, offering his hand to his uncle, who put his own therein and shook Philippe's, "you can do what you please; I shall have nothing to say against it so long as the honor of the Bridaus is not attacked."

Gilet was able to examine the lieutenant-colonel at his leisure, for Philippe, with visible affectation, avoided looking at him.   Although the blood was boiling in his veins, Max was too deeply interested in conducting himself with the prudence of great politicians, which sometimes resembles cowardice, to take fire like a young man; therefore he maintained a cold and calm demeanor.

"It will not look well, monsieur," said Flore, "to live on sixty francs a month under your uncle's nose, when he has forty thousand francs a year, and has behaved so generously to Monsieur le Commandant Gilet here, his natural brother—"

"Yes, Philippe," said the goodman, "we will see about that."

Upon Flore's introduction, Philippe bowed almost timidly to Gilet.

"I have some pictures to return to you, uncle; they are at Monsieur Hochon's; you will do me the favor to come and identify them some day."

With these last words uttered in an off-hand manner, Lieutenant-Colonel Philippe Bridau took his leave. His visit left in Flore's mind, as well as in Gilet's, an even deeper impression than that caused by the first sight of the redoubtable trooper. As soon as Philippe had closed the door with the natural violence of a disinherited heir, Flore and Gilet hid themselves behind the curtains to watch him as he crossed the square to Monsieur Hochon's.

"What a vagabond!" said Flore, with an inquiring glance at Gilet.

"Yes, unfortunately there were a few fellows of that stamp in the Emperor's armies; I did for seven of them on the hulks," replied Gilet.

"I hope, Max, that you won't pick a quarrel with this one," said Mademoiselle Brazier.

"Oh! he's a mangy dog who wants a bone," Max rejoined, addressing Père Rouget. "If his uncle has confidence in me, he will get rid of him by giving him a little something; for he won't leave you alone, Papa Rouget."

"He smells very strong of tobacco," said the old man.

"He smells your crowns, too," said Flore peremptorily. "My opinion is that you should refuse to receive him."

"I ask nothing better," said Rouget.

"Monsieur," said Gritte, entering the room where the whole Hochon family were assembled after breakfast, "here is the Monsieur Bridau you were speaking about."

Philippe made his entry with due courtesy, amid a profound silence due to general curiosity. Madame Hochon shuddered from head to foot as her eyes fell upon the author of all Agathe's sorrow and the assassin of good Madame Descoings. Adolphine also was alarmed. Baruch and François exchanged a glance of surprise. Old Hochon retained his self-possession and offered Madame Bridau's son a seat.

"I come to ask your assistance, monsieur," said Philippe; "for I must make my arrangements to live here for five years on the sixty francs per month which France gives me."

"It can be done," said the octogenarian.

Philippe talked of indifferent matters, his bearing being unexceptionable. He described as an eagle among his kind, the journalist Lousteau, the old lady's nephew, and established himself at once in her good graces by informing her that the name of Lousteau would become famous. He did not hesitate to acknowledge the errors of his life. In reply to a friendly reproof administered by Madame Hochon in an undertone, he said that he had reflected deeply in prison, and promised to be a very different man in future.

At a suggestion from Philippe, Monsieur Hochon went out with him. When the miser and the ex-trooper were on Boulevard Baron, where no one could overhear them, the latter began:

"Monsieur, if you agree with me, we will never talk about business or persons except when we are walking out of doors or are in some place where we can talk without being overhead. Master Desroches impressed upon me very forcibly the influence of idle gossip in a small town. I prefer therefore that you should not be suspected of assisting me with your advice, although Desroches bade me seek it and I beg you not to withhold it. We have a cunning enemy to deal with, and we must omit no precaution that may help us to get rid of him. And, first of all, you will excuse me if I do not call upon you again. A little apparent coolness between us, and you will be held blameless of any influence on my conduct. When I require to consult you, I will cross the square at half-past nine, just as you finish

23

breakfast. If you see me holding my cane at the carry, it will mean that we must meet, by accident, in some place that you will indicate to me."

"All this seems to me to denote a sagacious man, and one who intends to succeed," said the old man.

"And I shall succeed, monsieur. First of all, give me the names of the soldiers of the old army who have come back here, who are not partisans of Maxence Gilet and with whom I can safely become intimate."

"In the first place, there's a captain of artillery of the Guard, Monsieur Mignonnet, a graduate of the Ecole Polytechnique, about forty years old, who lives in a very modest way; he is a man of honor and a pronounced opponent of Max, whose conduct he considers unbecoming a true soldier."

"Good!" said the lieutenant-colonel.

"There aren't many soldiers of that stamp," continued Hochon; "I can think of only one other, a former captain of cavalry."

"That is my branch of the service," said Philippe. "Was he in the Guard?"

"Yes," was the reply. "In 1810, Carpentier was quartermaster-general in the dragoons; he left them to enter a line regiment as sublieutenant, and he rose to be a captain."

"Perhaps Giroudeau will know him," thought Philippe.

"Carpentier took the place Maxence didn't care for, at the mayor's office, and he is a friend of Commandant Mignonnet."

"What can I do to earn a living here?"

"I believe there is to be established here a branch office of the mutual assurance company of the Department of the Cher, and you might get a place in that; but it will be fifty francs a month at most."

"That will be enough for me."

Within a week Philippe had a new coat, waistcoat and trousers of good Elbeuf cloth, purchased on credit, to be paid for by monthly instalments; also boots, kid gloves and a hat. He received from Paris, through Giroudeau, linen, his weapons and a letter to Carpentier, who had served under the ex-captain of dragoons.—This letter procured Philippe the devoted friendship of Carpentier, who presented him to Commandant Mignonnet as a man of the highest merit and the most admirable character. Philippe won the admiration of those two worthy officers by some confidential disclosures concerning the recent conspiracy, which was, as everyone knows, the last attempt of the old army against the Bourbons, for the trial of the sergeants of La Rochelle belongs to a different class.

After 1822, the old soldiers, enlightened by the outcome of the conspiracy of August 19, 1820, and by the Berton and Caron affairs, were content to let events take their course. This latest conspiracy, the younger brother of that of the nineteenth of August, was substantially the same thing renewed, with better chances of success. Like the other, it was entirely unknown to the government. When their project was discovered, the conspirators had the good sense to pare it down to the paltry proportions of a mere barracks plot.   This conspiracy, in which several regiments of cavalry, infantry and artillery were involved, had the north of France for its theatre.   The fortified towns on the frontier were to be taken at a single blow.   In case of success, the treaties of 1815 would have been nullified by a speedy federation with Belgium, to be snatched from the Holy Alliance by virtue of a military compact entered into between soldiers.   Two thrones would have foundered in a moment in that sudden hurricane.   Instead of this formidable plan, devised by shrewd brains, and in which divers exalted personages were concerned, only a few unimportant details were laid before the court.   Philippe Bridau consented to shield his leaders, who disappeared just as the plot was discovered, whether by treachery, or by pure chance, and who, having seats in the Chambers, had promised their co-operation only to forward the success of the affair at the seat of government.   To describe the plan, which the admissions of the liberals, since 1830, have disclosed in all its extent, and in its vast ramifications, which were hidden from the inferior conspirators, would be to trench upon the domain of history, and to digress too far.   This brief summary will suffice to show the double rôle undertaken by Philippe.   The Emperor's former orderly was to direct a movement in Paris designed simply to mask the real conspiracy and to keep the government's hands

full in the centre of the kingdom when it should
burst out in the North. Philippe was then instructed to break the chain between the two plots
by betraying only the secrets of secondary importance; so it was that the lamentable conclusion of
the affair, to which his costume and his state of
health bore witness, assisted materially in min-
imizing and lessening the importance of the enterprise in the eyes of the authorities. This rôle
harmonized with the precarious plight of the un-
principled gambler. When he found himself astride
the two parties, the crafty Philippe played the
saint with the king's government and retained the
esteem of the men of high station in his own party,
reserving the right, however, to follow, at a later
period, that one of the two paths which seemed the
more advantageous to himself.

These revelations as to the vast extent of the plot
and as to the participation of some of the judges,
made of Philippe, in the eyes of Carpentier and
Mignonnet, a man of the highest distinction, for his
devotion showed him to be a politician worthy of
the glorious days of the Convention. Thus the
cunning Bonapartist became in a few days the close
friend of the two officers, and the general esteem in
which they were held extended to him. He soon
obtained, through their recommendation, the place
mentioned by old Hochon in the mutual assurance
office. His duties were to keep lists, as in a tax-
collector's office, to insert names and figures in
printed blanks and to fill out insurance policies, all

of which did not occupy three hours a day. Mignonnet and Carpentier procured the admission of
Issoudun's guest to their club, where his bearing
and his manners, harmonizing as they did with the
high opinion Mignonnet and Carpentier expressed
of this chief of a conspiracy, won for him the
respect often accorded to a deceitful exterior.

Philippe, whose conduct was the result of profound calculation, had reflected during his life in
prison upon the disadvantages of a dissolute career.
He did not require the seed sown by Desroches,
therefore, to realize the necessity of winning the
esteem of the bourgeoisie by an upright, decent,
regular life.   Delighted with the opportunity to
satirize Max by behaving himself *à la Mignonnet*,
he essayed to lull his suspicions to sleep by deceiv-
ing him as to his character.   His plan was to create
the impression that he was himself a fool, by ex-
hibiting great generosity and unselfishness, while
he was spreading his nets about his adversary,
with a covetous eye always fixed upon his uncle's
fortune; whereas his mother and brother, who were
genuinely unselfish, generous and noble, had been
taxed with scheming when they were acting with
the most artless simplicity.   Philippe's cupidity
was inflamed by the proportions of his uncle's
fortune, which Monsieur Hochon dilated upon to
him.   In his first secret interview with the octogenarian, they had agreed perfectly as to the
advisability of not arousing Max's suspicion; for
everything would be lost if Flore and Max should

take their victim away, if it were only as far as
Bourges.

The colonel dined once a week at Captain Mignonnet's, again at Carpentier's and on Thursdays
with Monsieur Hochon. After he had been three
weeks in Issoudun he was invited to several other
houses, and soon had hardly anything but his breakfast to pay for. Wherever he went, he never mentioned his uncle or La Rabouilleuse or Gilet
unless he desired to learn something concerning the
visit of his mother and brother. The three officers,
who were the only ones in town who wore a decoration, Philippe alone having the advantage of the
rosette, which gave him a marked superiority in
everybody's eyes in the provinces, always walked
together just before dinner, forming, according to a
common expression, *a band apart.* His reserve,
his tranquillity, his general attitude, produced an
excellent effect in Issoudun. All Max's adherents
looked upon Philippe as a *sabreur,* a term by which
soldiers accord their superior officers the most
ordinary form of physical courage, and deny them
the requisite capacity for command.

"He's a very honorable man," said Goddet
senior to Max.

"Bah!" was the reply, "his conduct before the
court proclaims him either a dupe or a spy; and he
is, as you say, stupid enough to be the dupe of men
who play for high stakes."

After obtaining his place in the insurance office,
Philippe, being informed of the current gossip, tried

to keep the town as much in the dark as possible concerning certain matters; he took up his quarters, therefore, in a house with a large garden at the farthest extremity of Faubourg Saint-Paterne. He was able to practise fencing there in the utmost secrecy with Carpentier, who had been a fencing-master in the line before entering the Guard. Having thus secretly recovered his former skill, Philippe learned from Carpentier certain secrets which made it possible for him to look forward without apprehension to a contest with an adversary of the first order. He thereupon began to practise with the pistol with Mignonnet and Carpentier, pretending that it was for amusement, but really to lead Maxence to believe that in case of a duel, he relied upon that weapon. When Philippe met Gilet, he waited for him to bow and responded by raising the brim of his hat cavalierly, as a colonel responds to the salute of a common soldier. Maxence Gilet made no sign of impatience or displeasure; he never breathed a word upon the subject at La Cognette's, where he still gave supper-parties; for, since Fario's assault, the practical jokes had been provisionally suspended.

After a certain time, Lieutenant-Colonel Bridau's contempt for Commandant Gilet became an accepted fact which was quietly discussed among themselves by three or four of the Knights of Idleness, who were not such close friends of Max as Baruch, François and three or four others. There was a general feeling of astonishment that the hot-tempered, violent

Max should conduct himself with so much self-restraint. No one in Issoudun, not even Potel or Renard, dared broach this delicate subject to Gilet. Potel who was deeply concerned at this public misunderstanding between two heroes of the Garde Impériale, declared that Max was quite capable of weaving a web in which the colonel would be caught. In Potel's judgment, they might expect something new and startling, in view of what Max had done to drive away the mother and the brother, for the Fario affair was no longer a mystery. Monsieur Hochon had not failed to explain Gilet's atrocious stratagem to the old people of the town. Moreover, Monsieur Mouilleron, the hero of a bit of bourgeois gossip, had whispered the name of Gilet's assassin in confidence, with a view to ascertain the causes of Fario's hostility to Max, so that the authorities might be on the alert for future occurrences. Thus it came about that, in conversation as to the lieutenant-colonel's situation with reference to Max, and in the endeavor to anticipate the results of their antagonism, the townspeople set them down in advance as enemies. Philippe, who was anxious to learn all the details of his brother's arrest and to glean all possible information concerning the antecedents of Gilet and La Rabouilleuse, eventually became quite intimate with this neighbor Fario. Having made a careful study of the Spaniard, Philippe believed that he could safely trust a man of his temper. The two men found themselves so

thoroughly in accord in their hatred that Fario
placed himself at Philippe's disposal and told him
all he knew concerning the Knights of Idleness.
Philippe promised, in case he should succeed in
acquiring the influence over his uncle then exerted
by Gilet, to indemnify Fario for his losses, and in
that way he procured a devoted partisan. Thus
Maxence was confronted by a redoubtable foe; he
found *his match*, as they say in the province.
Excited by the current rumors, the town of Issoudun
looked forward to a combat between these two men,
who, we must not forget, mutually despised each
other.

In the latter part of November, Philippe met
Monsieur Hochon one day about noon, in the
Avenue de Frapesle.

"I have discovered," he said, "that your grandsons Baruch and François are Maxence Gilet's intimate friends. The rascals take part in all the
nocturnal pranks that are played in the town. So
Maxence learned from them everything that was
said at your house while my brother and my
mother were staying there."

"What proof have you of such astounding statements?"

"I heard them talking last night as they came
out of a wine-shop. Each of your grandsons owes
Gilet a thousand crowns. The villain told the poor
boys to try and discover our intentions; he reminded them that you had invented the scheme of
surrounding my uncle with a crowd of priests, and

said that no one but you could be advising me, for luckily he takes me for a mere swashbuckler."

"My grandsons, you say?"

"Watch them," replied Philippe; "you'll see them coming across Place Saint-Jean at two or three o'clock in the morning, as drunk as lords, and with Maxence for their companion."

"So that's why my rascals are so abstemious!" exclaimed Monsieur Hochon.

"Fario posted me concerning the way they pass their nights," said Philippe; "except for him I never should have guessed it. My uncle is ground down by the most horrible sort of tyranny, judging from the few words my Spaniard heard Maxence say to your children. I suspect that he and La Rabouilleuse have formed a plan to *prig* the investment in the Funds, and then, after they have plucked that wing from their pigeon, to go off somewhere and get married. It's high time for us to find out what is going on in my uncle's family; but I don't know how to go about it."

"I will think it over," said the old man.

With that, seeing that somebody was coming toward them, they separated.

*

Never at any time in his whole life had Jean-Jacques Rouget suffered as he had suffered since his nephew Philippe's first visit. Flore was alarmed by the presentiment that some peril was hovering over Maxence. Weary of her master, and fearing that he would live to be very old, when she saw how stubbornly he resisted her criminal practices, she invented the very simple plan of leaving the province and marrying Max in Paris, after inducing the old man to give her the certificate for fifty thousand francs a year of his investment in the Funds. The old bachelor, impelled neither by regard for the interest of his heirs-at-law, nor by personal avarice, but by his passion, refused to give Flore the certificate, giving as his reason that she was his sole legatee. The miserable wretch knew how Flore loved Max, and he felt that he would be abandoned as soon as she was rich enough to marry. When Flore, after employing her most affectionate cajoleries, was still met with a refusal, she resorted to more rigorous treatment; she refused to speak to her master, and made La Védie wait upon him; one morning the cook found the old man's eyes red with the tears that he had shed during the night. For a week Père Rouget breakfasted alone, and God only knows how! So it was that when Philippe, on the

(365)

day following his conversation with Monsieur Hochon, paid his second visit to his uncle, he found him greatly changed. Flore sat beside the old man, glanced affectionately at him, spoke sweetly to him, and so overdid her part that Philippe divined the perils of the situation from such an exhibition of solicitude in his presence. Gilet, whose policy it was to avoid any sort of collision with Philippe, did not appear. Having scrutinized Père Rouget and Flore with a glance of keen observation, the colonel deemed it necessary to strike a decisive blow.

"Good-morning, my dear uncle," he said rising, and with a wave of his hand signifying his purpose to take his leave.

"Oh! don't go yet," cried the old man, his spirits revived by Flore's false good-humor. "Dine with us, Philippe."

"Yes, if you will come out and walk with me for an hour."

"Monsieur is not at all well," said Mademoiselle Brazier. "He refused just now to go to drive," she added, turning to the goodman, and gazing at him with the fixed stare with which we overawe madmen.

Philippe seized Flore's arm, compelled her to look him in the face and gazed at her as fixedly as she had gazed at her victim.

"Tell me, mademoiselle," he said, "am I to understand that my uncle is not at liberty to go to walk alone with me?"

"Why, of course he is, monsieur," replied Flore, who could hardly say anything else.

"Very well, come, uncle.—Give him his hat and cane, mademoiselle—"

"But he doesn't usually go out without me.—Do you, monsieur?"

"Yes, Philippe, yes, I always need her—"

"It would be much better to drive," said Flore.

"Yes, let us drive," cried the old man, in his anxiety to reconcile his two tyrants.

"You will come on foot and with me, uncle, or I will come here no more; for in that case the town of Issoudun is right: you are under the domination of Mademoiselle Flore Brazier.—That my uncle should love you is very natural!" he resumed with a stern glance at Flore. "That you should not love him is also in the natural order of things. But that you should make the good old man miserable—I draw the line at that! If you want a fortune you must earn it.—Are you coming, uncle?"

Philippe saw the heartrending hesitation on the poor idiot's face as he looked from Flore to his nephew.

"Ah! that's how it is!" continued Philippe. "Very well, adieu, uncle.—As to you, mademoiselle, I kiss your hands."

He turned quickly when he reached the door and surprised Flore in the act of threatening his uncle with a gesture.

"Uncle," said he, "if you conclude to go to walk with me I will meet you at your door; I am going

to call on Monsieur Hochon for ten minutes.—If we
don't go to walk, I undertake to send a number of
people walking about their business."

And Philippe crossed Place Saint-Jean to Monsieur Hochon's.

The reader will readily imagine the scene that
had followed Philippe's revelation to Monsieur
Hochon. At nine o'clock old Monsieur Héron appeared, armed with a bundle of papers, and found a
fire burning in the living-room, which the old man
had lighted, contrary to his usual custom. Madame
Hochon, fully dressed at that early hour, occupied
her armchair in the chimney corner. The two
grandsons, warned by Adolphine of the storm that
had been gathering over their heads since the preceding day, were forbidden to leave the house.
Entering the room at a summons from Gritte, they
were terror-stricken at the solemn state affected by
their grandparents, whose wrath had been rumbling
over them for twenty-four hours.

"Don't leave your seat for them," said Hochon
to the notary, "for they're miserable fellows, unde-
serving of pardon."

"Oh! grandpapa!" said François.

"Hold your tongue!" retorted the solemn old
man; "I know all about your nocturnal life and
your intimacy with Monsieur Maxence Gilet; but
you won't meet him any more at La Cognette's at
one o'clock in the morning, for you won't leave this
house, either of you, except to go to the places
where you belong. Ah! so you ruined Fario, did

you?—And you have barely escaped having to go before the assizes time and time again, eh?—Hold your tongue," he said, seeing that Baruch opened his mouth. "You both owe money to Monsieur Gilet, who has been supplying it to you for your orgies, for the last six years. Listen, both of you, to my accounts as guardian, and then we will talk. You will see from these documents whether you can make a fool of me and mock at the family and its laws by betraying to a Monsieur Maxence Gilet what is said and done here.—For a thousand crowns, you become spies; for ten thousand you would do murder, I suppose?—Indeed, haven't you already well-nigh killed Madame Bridau? for Monsieur Gilet was perfectly well aware that it was Fario who stabbed him, when he accused my guest, Joseph Bridau. If that gallows-bird committed that crime, it was because he had learned from you of Madame Agathe's purpose to remain here. You, my grandsons, spies for such a blackguard! You, midnight marauders!—Didn't you know that your worthy chief, in 1806, at the outset of his career, killed a poor young creature? I don't choose to have assassins or thieves in my family, so you can pack your trunks and go and get yourselves hanged somewhere else!"

The young men became as white and motionless as plaster statues.

"Go on, Monsieur Héron," said the miser, turning to the notary.

The old man proceeded to read a guardianship

24

account, from which it appeared that the net unencumbered fortune of the two Borniche children amounted to seventy thousand francs, which was the amount of their mother's marriage portion; but Monsieur Hochon had procured loans to a considerable amount for his daughter, and was now in a position to control a portion of the fortune of her children, in the name of the lenders. The amount due to Baruch was thus reduced to twenty thousand francs.

"You're a rich man," said his grandfather; "take your fortune and go your own way! I am at liberty to give my own property and Madame Hochon's, who agrees with me entirely in this matter, to whomever I please, to our dear Adolphine; yes, she shall marry the son of a peer of France, if we choose, for she will have all we possess."

"A very handsome fortune!" said Monsieur Héron.

"Monsieur Maxence Gilet will make it all up to you," said Madame Hochon.

"To think of heaping up twenty-sou pieces for such rake-hells!" cried Monsieur Hochon.

"Forgive me!" stammered Baruch.

"*Forgive me and I'll do it again!*" sneered the old man, imitating a child's voice. "If I forgive you, you'll go and tell Monsieur Gilet what has happened, so that he can be on his guard—No, no, my little gentlemen. I have means of finding out how you behave. As you act, so will I act. Not by your good conduct for a single day or a single month shall I judge you, but by your conduct for a number of years!—I have a nimble foot, a keen eye and good health. I hope to live long enough yet to know what path you choose to walk in.—And, first of all, Monsieur le Capitaliste, you will go to Paris to study banking with Monsieur Mongenod. Woe to you, if you don't walk straight: you will have a keen eye upon you. Your funds are with Messieurs Mongenod and Son; here is a draft upon them for the amount. Be kind enough to discharge me by signing my guardianship account, which ends with a receipt," he said, taking the account from Héron's hands and handing it to Baruch.—"As for you, François Hochon," said the old man, turning to his other grandson, "you owe me money instead of having any due to you.—Monsieur Héron, read him his account; it is clear—very clear."

The account was read amid profound silence.

"You will go to Poitiers with six hundred francs a year, to study law," said the grandfather when the notary had finished. "I had contemplated an enviable future for you; now you must become an advocate and earn your living.—Ah! my scoundrels, you fooled me for six years! understand that it took me just one hour to catch you up and pay off old scores: I wear seven-league boots."

Just as Monsieur Héron was leaving the house with the documents duly signed, Gritte announced Monsieur le Colonel Philippe Bridau. Madame Hochon left the room with her two grandsons, whom she took to her bedroom, to confess them, as old

Hochon remarked, and to ascertain what effect this scene had produced upon them.

Philippe and the old man stood in a window-recess and conversed in undertones.

"I have thought much concerning the condition of your affairs," said Monsieur Hochon, pointing toward the Rouget house. "I have just been talking the matter over with Monsieur Héron. The fifty thousand a year in the Funds can be transferred only by the holder himself or his lawfully authorized attorney; now, since you have been in Issoudun, your uncle has executed no power of attorney in any notary's office here; and as he has not left the town, he can't have executed one elsewhere. If he gives a power of attorney here, we shall know it instantly; if he gives one somewhere else, we shall also know it, for it must be registered, and worthy Monsieur Héron has a way of being notified of it. Therefore, if the goodman leaves Issoudun, have him followed, find out where he goes, and we will find a way to learn what he does there."

"The power of attorney hasn't been given yet," said Philippe; "they are trying to get it, but I hope to prevent its being given at all; and—it—shall—not—be—giv—en!" he cried, as he saw his uncle appear in the doorway, and he called Monsieur Hochon's attention to him, describing succinctly the incidents, great and small, of his visit. "Maxence is afraid of me, but he can't avoid me. Mignonnet tells me that all the officers of the old army in Issoudun celebrate the anniversary of the Emperor's coronation every year; so that, in two days, Maxence and I are certain to meet."

"If he has the power of attorney on the morning of December first, he will take the post for Paris and let the anniversary be celebrated without him—"

"Bah! to get it they must keep my uncle in his room; but I have the look that awes idiots," said Philippe, making Monsieur Hochon tremble at a ferocious glare.

"If they have consented that he should go to walk with you, Maxence must have found some way of winning the game," remarked the old miser.

"Oh! Fario is on the watch," said Philippe, "and he isn't the only one. The Spaniard discovered in the outskirts of Vatan, one of my old soldiers to whom I rendered some slight service. No one has the least suspicion that Benjamin Bourdet is under the orders of my Spaniard, who has placed one of his horses at Benjamin's service."

"If you kill the monster who led my grandsons astray, you will certainly do a good deed."

"To-day, thanks to me, all Issoudun knows what Monsieur Gilet has been doing at night for the last six years," said Philippe. "And the gossips, as you call them, have brought their guns to bear upon him. Morally speaking, he is ruined!"

As soon as Philippe left his uncle's house, Flore went to Max's room and described the audacious nephew's visit to the least detail.

"What's to be done?" said she.

"Before resorting to the last means of all, which

will be to fight with that tall corpse," Maxence replied, "we must try a *grand coup* and play double or quits. Let our old fool go with his nephew."

"But the great cur won't beat about the bush," cried Flore; "he'll call things by their names."

"Listen to me," said Max in a strident voice. "Do you think I haven't listened at doors and reflected on our position? Order a horse and carriage from Père Cognet; you must have them instantly! let everything be ready in five minutes. Put all your belongings inside, take La Védie and drive as fast as you can to Vatan; take up your quarters there as if you intended to remain, and take with you the twenty thousand francs he has in his secretary. If I bring the goodman to you at Vatan, don't consent to return until the power of attorney is signed. Then I will steer for Paris while you are on your way back to Issoudun. When Jean-Jacques returns from his walk and doesn't find you here, he'll lose his head and insist on running after you—Very good, then I will take it on myself to speak to him."

While this scheme was being matured Philippe walked away, arm-in-arm with his uncle, to Boulevard Baron.

"The two great politicians are face to face at last," said old Hochon to himself, as he looked after the colonel and his uncle. "I am curious to see the end of this game for a stake of ninety thousand francs a year."

"My dear uncle," said Philippe, whose language

bore the imprint of his associations in Paris, "you love this girl, and you're devilish right, for she's enticingly lovely! Instead of coddling you, she treats you like a footman, and that's very simple too; she would like to see you six feet under ground, so that she could marry Max, whom she worships—"

"Yes, I know that, Philippe, but I love her all the same."

"Very well; by the sorrows of my mother, who is your own sister," rejoined Philippe, "I have sworn to make your Rabouilleuse as supple as a glove in your hands, just as she must have been before that sneak, who isn't worthy to have served in the Garde Impériale, billeted himself at your house."

"Oh! if you should do that!—" said the old man.

"It's a very simple matter," Philippe replied, cutting his uncle short; "I'll kill your Max like a dog—But, only on one condition," he added.

"What is that?" asked old Rouget, gazing stupidly at his nephew.

"Don't sign the power of attorney they're asking you for, until December 3d; put them off till then. The two wretches want leave to sell your certificate for fifty thousand francs a year for the sole purpose of going to Paris to get married, and enjoying themselves with your million."

"I'm very much afraid so," replied Rouget.

"Very well, whatever they do to you, postpone signing the power of attorney until next week."

"Yes; but when Flore speaks to me she excites me so that I lose my mind. Why, when she looks at me in a certain way, her blue eyes are like paradise to me, and I have no control over myself, especially when she's been cross to me for several days."

"Well, if she is sugary with you, content yourself with promising her the power of attorney and let me know the day before you're to sign it. That will be enough for me: Maxence shall not be your attorney, or he will have killed me first. If I kill him, you will take me into your house, and then I'll make that pretty girl obey your finger and your eye. Yes, Flore shall love you, by God's thunder! or, if you're not satisfied with her, I'll cowhide her!"

"Oh! I will never allow that. A blow struck at Flore would cut me to the heart."

"But I tell you it's the only way of governing women and horses. A man makes himself feared and loved and respected in that way. That is what I wanted to whisper into the drum of your ear.— Good-morning, messieurs," he said to Mignonnet and Carpentier; "I'm taking my uncle out to walk, as you see, and trying to form his mind; for we live in an age when children are obliged to attend to the education of their grandparents."

Bows were exchanged on both sides.

"You see in my dear uncle the effects of an unhappy passion," continued the colonel. "They want to strip him of his fortune and leave him lying by the roadside like Ali Baba; you know whom I mean. The goodman knows all about the plot, but he hasn't the strength of mind to do without *nanan* for a few days in order to defeat it."

Philippe explained his uncle's position clearly.

"Messieurs," he concluded, "you see that there are not two ways of delivering my uncle; Colonel Bridau must kill Commandant Gilet or Commandant Gilet must kill Colonel Bridau. We celebrate the Emperor's coronation the day after to-morrow; I rely upon you to arrange the seats at the banquet so that I shall be opposite Commandant Gilet. You will do me the honor to be my seconds, I trust."

"We will elect you president and sit on each side of you. Max, as vice-president, will be your *vis-à-vis*," said Mignonnet.

"The hound will have Commandant Potel and Captain Renard on his side," said Carpentier. "Notwithstanding all the stories about his nocturnal raids, those two excellent men have been his seconds before and they will be faithful to him."

"You see, uncle," said Philippe, "how the thing is ripening; so don't sign before December 3d, for on the next day you will be free, happy, beloved by Flore, and without your court of aids."

"You don't know him, nephew," said the old man in dismay. "Max has killed nine men in duels."

"Yes, but not when the theft of a hundred thousand francs a year was involved."

"An evil conscience spoils the eye," observed Mignonnet sententiously.

"A few days hence," said Philippe, "you and La Rabouilleuse will be living together like a pair of turtle-doves, when her grief has worn itself out; for she will twist about like a worm, she will yelp and burst into tears; "but—just let the water flow!"

The two officers supported Philippe's arguments and did their utmost to inspire courage in Père Rouget, with whom they walked for nearly two hours. At last Philippe brought his uncle back to the house, saying to him as they parted:

"Don't make up your mind to anything without me. I know all about women; I paid for one who cost me more than Flore will ever cost you!—She taught me how to behave with the fair sex for the rest of my life. Women are naughty children, they are inferior to man, and you must make them afraid of you; for the worst thing that can happen to us is to be governed by the brutes!"

It was about two o'clock when the goodman returned home. Kouski opened the door; he was weeping, or, at all events, following the orders he had received from Maxence, he was pretending to weep.

"What's the matter?" asked Jean-Jacques.

"Oh! monsieur, madame has gone away with La Védie!"

"Go—one!" exclaimed the old man in a choking voice.

The blow was so severe that Rouget sat down on the stairs. A moment later, he rose, looked into

the living-room and the kitchen, went up to his
bedroom, searched all the rooms, returned to the
living-room, threw himself into an armchair and
burst into tears.

"Where is she?" he sobbed. "Where is she?
Where is Max?"

"I don't know," replied Kouski; "the commandant went out without saying anything to
me."

Gilet, like the very clever politician he was, had
deemed it advisable to take a stroll through the
town. By leaving the old man alone with his
despair, he would cause him to feel his desolation
more keenly and thus render him docile to his advice. But, in order to make sure that Philippe
should not comfort his uncle at that crisis, Max had
instructed Kouski to admit no one. With Flore
absent the old man was without rein or bit and the
situation would thus become extremely critical. As
he walked through the town Maxence Gilet was
avoided by several persons, who, twenty-four hours
before, would have been very eager to press his
hand. There was a general reaction against him.
The exploits of the Knights of Idleness were on
every tongue. The story of Joseph Bridau's arrest,
elucidated at last, disgraced Max, whose life and
conduct received their reward in a single day. He
met Commandant Potel, who was looking for him,
and who seemed to be intensely excited.

"What's the matter, Potel?"

"My dear fellow, the Garde Impériale is being

cried down all over town! The *pékins* are pointing their fingers at you, and that cuts me to the
quick."

"What do they complain of?" queried Max.

"Of what you've been doing to them at nights."

"As if a fellow couldn't amuse himself a little
bit!"

"But that's not all," said Potel.

Potel belonged to the same class of officers as the
man who said to a burgomaster: "Oh! we'll pay
you for your town if we burn it!" Therefore he
was very little shocked by the practical jokes of the
Knights of Idleness.

"What else?" said Gilet.

"The Guard is against the Guard! that's what
breaks my heart. Bridau's the man who has set
all these bourgeois against you. The Guard against
the Guard!—no, that's not as it should be! You
can't draw back, Max, so we must line up against
Bridau. Look you, I longed to pick a quarrel with
that long-legged hound and bring him down; for
then the bourgeois wouldn't have seen the Guard
against the Guard. In camp, I haven't a word to
say: two of the Guard fall out and they fight; there
are no *pékins* there to laugh at them. No, that
lanky rascal never served in the Guard. An officer
of the Guard would never act so before a parcel of
bourgeois, against another officer of the Guard!
Ah! the Guard is pointed at, and in Issoudun of all
places! where it was held in honor!—"

"Nonsense, Potel, don't you worry at all," replied

Maxence. "Even if you shouldn't see me at the banquet on the anniversary—"

"What! you won't be at Lacroix's the day after to-morrow?" cried Potel, interrupting his friend. "Why, do you want to be looked upon as a coward, to act as if you were avoiding Bridau? No, no! The foot-grenadiers of the Guard mustn't fall back before the dragoons of the Guard. Arrange your business some other way, and be there!"

"Still another one to do away with," said Max. "All right; I think I can be there and attend to my business too!—For," he said to himself, "the power of attorney mustn't be in my name. As old Héron said, that would look too much like robbery."

The lion, involved in the meshes of the net spread by Philippe Bridau, gnashed his teeth with rage; he avoided the glance of everybody he met and returned home by Boulevard Vilatte, saying to himself:

"Before I fight, I shall have the funds. If I die, at all events Philippe won't have the certificate. I shall have had it transferred to Flore's name. According to my instructions the child will go straight to Paris, and if she chooses she can marry the son of some marshal of the Empire who has been deprived of his bâton. I'll have the power of attorney made in Baruch's name, and he will transfer the certificate only on my order."

We must do Max the justice to say that he was never more calm outwardly than when his blood and his ideas were boiling. Never were the qualities

that go to make a great general exhibited in a
higher degree in a soldier. If his career had not
been cut short by his imprisonment, the Emperor
would certainly have found in this youth one of
the men who are so essential in carrying out vast
enterprises. As he entered the living-room where
the victim of all these tragic-comic scenes still sat
weeping, Max inquired the cause of his despair;
he feigned astonishment, he knew nothing at all,
he learned with well counterfeited surprise of Flore's
departure, he questioned Kouski to obtain some information as to the purpose of this inexplicable
journey.

"Madame told me," said Kouski, "to tell monsieur
that she had taken the twenty thousand francs that
were in his secretary, thinking that monsieur would
not refuse her that sum by way of wages for twenty-
two years."

"Wages?" said Rouget.

"Yes," Kouski replied. "'Oh! I shall never
come back again!' she said to La Védie as they
went away; for poor La Védie, who is very much
attached to monsieur, remonstrated with her. 'No,
no!' she said, 'he hasn't the least affection for me,
he let his nephew treat me like the lowest of the
low!'—And she wept—hot tears."

"Oh! I snap my fingers at Philippe!" cried the
old man, whom Max was watching closely. "Where
is Flore? How can we find out where she is?"

"Philippe, whose advice you follow, will assist
you," replied Max coldly.

"Philippe!" said the old man, "what can he do about the poor child?—You're the only one, my dear Max, who can find Flore; she will follow you and you will bring her back to me—"

"I don't wish to act in opposition to Monsieur Bridau," said Max.

"*Parbleu!*" cried Rouget, "if that's what embarrasses you, why he promised me that he'd kill you.—"

"Aha!" exclaimed Gilet, with a laugh, "we'll see about that."

"My boy," said the old man, "find Flore and tell her I'll do whatever she wants."

"They must have seen her pass somewhere in the town," said Maxence to Kouski; "serve the dinner, put everything on the table, and go and inquire from place to place, so that you can tell us at dessert what road Mademoiselle Brazier took."

This order momentarily quieted the poor man, who was groaning like a child who has lost his nurse. At that moment Maxence, whom Rouget hated as the cause of all his misfortunes, seemed to him an angel. Such a passion as Rouget's for Flore bears an astonishing resemblance to the passions of childhood. At six o'clock, the Pole, who had simply taken a walk, returned and announced that La Rabouilleuse had taken the Vatan road.

"Madame is returning to her own people, that is clear," said Kouski.

"Would you like to go to Vatan to-night?" Max asked the old man. "It's a bad road, but Kouski's a good driver, and you can make it up with her at eight o'clock better than to-morrow morning."

"Let us go!" cried Rouget.

"Harness the horse quietly and try not to let the town know anything of all this business, for Monsieur Rouget's honor. Saddle my horse, I will ride ahead," he said in Kouski's ear.

*

Monsieur Hochon had already sent word of Mademoiselle Brazier's departure to Philippe Bridau, who at once left the table at Mignonnet's and hurried to Place Saint-Jean; for he instantly divined the purpose of this clever strategy. When Philippe made his appearance at his uncle's house, Kouski answered from a window on the first floor that Monsieur Rouget could receive nobody.

"Fario," said Philippe to the Spaniard, who was walking on Grande-Narette, "tell Benjamin to have his horse ready; it is very important that I should know what my uncle and Maxence do."

"They're harnessing the horse to the berlin," said Fario, who was keeping watch on Rouget's house.

"If they go to Vatan," said Philippe, "find me another horse, and return with Benjamin to Monsieur Mignonnet's."

"What do you intend to do?" said Monsieur Hochon, coming out of his house when he saw Philippe and Fario on the square.

"The talent of a general, my dear Monsieur Hochon, consists not merely in closely watching the movements of the enemy, but also in divining his intentions from his movements, and in always modifying his plan as soon as the enemy disturbs it

25   (385)

by an unforeseen step. Now, if my uncle and Maxence go away together in the berlin, they are going
to Vatan; Maxence has promised to reconcile him
to Flore, who *fugit ad salices!*—that is a manœuvre
of General Virgil. If affairs take that course, I
don't know what I shall do; but I shall have the
night to think about it, for my uncle won't sign the
power at ten o'clock at night; the notaries are all
in bed. If, as the stamping of a second horse sug-
gests to my mind, Max rides on ahead of my uncle
to give Flore her instructions—which seems necessary and probable—the villain is lost! you will see
how we old soldiers take our revenge in the game
of inheritances.—And as I need a second for this
last hand in the game, I return to Mignonnet's to
make arrangements with my friend Carpentier."

Having pressed Monsieur Hochon's hand, Philippe
descended Petite-Narette on his way to Commandant Mignonnet's. Ten minutes later Monsieur
Hochon saw Maxence ride away at a fast trot, and
his old man's curiosity was so strongly aroused
that he remained standing at the window of the
living-room, waiting for the rumbling of the old
demi-fortune, which soon appeared. Jean-Jacques's
impatience led him to follow Maxence at an interval
of twenty minutes. Kouski, acting doubtless by
his master's orders, drove at a footpace, at least in
the town.

"If they are going to Paris, all is lost!" said
Monsieur Hochon to himself.

At that moment a small boy from Faubourg de

Rome appeared at Monsieur Hochon's with a letter
for Baruch. The two grandsons, in disgrace since
the morning, had voluntarily remained within doors.
As they reflected upon their future, they realized
how much depended upon standing well with their
grandparents. Baruch was well aware of his
grandfather Hochon's influence over his grandfather and grandmother Borniche; Monsieur Hochon
would not fail to turn all the Borniche property in
Adolphine's direction, if his conduct justified them
in resting their hopes upon the grand marriage with
which he had been threatened that very morning.
Baruch, being richer than François, had more to
lose; therefore he was for absolute submission upon
no other conditions than the payment of their debts
to Max. As to François, his future was in his
grandfather's hands; he had no hope of fortune
except from him, and according to the guardianship
account he was his debtor. Solemn promises were
therefore made by the two young men, whose
repentance was stimulated by their endangered
prospects, and Madame Hochon reassured them as
to their debts to Max.

"You have made fools of yourselves," she said;
"make up for it by behaving yourselves and Monsieur Hochon will calm down."

And so, when François had read the letter over
Baruch's shoulder, he said in his ear:

"Ask grandpapa's advice."

"Look at this," said Baruch, carrying the letter
to the old man.

"Read it to me, I haven't my glasses."

"MY DEAR FRIEND,

"I trust that you will not hesitate, considering the serious plight in which I find myself, to confer a favor on me by consenting to act as Monsieur Rouget's attorney. Be at Vatan at nine o'clock to-morrow. I shall probably send you to Paris, but don't be alarmed; I will give you money for the journey and join you there very soon, for I am almost sure that I shall have to leave Issoudun on the third of December. Adieu : I rely upon your friendship, do you rely upon that of your friend,

"MAXENCE."

"God be praised!" exclaimed Monsieur Hochon, "that imbecile's money is saved from the claws of those devils!"

"It will be, if you say so," said Madame Hochon, "and I thank God, who has doubtless listened to my prayers. The triumph of the wicked is always fleeting."

"You will go to Vatan, you will accept Monsieur Rouget's power of attorney," said the old man to Baruch. "They propose to transfer fifty thousand francs a year to the name of Mademoiselle Brazier. You will start for Paris; but you will stop at Orléans and await a line from me there. Take a room at the last inn on Faubourg Bannier, even if it's no more than a teamsters' inn, and don't let any person whomsoever know where you lodge."

"Listen!" said François, who had rushed to the window upon hearing the wheels of a carriage on Grande-Narette, "here's something new; Père

Rouget and Monsieur Philippe Bridau are returning together in the calèche, with Benjamin and Monsieur Carpentier following on horseback!"

"I'll go over there," cried Monsieur Hochon, whose curiosity carried the day over every other feeling.

Monsieur Hochon found old Rouget in his room, writing the following letter at his nephew's dictation:

" MADEMOISELLE,

"If you do not return to my house immediately upon receipt of this letter, your conduct will denote so much ingratitude for my kindness to you, that I shall revoke the will I have made in your favor and give my fortune to my nephew Philippe. You will understand too that Monsieur Gilet can no longer be an inmate of my house, as he is with you at Vatan. I entrust this letter to Monsieur le Capitaine Carpentier, and I trust that you will listen to his advice, for he will speak to you in the name of

" Your affectionate
" J.-J. ROUGET."

"Captain Carpentier and I *met* my uncle, who was foolish enough to start for Vatan in pursuit of Mademoiselle Brazier and Commandant Gilet," said Philippe with profound irony to Monsieur Hochon. "I made my uncle understand that he was running head-foremost into a trap; won't the girl desert him as soon as he has signed the power of attorney she demands so that she can sell to herself a certificate for fifty thousand francs a year? By writing this letter, won't he see the fair fugitive under his roof again this very night?—I undertake to make Mademoiselle Brazier as pliable as a reed for the rest of his days, if my uncle will allow me to take the place of Monsieur Gilet, who seems to me more than out of place here. Am I right?—and yet my uncle is complaining!"

"Neighbor," said Monsieur Hochon, "you have taken the best means to obtain peace in your house. If you take my advice you will destroy your will, and then you will find Flore will be the same to you that she was in the beginning."

"No, for she will never forgive me the pain I am going to cause her," said the old man, weeping; "she will never love me again."

"She shall love you, and love you well; I'll answer for it," said Philippe.

"Pray open your eyes!" said Monsieur Hochon to Rouget. "They mean to strip you and desert you—"

"Ah! if I were sure of it!" cried the imbecile.

"See, here's a letter Maxence wrote to my grandson Borniche," said old Hochon. "Read it!"

"What a horrible thing!" cried Carpentier, as Rouget read the letter aloud, weeping as he read.

"Is that definite enough, uncle?" queried Philippe. "Hold the girl by her selfish interests, I tell you, and she will adore you—as much as anyone could; willingly or unwillingly."

"She's too fond of Maxence, she will leave me," said the old man, in evident alarm.

"But, uncle, either Max or I won't leave any

footprints on the streets of Issoudun after the day after to-morrow."

"Very well, go, Monsieur Carpentier," said the goodman; "if you promise me that she will come back, go! You're an honest man; tell her whatever you think you ought to tell her in my name—"

"Captain Carpentier will whisper in her ear that I have sent to Paris for a young woman whose youth and beauty are decidedly dainty," said Philippe, "and the hussy will come back at full speed!"

The captain started, driving the old calèche himself; he was accompanied by Benjamin on horseback, for Kouski was not to be found. Although threatened by the two officers with prosecution and the loss of his place, the Pole had fled to Vatan on a hired horse, to inform Maxence and Flore of their adversary's *coup de main.* Carpentier, when he had accomplished his mission, was to take Benjamin's horse, as he did not choose to return with La Rabouilleuse.

When he learned of Kouski's flight, Philippe said to Benjamin:

"You will take the Pole's place here from this evening. So try to cling behind the calèche, without Flore's knowledge, in order to arrive here at the same time that she does.—Things are coming round, Papa Hochon!" he added. "The banquet the day after to-morrow will be a joyful affair."

"Are you going to take up your quarters here?" asked the old miser.

"I have just told Fario to send me all my belongings. I shall sleep in the room that opens on the same landing as Gilet's; my uncle agrees."

"What will be the end of all this?" said the terrified Rouget.

"The end of it will be that Mademoiselle Flore Brazier will arrive here four hours hence, gentle as the Paschal Lamb," replied Monsieur Hochon.

"God grant it!" exclaimed the goodman, wiping away his tears.

"It is seven o'clock," said Philippe, "and the queen of your heart will be here about half-past eleven. You won't see Gilet again; won't you be as happy as the Pope?—If you want my triumph to be complete," Philippe whispered to Monsieur Hochon, "stay with us until that monkey arrives; you can help me to hold the goodman to his resolution, and, between us, we will make Mademoiselle La Rabouilleuse understand her real interests."

Monsieur Hochon bore Philippe company, recognizing the reasonableness of his request; but they both had much to do, for Père Rouget abandoned himself to childish lamentations, which did not cease until Philippe had repeated this argument ten times over:

"Uncle, if Flore returns and treats you kindly, you will acknowledge that I was right. You will be coddled to your heart's content, you will keep your consols, you will henceforth be guided by my advice and everything will go along as smoothly as if you were in paradise."

PHILIPPE TO FLORE

———

"*Kouski,*" *said Philippe, offering his hand to assist Flore to alight,* "*you are no longer in Monsieur Rouget's service, you will not sleep here to-night, so pack your trunks; Benjamin here takes your place.*"

"*Are you the master, pray?*" *queried Flore ironically.*

"*With your permission,*" *replied Philippe, pressing her hand in his as in a vice.* "*Come! we must both* rabouiller *our hearts.*"

When at half-past eleven, they heard the rumbling of the berlin on Grande-Narette, the question in all their minds was whether it was occupied or unoccupied. Rouget's face wore an expression of horrible agony, which was replaced by the predominant look of excessive joy when he caught sight of the two women as the carriage turned into the square.

"Kouski," said Philippe, offering his hand to assist Flore to alight, "you are no longer in Monsieur Rouget's service, you will not sleep here to-night, so pack your trunks; Benjamin here takes your place."

"Are you the master, pray?" queried Flore ironically.

"With your permission," replied Philippe, pressing her hand in his as in a vice. "Come! we must both *rabouiller* our hearts."

He led the bewildered woman a few steps away on Place Saint-Jean.

"My love, Gilet will be laid low by this arm the day after to-morrow," said the trooper, putting out his right hand, "or else his will make me lower my crest. If I die, you will be the mistress in my poor fool of an uncle's house: *bene sit!* If I remain on my stumps, walk straight and serve him up happiness number one. If you don't, why I know Rabouilleuses at Paris, who, without any disparagement to you, are prettier than you, for they're only seventeen; they will make my uncle extremely happy and will act in my interest. Begin your service to-night, for if the goodman isn't as gay as a lark to-morrow, I have just one word to say to you; listen carefully! There's only one way of killing a man without giving the law a chance to say a word, and that is to fight a duel with him; but I know three ways of getting rid of a woman. There you are, my girl!''

During this harangue, Flore trembled as if she were attacked with fever.

"Kill Max?—'' she said, glancing at Philippe in the moonlight.

"Come, here's my uncle—''

In truth, Père Rouget, despite Monsieur Hochon's remonstrances, came out into the street and took Flore by the hand, like a miser laying hold of his treasure; he returned to the house, led her to his own room, and locked himself in.

"This is Saint-Lambert's day; the man who leaves his place, loses it,'' said Benjamin to the Pole.

"My master will close all your mouths,'' Kouski replied, going off to join Max, who had taken up his quarters at the Hôtel de La Poste.

The next day, from nine o'clock to eleven, the women of the town were all talking with one another at their doors. The one subject of conversation was the extraordinary revolution in Père Rouget's household the night before. The substance of the conversations was the same everywhere.

"What will happen to-morrow, at the coronation dinner, between Max and Colonel Bridau?''

Philippe said a word or two to La Védie: "An annuity of six hundred francs, or turned out!" which rendered her neutral for the moment between two powers as formidable as Philippe and Flore.

Knowing that Max's life was in danger, Flore became even more amiable to old Rouget than in the early days of their housekeeping. Alas! in love, selfish deception is superior to the truth, and that is why so many men pay so dearly for their experience with clever deceivers. La Rabouilleuse did not appear until breakfast, when she came down with Rouget leaning on her arm. Tears stood in her eyes when she saw in Max's place the redoubtable trooper with his threatening blue eye, his coldly sinister face.

"What is the matter, mademoiselle?" he asked, after wishing his uncle good-morning.

"The matter is, nephew, that she can't endure the thought that you are going to fight with Commandant Gilet—"

"I haven't the slightest wish to kill this Gilet," Philippe replied; "he has only to leave Issoudun and sail for America with a stock of goods to sell, and I will be the first to advise you to give him the wherewithal to buy the best goods in the market, and to wish him a pleasant journey! He will make his fortune, and that will be much more honorable than playing practical jokes in Issoudun at night and raising the devil in your house."

"Well, isn't that proper?" said Rouget, glancing at Flore.

"To Ame-e-e-rica!" she replied, sobbing bitterly.

"It's better to be on your legs in New York than to rot in a wooden coat in France.—But you tell me that he's a skilful fighter; perhaps he'll kill me!" observed the colonel.

"Will you let me speak to him?" entreated Flore in an humble and submissive tone.

"Certainly; he's at liberty to come here and get his belongings; but I will stay with my uncle meanwhile, for I don't propose to leave the goodman again," Philippe replied.

"Védie," cried Flore, "run to La Poste, and tell the commandant that I beg him to—"

"To come and get everything that belongs to him," said Philippe, cutting her short.

"Yes, yes, Védie. That will be the best excuse for seeing me; I want to speak to him."

The girl's hatred was so held in check by her terror, the bewilderment which she, who had hitherto been flattered and fawned upon, experienced upon coming in contact with a strong and pitiless nature, was so great, that she accustomed herself to submit to Philippe, as poor Rouget had accustomed himself to submit to her. She anxiously awaited La Védie's return; but La Védie returned with a formal refusal from Max, who requested Mademoiselle Brazier to send his effects to the Hôtel de la Poste.

"Will you allow me to go and take them to him?" she asked Jean-Jacques.

"Yes, but you will return, won't you?" the old man replied.

"If mademoiselle has not returned at noon, you will give me your power of attorney to sell our consols at one o'clock," said Philippe, looking at Flore.—"Go with La Védie to save appearances, mademoiselle. We must henceforth take some care of my uncle's honor."

Flore could obtain nothing from Maxence. The commandant, in despair at having allowed himself to be ousted from his ignoble position in the sight of the whole town, was too proud to run away from Philippe. La Rabouilleuse combated his arguments with a suggestion that they should fly together to America; but Gilet, who did not want Flore without Père Rouget's fortune, but did not choose to show the girl his whole heart, persisted in his purpose to kill Philippe.

"We have been guilty of the most stupid folly," he said. "We must all three go to Paris to pass the winter; but how could we have imagined, when we first saw that cadaverous creature, that things would turn out this way? Events move with a rapidity that makes one's head swim. I took the colonel for one of the swashbucklers, who haven't two ideas in their heads; that was my mistake. As I didn't know enough at first to double on my tracks, I should be a coward now to retreat before the colonel; he has ruined me in the opinion of the town, and I can rehabilitate myself only by his death."

"Go to America with forty thousand francs; I'll

find a way to get rid of that savage, and I'll join
you there; that will be the wisest way—"

"What would people think of me?" he cried,
with the fear of the gossips in his mind. "No.
Why, I have buried nine men already. This fellow
doesn't seem to me to be very skilful: he went
from the school into the army, was in active service up to 1815, and then traveled in America; so
my lubber has never set foot in a fencing school,
while I am without an equal with the sabre! The
sabre is the weapon of his branch of the service, so
I shall seem to be generous by offering to fight with
it,—for I shall try to be the insulted party,—and
I'll finish him. Unquestionably that is the better
way. Don't you be alarmed: we shall be on top
after to-morrow."

Thus the absurd point of honor had more weight
with Max than the healthy promptings of prudence.
Flore returned home at one o'clock and shut herself
up in her room, to weep at her leisure. During
the whole day the gossips were in full cry in Issoudun, where a duel between Philippe and Maxence
was regarded as inevitable.

"Ah! Monsieur Hochon," said Mignonnet, who,
with Carpentier, met the old man walking on Boulevard Baron, "we are very uneasy, for Gilet is very
skilful with every sort of weapon."

"No matter if he is," replied the old provincial
diplomatist, "Philippe has managed this business
extremely well. And I wouldn't have believed that
such a great careless fellow would succeed so

quickly. The two youngsters have bowled along toward each other like two storms."

"Oh!" said Carpentier, "Philippe's a deep fellow; his conduct before the Court of Peers was a masterpiece of diplomacy."

"Well, Captain Renard," observed a bourgeois, "they say that wolves don't eat one another, but it seems that Max is going to have a brush with Colonel Bridau. That will be a serious matter, between two men of the Old Guard."

"You people laugh about it! Because the poor fellow had a little sport at night, you are all down on him," said Commandant Potel. "But Gilet's a man who can hardly stay in a hole like Issoudun, without something to occupy his mind."

"After all, messieurs," said a fourth, "Max and the colonel have played the game they were bound to play. Shouldn't the colonel avenge his brother Joseph? Don't you remember Max's treachery to that poor fellow?"

"Bah! an artist," said Renard.

"But Père Rouget's fortune is at stake. They say Monsieur Gilet was just about to lay hold of fifty thousand francs a year when the colonel took up his quarters at his uncle's."

"Gilet, steal anybody's money?—Look you, don't say that anywhere else, Monsieur Ganivet," cried Potel, "or we'll make you swallow your tongue, and without sauce!"

In all the bourgeois households prayers were offered for the excellent Colonel Bridau.

*

The next afternoon, about four o'clock, all the officers of the old army who lived in Issoudun or its neighborhood were walking on the Place du Marché, in front of the door of a café kept by one Lacroix, awaiting the arrival of Philippe Bridau. The banquet by which the anniversary of the coronation was to be commemorated was to begin at five o'clock, the military hour. The affair of Maxence and his summary ejection from Père Rouget's house was the topic of conversation in all the groups, for the private soldiers had conceived the idea of holding a reunion in a wineshop on the square. Among the officers, Potel and Renard were the only persons who tried to defend their friend.

"Is it our business to interfere with what takes place between two heirs?" said Renard.

"Max is weak with women," observed the cynical Potel.

"There will be swords unsheathed before long," said a former sub-lieutenant, who cultivated a marsh in Upper Baltan. "If Monsieur Maxence Gilet was foolish enough to come and live at Monsieur Rouget's, he would be a coward to allow himself to be driven out like a lackey without demanding satisfaction."

"Certainly," rejoined Mignonnet dryly. "A foolish act that doesn't succeed, becomes a crime."

Max, who joined the other old soldiers of Napoléon at that moment, was greeted with significant silence. Potel and Renard each took an arm of their friend, and walked a few steps away to talk with him. At the same moment Philippe appeared in the distance, in full feather, dragging his cane behind him with an imperturbable air, in striking contrast to the profound attention which Max was forced to give to the words of his two remaining friends. Mignonnet, Carpentier and some others shook hands with Philippe. This welcome, so different from that just accorded Max, completely put to flight the lingering thoughts of cowardice,—of prudence, if you please,—to which Flore's entreaties, and above all her caresses, had given birth when he was left to himself.

"We will fight," he said to Captain Renard, "and to the death! So say no more to me, but let me play my part."

After these last words, uttered in a feverish tone, the three Bonapartists returned to the group of officers. Max bowed first to Bridau, who returned his salute with the coldest glance imaginable.

"Come, messieurs, to the table!" exclaimed Commandant Potel.

"Let us drink to the imperishable glory of *Le Petit Tondu*, who is now in the paradise of heroes!" cried Renard.

One and all understood the purpose of the diminutive captain of *voltigeurs*, for they felt that the constraint would be less embarrassing at table. So

they hurried to the long, low dining-room of the Lacroix restaurant, the windows of which looked upon
the market place. Each guest promptly took his
place at the table, where, as Philippe had requested,
he and his adversary were seated facing each other.
Several young men of the town, mostly former
Knights of Idleness, much disturbed as to the probable outcome of the banquet, walked back and forth
discussing the critical position in which Philippe
had succeeded in placing Maxence Gilet. They
deplored the collision, while looking upon it and the
duel as inevitable. Everything passed off smoothly
until the dessert, although the two athletes, notwithstanding the excitement of the occasion, maintained a watchful attitude that indicated something
resembling uneasiness. Pending the beginning of
the quarrel, with which the minds of both must
have been filled, Philippe displayed admirable *sang-
froid* and Max a bewildering flow of spirits; but to
an experienced eye each was playing a part.

When the dessert was served, Philippe said:

"Fill your glasses, my friends. I claim the privilege of proposing the first toast."

"He said *my friends;* don't fill your glass," Renard
whispered to Max.

Max filled his glass.

"To the *Grande Armée!*" cried Philippe with
unfeigned enthusiasm.

"To the *Grande Armée!*" all the guests repeated
as with a single voice.

At that moment eleven private soldiers, among

whom were Benjamin and Kouski, appeared in the doorway, repeating: "To the *Grande Armée!*"

"Come in, my boys! we are going to drink *his* health," said Commandant Potel.

The old soldiers entered and took their places, standing behind the officers.

"You see that *he* isn't dead!" said Kouski to an old sergeant who had doubtless been lamenting the sufferings of the Emperor, ended at last.

"I claim the second toast," said Commandant Mignonnet.

The others pretended to eat to keep themselves in countenance. Mignonnet rose.

"To those who tried to restore *his* son!" he said.

All except Maxence bowed to Philippe Bridau and held out their glasses toward him.

"Listen to me," said Max, rising from his seat.

"It's Max! it's Max!" was heard from without.

Then profound silence reigned in the room and on the square, for Gilet's character led everyone to expect an insult.

"May we *all* meet here to celebrate the same anniversary next year!"

And he bowed to Philippe ironically.

"He's forming his lines," said Kouski to his neighbor.

"In Paris the police don't allow you to have banquets like this," said Commandant Potel to Philippe.

"Why the devil do you mention the police to Colonel Bridau?" said Max insolently.

"Commandant Potel had no malicious purpose in what *he* said!" retorted Philippe, with a bitter smile.

The silence became so profound that you could have heard a fly's wings.

"The police fear me enough," Philippe continued, "to send me to Issoudun, where I have had the pleasure of finding some old comrades; but you must admit that there are no great diversions here. For a man who didn't dislike pleasures, I am pretty badly off. However, I will save up my money for the young ladies, for I am not one of those who find consols in feather beds, and Mariette of the Opéra cost me enormous sums."

"Do you say that for my benefit, Monsieur le Colonel?" said Max, darting a glance at Philippe that was like an electric current.

"Take it as you choose, Commandant Gilet," retorted Philippe.

"Colonel, my two friends, Renard and Potel, will arrange matters to-morrow with—"

"With Mignonnet and Carpentier," said Philippe, cutting his adversary short, and indicating his two neighbors.

"Now," said Max, "let us go on with the toasts."

Neither of the two adversaries had departed from the ordinary tone of conversation; there was nothing solemn in the incident except the silence that prevailed while they were speaking.

"I say, you fellows," said Philippe, glancing at the private soldiers, "just remember that our affairs don't concern the bourgeois.—Not a word of what has taken place. It must remain a secret with the Old Guard."

"They will obey orders, colonel," said Renard; "I'll answer for them."

"Long live his son! May he reign over France!" cried Potel.

"Death to the Englishman!" cried Carpentier.

This toast was received with prodigious enthusiasm.

"Shame upon Hudson Lowe!" said Captain Renard.

The dessert passed off very smoothly, the libations were ample. The two adversaries and their four seconds made it a point of honor that this duel, in which an immense fortune was at stake, and in which the principals were men so distinguished for personal courage, should have nothing in common with ordinary disputes. Two *gentlemen* could not have borne themselves more properly than Max and Philippe. Thus the expectations of the young men and of the worthy bourgeois who stood in groups upon the square, were disappointed. All the guests, like true soldiers, observed the most profound secrecy as to the episode that occurred at dessert. At ten o'clock, each of the principals was informed that the weapon agreed upon was the sabre. The place selected for the meeting was the apse of the Capuchin church, and the time eight o'clock in the morning. Goddet, who, as a former surgeon-major, was one of the guests at the banquet, was requested to be present at the meeting. The seconds decided that the duel should not last more than ten minutes, whatever might happen.

At eleven o'clock at night, just as he was about to retire, Philippe, to his intense surprise, received a visit from Monsieur Hochon and his wife.

"We know what is going on," said the old lady with tears in her eyes, "and I have come to beg you not to go out to-morrow without saying your prayers.—Raise your eyes to God."

"Yes, madame," replied Philippe in obedience to a signal from old Hochon, who stood behind his wife.

"That is not all," said Agathe's godmother: "I put myself in your poor mother's place, and I have decided to give up my most precious possession; see!"

She held out to Philippe a tooth lying upon a piece of black velvet embroidered with gold, to which she had sewn two green ribbons, and replaced it in a bag after she had shown it to him.

"It's a relic of Sainte-Solange, the patron saint of Berri; I saved it in the Revolution; wear it on your breast to-morrow morning."

"Can that protect me from sword thrusts?" queried Philippe.

"Yes," was the reply.

"I can no more wear that affair upon me than I can wear a coat of mail!" cried Agathe's son.

"What does he say?" Madame Hochon asked her husband.

"He says that it's not allowed," replied old Hochon.

"Very well, then we'll say no more about it," said the old lady. "I will pray for you."

"Surely, madame, a prayer and a good thrust with the point can do no harm," said the colonel, going through the motion of running Monsieur Hochon through the heart.

The old lady insisted upon kissing Philippe's forehead. Then, as they went downstairs, she gave ten crowns, all the money she owned, to Benjamin, to bribe him to sew the relic into his master's trousers pocket. This Benjamin did, not because he believed in the virtue of the tooth, for he said that his master had a much better one with which to bite Gilet, but because he felt bound to execute a commission for which he was so handsomely paid. Madame Hochon withdrew, full of confidence in Sainte-Solange.

At eight o'clock on the following morning, December 3d, under a cloudy sky, Max, accompanied by his two seconds and the Pole, arrived at the little meadow which at that time surrounded the apse of the Capuchin church. They found Philippe and his seconds there, with Benjamin. Potel and Mignonnet measured twenty-four feet. At each end of that space the two soldiers with the assistance of a spade, drew a line. Under penalty of being branded as cowards, the combatants could not fall back beyond their respective lines; each of them was to stand upon his line

and advance at will when the seconds called:
"Go!"

"Shall we remove our coats?" Philippe coldly
asked Gilet.

"Willingly, colonel," Maxence replied, with the
assurance of a bully.

They stripped to their trousers; their flesh could
be seen through their thin shirts. They were
armed with regulation sabres, of the same weight,
about three pounds, and of the same length, three
feet; they took their places, holding the points
downward and awaiting the signal. The whole performance was marked by such calmness on both
sides that, notwithstanding the cold, their muscles
quivered no more than if they were made of bronze.
Goddet, the four seconds and the two soldiers felt
an involuntary thrill.

"They're fine fellows!"

This exclamation escaped from the mouth of
Commandant Potel.

Just as the signal: "Go!" was given, Maxence
noticed Fario's sinister face watching them through
the hole the knights had made in the church roof to
admit the pigeons into his storehouse. His eyes,
from which two streams of fire, hate and vengeance
seemed to pour, dazzled Max. The colonel walked
straight up to his adversary, putting himself on
guard in such a way as to seize the advantage. Ex-
perts in the art of killing know that the most skilful
of two adversaries will always "take the pole," to
use an expression which metaphorically describes

the effect of a high guard. This attitude, which
enables the duelist to watch his adversary's ap-
proach, is so sure an indication of a duelist of the
first order, that the consciousness of his own in-
feriority was borne in upon Max's mind and produced that confusion of forces which demoralizes a
gambler when he meets a master hand or a lucky
player, so that he plays with less than his usual
skill.

"Ah! the lascar!" said Max to himself, "he's an
old hand, I am lost!"

Max tried a windmill movement, handling his
weapon with the dexterity of a drum-major; he
hoped to confuse Philippe and to strike his sabre and
disarm him; but he saw, at the first onset, that the
colonel had a wrist of iron and as flexible as a steel
spring. Maxence found that he must try some
other plan, and he attempted to reflect, the unlucky
wretch! whereas Philippe, whose eyes shot forth
brighter gleams than the sabres, parried all his attacks with the *sang-froid* of a fencing-master with
his mask, giving an exhibition.

Between men as strong as the two combatants,
there occurs a phenomenon almost like that which
takes place among men of the lower classes in the
terrible combat called the *savate*. Victory depends
upon a false movement, upon an error in the calculation, swift as light, which one instinctively makes.
During a space of time which seems as brief to the
spectators as it seems long to the adversaries, the
struggle consists in close observation which absorbs

the energies of mind and body, concealed behind feints whose moderation and apparent timidity lead one to believe that neither of the two really wants to fight. Such a moment, followed by a rapid and decisive struggle, is one of terrible suspense to connoisseurs in dueling. At an ill-judged parry on Max's part, Philippe sent his sabre spinning out of his hand.

"Pick it up," he said, suspending operations; "I am not the man to kill a disarmed enemy."

It was the sublimity of atrocity. The grandeur of this conduct implied such superiority, that it was taken for the most adroit of all manœuvres by the spectators. In fact, when Max stood at guard once more, he had lost his self-possession and found himself still under the shadow of the high guard which threatens one while covering one's adversary; he attempted thereupon to atone for his shameful defeat by playing a bold game; he abandoned all thought of protecting himself, grasped his sabre with both hands and rushed furiously at Philippe, intending to wound him mortally while sacrificing his own life. Although Philippe received a blow which gashed his forehead and his cheek, he cleft Max's head obliquely with a terrible windmill stroke with which he sought to deaden the force of the blow Max aimed at him. These two frantic blows brought the battle to a close in the ninth minute. Fario left his post of observation and came down to feast his eyes upon his enemy in the convulsions of death, for Max was such a powerful man that his muscles writhed and twisted horribly.

Philippe was taken to his uncle's house.

Thus died a man who was destined to do great things, if he had remained amid the surroundings that were best suited to his character; a man treated by nature as a spoiled child, for she endowed him with courage, self-possession and political shrewdness of the Cæsar Borgia type. But education had not imparted to him that nobility of ideas and conduct without which nothing is possible in any career. He was not regretted, because of the underhand means adopted by his adversary, who was a worse man than he, to bring him into disrepute. His death put an end to the exploits of the Knights of Idleness, to the unbounded satisfaction of the town of Issoudun. Philippe was not molested on account of the duel, which seemed a manifestation of divine vengeance; the circumstances attending it attained wide currency throughout the neighborhood, and the conduct of both the participants was unanimously praised.

"They ought to have killed each other," said Monsieur Mouilleron; "it would have been a good riddance for the government."

Flore Brazier's position would have been very embarrassing, had it not been for the serious illness caused by Max's death; she had an attack of brain-fever, combined with a dangerous inflammation occasioned by the exciting events of the last three days; if she had enjoyed her usual health, perhaps she would have fled from the house where, in the room above hers, in Max's room and between Max's sheets, lay Max's murderer. She was between life and death for three months, attended by Monsieur Goddet, who was also in attendance upon Philippe.

As soon as Philippe could hold a pen, he wrote the following letters:

" To MONSIEUR DESROCHES, SOLICITOR:

"I have already killed the more venomous of the two beasts, but I did not do it without having my own head split open by a sabre cut; luckily, the rascal's hand was paralyzed. There remains another viper, with whom I propose to try and come to terms, for my uncle thinks as much of her as of his own gizzard. I was afraid that this Rabouilleuse, who is devilish pretty, by the way, would clear out, for my uncle would have followed her; but she had a sudden and serious attack of sickness that nailed her to her bed. If God wished to befriend me, He would recall that soul to His own bosom while it repents of its errors. Meanwhile I have on my side, thanks to Monsieur Hochon—the old trump—the physician, one Goddet, a good fellow, who opines that the inheritances of uncles are better placed in the hands of nephews than of such hussies. Monsieur Hochon, by the way, has some influence over a certain Papa Fichet, whose daughter is very rich, and whom Goddet would like as a wife for his son; so that the thousand-franc note he was allowed a glimpse of, as the prospective reward for curing my noddle, counts for little in his devotion. This Goddet, a former surgeon-major in the Third of the line, has also been made much of by two gallant officers, Mignonnet and Carpentier, who are my good friends, so that he preaches to his patient.

"'There's a God, after all, my child,' he says, feeling her pulse. 'You have been the cause of a great misfortune, and you must repair it. The finger of God is in it '—it's inconceivable how much people make the finger of God do !—'Religion is religion ; submit, resign yourself ; in the first place it will calm you, and it will cure you almost as well as my drugs. Above all, remain here and nurse your master. In short, forget and forgive ; that is the Christian law.'

" This Goddet has promised to keep La Rabouilleuse in bed three months. Insensibly, she will become used, perhaps, to living under the same roof with me. I have enlisted the cook in my interest. The abominable hag told her mistress that Max would have made her life very hard. She heard the dear departed say, so she told her, that, if he was compelled to marry Flore when the goodman died, he didn't propose to have his ambition balked by a strumpet. And the cook has reached the point of hinting to her mistress that Max would have got rid of her. So all goes well. My uncle, acting on Père Hochon's advice, has torn up his will."

" To MONSIEUR GIROUDEAU, care of MADEMOISELLE FLORENTINE, RUE DE VENDÔME, AU MARAIS :

" MY OLD COMRADE,

" Find out if that little rat of a Césarine is engaged, and try to have her all ready to come to Issoudun as soon as I send for her. Then let the hussy come by the next coach. She must be gotten up in decent shape and drop everything that smells of the wings : for she must appear in the province as the daughter of a gallant soldier, dead on the field of honor. So plenty of morality, boarding-school clothes, and virtue of the first quality : such are the orders. If I need Césarine, and if she succeeds, there will be fifty thousand francs for her at my uncle's death ; if she is engaged, explain the matter to Florentine ; and between you find me some *figurante* capable of playing the part. I had my skull grazed in my duel with my devourer of inheritances, who has turned up his toes. I'll tell you about the stroke ! Ah ! old boy, we shall see some fine days and we'll have some sport yet, or the

Other won't be the Other. If you can send me five hundred cartridges, I can use them. Adieu, my old comrade. Light your cigar with my letter. It is understood that the officer's daughter is to come from Châteauroux, and to pretend to want assistance. I hope, however, that I shall not have to resort to this dangerous method. Remember me to Mariette and all our friends."

Agathe, informed by a letter from Madame Hochon, hurried to Issoudun, and was received by her brother, who gave her Philippe's former room. The poor mother, whose love for the son she had cursed was instantly renewed in all its force, enjoyed a few happy days listening to the bourgeoisie of the town sing the colonel's praises.

"After all, my love," said Madame Hochon on the day of her arrival, "youth must have its fling. The frivolous actions of the soldiers of the Emperor's day cannot be repeated by young men under their father's eye. Ah! if you knew all the tricks that wretched Max perpetrated here, at night!—Issoudun, thanks to your son, breathes and sleeps in peace. Philippe came to his senses a little late, but he came; as he said to us, three months in prison at the Luxembourg make one's head clearer; his behavior here has delighted Monsieur Hochon, and he enjoys general consideration. If your son can remain away from the temptations of Paris for some little time, he will end by being a great comfort to you."

When she heard these consoling words, Agathe raised her eyes, filled with tears of happiness, to her godmother's face.

Philippe played the saint with his mother, for he
needed her. The clever tactician preferred not to
have recourse to Césarine unless he should prove to
be an object of horror to Mademoiselle Brazier.
Recognizing in Flore an admirable instrument fashioned by Max, a habit adopted by his uncle, he desired to use her rather than a Parisian who might
induce the goodman to marry her. Just as Fouché
advised Louis XVIII. to sleep between Napoléon's
sheets instead of granting a *Charter*, Philippe desired to remain between Gilet's sheets; but he was
disinclined also to lessen the good reputation he
had made for himself in Berri; now, to continue to
play Max's rôle with La Rabouilleuse would be
quite as odious a performance on her part as on his.
He could, without dishonoring himself, live in his
uncle's house and at his uncle's expense, by virtue
of the laws of nepotism; but he could not have
Flore unless she were rehabilitated. In the midst of
so many difficulties, spurred on by the hope of
gaining possession of the inheritance, he conceived
the admirable idea of making La Rabouilleuse his
aunt. And so, with that latent design, he bade his
mother go to see the girl and show her some affection, treating her as she would a sister-in-law.

"I must confess, my dear mother," he said, assuming a hypocritical expression as he glanced at
Monsieur and Madame Hochon, who had come to
call upon dear Agathe, "that my uncle's manner of
life is far from becoming, and he would need do no
more than regularize it to obtain for Mademoiselle

Brazier the esteem of the town. Would it not be better for her to be Madame Rouget than the servant-mistress of an old bachelor? Isn't it simpler to acquire definite rights by a contract of marriage than to threaten a whole family with exheredation? If you and Monsieur Hochon and some good priest would talk the matter over, we might put an end to a scandal which distresses virtuous people. And then Mademoiselle Brazier would be happy to be greeted by you as a sister and by myself as an aunt.''

The next day, Agathe and Madame Hochon visited Mademoiselle Flore's bedside and made known to her and to Rouget, Philippe's praiseworthy sentiments. The colonel was spoken of throughout all Issoudun as an excellent man of noble character, especially because of his conduct toward Flore. For a month La Rabouilleuse listened to Monsieur Goddet, her physician—this man whose influence over the mind of his patient was so great!—the respectable Madame Hochon, impelled by religious sentiments, and the gentle and pious Agathe, setting forth all the advantages of a marriage with Rouget. When, captivated by the thought of becoming Madame Rouget, a worthy and honest bourgeoise, she expressed an earnest desire to recover her health, in order that the marriage might take place, it was not difficult to make her understand that she could not enter the old Rouget family with the intention of turning Philippe out of doors.

"After all," said Goddet to her one day, "don't

27

you owe your good fortune to him? Max would
never have let you marry Père Rouget. And
then," he whispered, "if you have children, you
will avenge Max, won't you? for the Bridaus will
be disinherited."

And so, two months after the fatal event, in February, 1823, the invalid, advised to do so by all who
surrounded her, and implored by Rouget, consented
to receive Philippe, whose scar made her weep, but
whose manners, which he had softened for her benefit and made almost affectionate, calmed her. At
Philippe's request, he was left alone with his future
aunt.

"My dear child," said the soldier, "I was the
first one to advise your marriage to my uncle; and
if you consent, it shall take place as soon as your
health is restored—"

"So they have told me," she replied.

"It is natural that, since circumstances have
compelled me to inflict pain upon you, I should wish
to do all that I possibly can for your good. Wealth,
esteem and a family are worth more than what you
have lost. With my uncle dead, you would not long
have been that fellow's wife, for I have learned
from his friends that he had not a pleasant fate in
contemplation for you. Come, my dear girl, let us
make terms; we will all live happily together.
You shall be my aunt, and *nothing but my aunt.*
You will take care that my uncle doesn't forget me
in his will; on my side, you will see what sort
of treatment I will obtain for you in the marriage

contract.—Calm yourself, think it over, and we will talk of it again. You see, the most sensible people, the whole town, advise you to put an end to an illegal state of things, and no one thinks ill of you for receiving me. Everybody understands that, in real life, self-interest goes before sentiment. On the day of your marriage, you will be lovelier than you have ever been. Your sickness, by making you pale, has given you an air of distinction. If my uncle didn't love you madly," he said, rising and kissing her hand, "on my word, you should be the wife of Colonel Bridau."

Philippe left the room, leaving his last words to awaken in Flore's mind a vague idea of revenge which delighted the girl, who was almost happy to have seen that redoubtable individual at her feet. Philippe had played on a small scale the scene Richard III. plays with the queen he has just made a widow. A study of this scene shows that the scheming concealed beneath a sentiment penetrates far into the heart and dissipates the most genuine sorrow. That is how it happens that in private life nature indulges in antics which, in works of genius, are the culmination of art; her instrument is *selfishness*, which is the genius of wealth.

Early in the month of April, 1823, Jean-Jacques Rouget's living-room was the scene of a magnificent dinner-party, given on the occasion of the execution of the marriage contract of Mademoiselle Flore Brazier and the old bachelor, an event that surprised nobody. The guests were the notary, Monsieur Héron; the four witnesses, Messieurs Mignonnet, Carpentier, Hochon and Goddet senior; the mayor and the curé; Agathe Bridau and Madame Hochon and her friend Madame Borniche, the two old ladies who ruled society in Issoudun. The bride-elect was very grateful to Philippe for obtaining this concession from the old ladies, who intended it as a token of the approbation it was proper to bestow upon a repentant girl. Flore was dazzlingly beautiful. The curé, who for a fortnight past had been instructing the ignorant Rabouilleuse, was to administer the sacrament to her for the first time on the following day. This marriage was the theme of the following religious article, published in the *Journal du Cher* at Bourges, and in the *Journal de l'Indre* at Châteauroux:

"Issoudun.

"The religious movement is making progress in Berri. All the friends of the Church and the virtuous people of this town were witnesses yesterday of a ceremony by which one of the principal landed proprietors in the province put

an end to a scandalous condition of affairs which dated back
to the time when religion was without influence in our country
districts.   This result, due to the enlightened zeal of the
ecclesiastics of our town, will find imitators, we trust, and
will put an end to the burning scandal of unconsecrated mar-
riages, contracted during the most disastrous period of the
revolutionary régime.

" There is this noteworthy fact in relation to the occurrence
of which we speak, namely, that it was brought about by the
persistent entreaties of a colonel belonging to the old army
sent to our town by decree of the Court of Peers, who may
lose his uncle's inheritance by reason of this marriage.   Such
disinterestedness is rare enough in our day to merit publicity."

In the contract, Rouget acknowledged a supposititious marriage-portion of a hundred thousand
francs, and assured Flore an annuity of thirty thousand francs after his death.   After the wedding,
which was a sumptuous affair, Agathe returned to
Paris the happiest of mothers, and told Desroches
and Joseph what she called the good news.

"Your son is too deep not to get his hands upon
that inheritance," the solicitor replied, when he had
heard Madame Bridau to the end.   "You and poor
Joseph here will never touch a sou of your brother's
fortune."

"So you too, like Joseph, will always be unjust
to the poor boy?" said the mother.   "His conduct
before the Court of Peers was the conduct of a great
politician, and he succeeded in saving many heads!
—Philippe's errors come from the non-use of his
great faculties; but he realizes now how such faults
in conduct injure a man who wishes to succeed;

and he is ambitious, I am sure of it; nor am I the only one who predicts a great future for him. Monsieur Hochon firmly believes that Philippe has an enviable destiny in store."

"Oh! if he chooses to devote his exceedingly perverse intellect to making a fortune, he will succeed, for he is capable of anything, and such people always get ahead quickly," said Desroches.

"Why should he not succeed by honorable methods?" demanded Madame Bridau.

"You will see," said Desroches. "Lucky or unlucky, Philippe will always be the man of Rue Mazarine, the assassin of Madame Descoings, the domestic thief; but, never fear, he will appear perfectly honest to the world!"

On the day following the marriage, after breakfast, Philippe took Madame Rouget by the arm, when his uncle had left the room to go and dress, for the newly married pair had come downstairs, Flore in her *peignoir* and the old man in his dressing-gown.

"Aunt-in-law," he said, leading her into a window-recess, "you are now one of the family. Thanks to me, all the notaries have done the business. Now listen! no nonsense. I hope that we shall play a fair game. I know what tricks you might play upon me, and you will be watched more closely than by a duenna. You shall never go out except on my arm and you shall never leave me. As for what may take place in the house, *sacrebleu!* I will look out for that like a spider in the centre of his web. Here is something that will prove to you that I might, while you were in your bed, unable to move hand or foot, have turned you out of doors without a sou. Read!"

And he handed the stupefied Flore the following letter:

"MY DEAR BOY,

"Florentine, who has just made her début at the new quarters of the Opéra, in a *pas de trois* with Mariette and Tullia, has had you constantly in mind, and so has Florine, who has finally thrown over Lousteau and taken up with Nathan. Those two sly pusses have found for you the sweetest creature in the world, a girl of seventeen, lovely as an Englishwoman, with the virtuous air of a *lady* at her little tricks, crafty as Desroches, faithful as Godeschal; and Mariette has trained her, wishing you good luck. There isn't a woman in the world who can hold her own against this little angel, who has a devil hidden under her skin; she will be up to playing any part, coddling your uncle and driving him mad with love. She has poor Coralie's celestial expression; she knows how to weep, she has a voice that will extract a thousand-franc note from the hardest heart, and the hussy absorbs champagne better than any of us. She's a precious subject; she is under obligations to Mariette and anxious to square accounts with her. Having drunk up the fortunes of two Englishmen, a Russian and a Roman prince, Mademoiselle Esther is at this moment in most distressingly straitened circumstances; if you give her ten thousand francs, she will be quite content. She has just remarked, laughingly: 'You know, I've never had a slap at a bourgeois; it will keep my hand in!' She is well-known to Finot, Bixiou, Des Lupeaulx, to all our set in fact. Ah! if there were any fortunes left in France, she would be the greatest courtesan of modern times. My editorial sanctum is redolent of Bixiou, Finot and Nathan, who are now disporting themselves with the aforesaid Esther

in the most magnificent apartment imaginable, furnished for
Florine by old Lord Dudley, De Marsay's real father, whom
the clever actress has *hooked*, thanks to the costume of her
latest part.   Tullia is still with the Duc de Rhétoré, Mariette
is still with the Duc de Maufrigneuse; between them they
will obtain your release from surveillance on the king's birthday.   Try to have your uncle safely under ground before next
Saint-Louis's day, come back to Paris with your inheritance,
and you can spend a little of it with Esther and your old
friends, who sign in a body to recall themselves to your
memory.

"NATHAN, FLORINE, BIXIOU, FINOT, MARIETTE,
        FLORENTINE, GIROUDEAU, TULLIA."

The letter, as it trembled in Madame Rouget's
hands, betrayed her terror, mental and physical.
The aunt did not dare to look at her nephew, whose
eyes fixed upon her a terrible expression.

"I have confidence in you, as you see," he said;
"but I demand something in return.   I have made
you my aunt in order to be able to marry you some
day.   You are as good as Esther so far as my uncle
is concerned.   In a year from this time we ought to
be at Paris, the only place where beauty can really
live.   You will enjoy yourself there a little better
than here, for it is a perpetual carnival.   I shall
return to the army and become a general, and then
you will be a great lady.   There's your future,
work to bring it about—But I must have a pledge of
our alliance.   You will procure for me, within a
month, a general power of attorney from my uncle,
on the pretext of relieving yourself as well as him,
of the care of his fortune.   A month later, I must

have a special power of attorney to transfer his property in the Funds. Once they are in my name, we
shall have an equal interest in being married some
day. All this, my fair aunt, is clear and explicit.
Between us there must be nothing ambiguous. I
may marry my aunt after a year of widowhood,
whereas I could not marry a dishonored strumpet."

He left the room without awaiting a reply. When
La Védie entered a quarter of an hour later, to clear
the table, she found her mistress pale and perspir-
ing, notwithstanding the season. Flore felt as if
she had fallen over a precipice, she saw nothing but
shadows in her future, and among those shadows,
as if in the far-off recesses of a cavern, she saw
indistinctly the shapes of monstrous things, which
terrified her. She felt the cold dampness of underground vaults. She had an instinctive fear of the
man, and yet a voice called out to her that she deserved to have him for her master. She could do
nothing against her destiny.

Flore Brazier had, for decency's sake, an apartment of her own in Père Rouget's house; but Madame Rouget belonged to her husband, and thus
she found herself deprived of the precious liberty
of action that a servant-mistress retains. In her
lamentable plight she conceived the hope of having
a child; but, during the last five years, she had
made Jean-Jacques Rouget the most feeble of old
men. The marriage was destined to have the result that followed the second marriage of Louis XII.
Furthermore, the constant surveillance of such a

man as Philippe, who had nothing to do, having given up his place, made any sort of vengeance impossible. Benjamin was an innocent and devoted spy. La Védie trembled before Philippe. Flore realized that she was alone and without resource! Last of all she was afraid that she should die; without any clear idea of the probable method to be adopted by Philippe to kill her, she foresaw that the slightest suspicion of pregnancy would be her death-warrant: the sound of his voice, the veiled gleam of his gambler's glance, the slightest movements of the soldier, who treated her with the most polished brutality, made her shudder. As to the power of attorney demanded by the ferocious colonel, who was a hero in the eyes of all Issoudun, he had it the moment he required it; for Flore fell under this man's domination as France had fallen under the domination of Napoléon. Like the moth whose legs are caught in the melting wax of a candle, Rouget speedily wasted his last remaining strength. In the presence of his dying agony his nephew was as cold and impassive as the diplomatists, in 1814, during the convulsions of imperial France.

Philippe, who had little faith in Napoléon II., thereupon wrote to the Minister of War the following letter, which Mariette induced the Duc de Maufrigneuse to deliver:

" MONSEIGNEUR,

" Napoléon is no more; I was in duty bound to remain faithful to him after I had taken the oath of allegiance to him ;

now I am at liberty to offer my services to His Majesty. If
Your Excellency will condescend to explain my conduct to His
Majesty, the king will deem it conformable to the laws of
honor if not to those of the realm. The king, who considered
it not unnatural that his aide-de-camp, General Rapp, should
weep for his former master, will, without doubt, be indulgent
to me ; Napoléon was my benefactor.

"I therefore beg Your Excellency to take into consideration
my request for employment in my former rank, hereby assuring you of my entire submission. It is enough to say to you,
Monseigneur, that the king will find in me a most faithful
subject.

"Deign to acccept the homage of the respect with which I
have the honor to be

"Your Excellency's most obedient and most humble servant,

                              "PHILIPPE BRIDAU,
    "*Formerly Captain in the Dragoons of the Guard, officer of the
Legion of Honor, now under police surveillance at Issoudun.*"

To this letter was added a request for permission
to visit Paris on family affairs, to which Monsieur
Mouilleron annexed letters from the mayor, the
sub-prefect and the commissioner of police of Issoudun, all of whom spoke in the highest terms of
Philippe, referring particularly to the article relat-
ing to the subject of his uncle's marriage.

A fortnight later, just at the opening of the Exposition, Philippe received the desired permission,
together with a letter in which the Minister of War
informed him that, by the king's orders, he was
restored to the army list as a lieutenant-colonel, as
an initial favor.

Philippe came to Paris with his aunt and old

Rouget, whom he escorted to the Treasury, three days after his arrival, to sign the transfer of the certificate, which thereupon became his property. The dying man, as well as La Rabouilleuse, were plunged by their nephew into the life of unbridled pleasure led by the dangerous coterie of indefatigable actresses, journalists, artists and women of equivocal character, among whom Philippe had already wasted his youth, and where old Rouget found Rabouilleuses enough to be the death of him. Giroudeau undertook to arrange for Père Rouget the kind of death made memorable at a later period, it was said, by a marshal of France. Lolotte, one of the loveliest supernumeraries at the Opéra, was the old man's amiable assassin. He died after a splendid supper given by Florentine, so that it was no easy matter to decide whether the supper or Mademoiselle Lolotte finished the old Berrichon. Lolotte attributed his death to a slice of pâté de foie gras; and as the Strasbourg article could not reply, it was held to be proved that the goodman died of indigestion. Madame Rouget found herself in her element in that exceedingly free-and-easy society; but Philippe gave her Mariette for a chaperon, and she prevented the widow, whose period of mourning was embellished by some few passages of gallantry, from making a fool of herself.

In October, 1823, Philippe returned to Issoudun, provided with a power of attorney from his aunt, to settle his uncle's estate, an operation which was speedily performed; for he was back in Paris in

March, 1824, with sixteen hundred thousand francs, the net assets of his late uncle, over and above the valuable pictures which had never left old Hochon's house. Philippe placed his funds with the house of Mongenod and Son, where young Baruch Borniche was employed, old Hochon having given him convincing proofs of their solvency and honorable methods. The house took the sixteen hundred thousand francs at six per cent interest, on condition that three months' notice should be given of the proposed withdrawal of the funds.

One fine day Philippe came to request his mother to be present at his wedding, the witnesses being Giroudeau, Finot, Nathan and Bixiou. By the contract, the widow Rouget, whose contribution consisted of a million francs, gave all her property to her husband in case she should die without children. There were no invitations, no breakfast, no display, for Philippe had his plans; he installed his wife on Rue Saint-Georges, in an apartment that Lolotte sold to him all furnished, which Madame Bridau the younger thought delightful, and in which her husband rarely set foot. Without the knowledge of any of his friends, Philippe purchased, for two hundred and fifty thousand francs, a magnificent mansion on Rue de Clichy, at a time when no one suspected the value that property in that quarter would some day acquire; he paid a hundred and fifty thousand francs in cash out of his income, and took two years to pay the remainder. He spent enormous sums in interior decorations and furniture, devoting his whole income to that purpose for two years. The superb pictures, which, when renovated, were valued at three hundred thousand francs, shone there in all their glory.

The accession of Charles X. had raised to greater favor than before, the family of the Duc de Chaulieu, whose eldest son, the Duc de Rhétoré, frequently saw Philippe at Tullia's. Under Charles X., the elder branch of the Bourbons fancied itself definitively seated upon the throne, and followed the advice previously given by Maréchal Gouvion-Saint-Cyr to win over the soldiers of the Empire. Philippe, who undoubtedly made certain useful disclosures concerning the conspiracies of 1820 and 1822, was appointed lieutenant-colonel in the regiment of the Duc de Maufrigneuse. That fascinating great nobleman deemed himself in honor bound to patronize a man from whom he had stolen Mariette. The *corps de ballet* was not uninfluential in the matter of this appointment. Moreover it had been decided by Charles the Tenth's secret council in their wisdom, that Monseigneur le Dauphin should be made to adopt a slight tinge of liberalism. Thus Monsieur Philippe, become, so to speak, the gentleman-in-waiting to the Duc de Maufrigneuse, was presented not only to the Dauphin, but to the Dauphiness, who was not ill-disposed toward unpolished characters and soldiers of tried loyalty. Philippe gauged very accurately the part the Dauphin had to play, and he took advantage of the first manifestation of his sham liberalism, to secure an appointment as aide-de-camp to a marshal who stood extremely well at court.

In January, 1827, Philippe, who had passed into the Garde Royale as lieutenant-colonel in the regiment that the Duc de Maufrigneuse then commanded in that organization, solicited the favor of being ennobled. Under the Restoration, letters-patent of nobility had become a quasi-right of plebeians who served in the Guard. Colonel Bridau, who had recently purchased the estate of Brambourg, requested the favor of making it into a *majorat*, and assuming the title of count. He obtained this favor by making the most of his connections in the highest society, where he displayed the utmost magnificence in the way of carriages and liveries, and appeared in fact in the guise of a great nobleman. As soon as Philippe, who was lieutenant-colonel of the finest cavalry regiment in the Guard, saw his name entered in the Royal Almanac as Comte de Brambourg, he began to frequent the house of the lieutenant-general of artillery, Comte de Soulanges, paying court to the youngest daughter, Mademoiselle Amélie de Soulanges. Insatiable by nature, and supported by the mistresses of all the men of influence, Philippe solicited the honor of being one of the aides-de-camp of Monseigneur le Dauphin. He had the audacity to say to the Dauphiness that "an old officer, wounded upon several battle-fields, who had served through the great war, might well be, if occasion offered, of some service to Monseigneur." Philippe, who could assume the tone of all

varieties of the courtier, was, in this superior
sphere, all that it was requisite that he should be,
just as he had made himself another Mignonnet at
Issoudun. He had a magnificent establishment;
he gave entertainments and splendid dinners, admitting none of his former friends to his superb
mansion, for they might have endangered his future.
He was equally hard-hearted to his companions in
debauchery. He abruptly refused Bixiou's request
that he would say a word in favor of Giroudeau,
who wished to re-enter the service when Florentine
cast him off.

"He's a man of no morals!" said Philippe.

"Ah! that's what he said about me," cried Giroudeau, "when I got rid of his uncle for him!"

"We'll pay him back," said Bixiou.

Philippe desired to marry Mademoiselle Amélie
de Soulanges, to rise to the rank of general, and to
command a regiment in the Garde Royale. He
asked for so many things that they made him a commander in the Legion of Honor and a commander
in the Order of Saint-Louis to close his mouth.
One evening, Agathe and Joseph, as they were returning home on foot in the rain, saw Philippe
drive by in full uniform, his breast covered with
orders, sitting back in the corner of his beautiful
coupé, lined with yellow silk, and with his coat of
arms surmounted by a count's coronet engraved on
the door, while on his way to a party at the Elysée-
Bourbon; he spattered mud upon his mother and
brother as he saluted them with a patronizing nod.

28

"How the rascal goes! how he goes!" said Joseph to his mother. "Nevertheless, he ought to send us something besides mud in our faces."

"He occupies such a fine, exalted position, that we mustn't bear him a grudge for forgetting us," said Madame Bridau. "Ascending such a steep incline, he has so many obligations to fulfil, so many sacrifices to make, that he may very well be unable to come and see us, even though he thinks of us."

"My dear fellow," said the Duc de Maufrigneuse one evening to the new Comte de Brambourg, "I am sure that your request will be taken in good part; but, before you marry Amélie de Soulanges, you must be free. What have you done with your wife?"

"My wife?—" Philippe answered, with a gesture, a glance and an accent which were subsequently adopted by Frédérick Lemaître in one of his most terrible parts. "Alas! I have the melancholy certainty that I must lose her. She hasn't a week to live. Ah! my dear duke, you don't know what a *mésalliance* means! a woman who was a cook, who has the tastes of a cook, and who disgraces me—I am much to be pitied. But I have had the honor to explain my position to Madame la Dauphine. At the time, it was a question of rescuing a million of money which my uncle had left to this creature by his will. Luckily my wife has taken to drink; at her death, I shall come into possession of a million now placed with the Mongenod house; I have also thirty thousand francs in the five per cents, and my *majorat*, which is worth forty thousand a year. If, as everything leads him to expect, Monsieur de Soulanges receives a marshal's bâton, I am in a fair way, with my title of Comte de Brambourg, to become a general and a peer of France. That will be a suitable retiring pension for an aide-de-camp of the Dauphin."

After the Salon of 1823, the king's first painter, one of the most estimable men of the day, had obtained for Joseph's mother a lottery office in the neighborhood of the Market. Later, Agathe was luckily able to make an exchange, without any extra payment, with the proprietor of an office on Rue de Seine, in a house in which Joseph hired a studio. The widow now had a manager of her own and was no longer a burden to her son. Even as late as 1828, although she was directress of one of the best lottery offices, a position which she owed to Joseph's renown, Madame Bridau still refused to believe in that renown, which was hotly disputed, as all true renown is. The great painter, still at odds with his passions, needed a great deal of money; he did not earn enough to support the style of living which his social connections imposed upon him, as well as his distinguished position in the younger school. Although powerfully supported by his friends of the club and by Mademoiselle des Touches, he did not please the bourgeois fancy. That class, from which the money comes to-day, never unties its purse-strings for disputed talents, and Joseph had against him the classicists, the Institute, and the critics who were dependent upon those two powers. Lastly, the Comte de Brambourg expressed amazement when anyone mentioned Joseph to him.

The brave-hearted artist had few orders, although he was upheld by Gros and by Gérard, who obtained the Cross for him at the salon of 1827. If the Ministry of the Interior and the king's household were with difficulty induced to take his large canvases, the dealers and rich foreigners burdened themselves still less with them. Moreover, Joseph, as we know, is a little too much inclined to indulge his fancy, and the result is an inequality in his work which his enemies take advantage of to deny his talent.

"Great painting is in a very bad way," said his friend Pierre Grassou, who made daubs to suit the taste of the bourgeoisie, whose apartments are too small for large paintings.

"You ought to have a whole cathedral to paint," Schinner said to him; "you would reduce criticism to silence by a monumental work."

These observations, which terrified poor Agathe, confirmed her in the judgment she had formed at first concerning Joseph and Philippe. The facts justified this mother, who had never ceased to be a provincial. Philippe, her favorite child, was the great man of the family, was he not? she saw in his early misdemeanors the errors of genius; Joseph, to the merit of whose productions she was insensible, for she saw too much of them in their swaddling-clothes to admire them when finished, seemed to her no farther advanced in 1828 than in 1816. Poor Joseph owed money, he bent beneath the burden of his debts, *he had adopted an ungrateful profession which brought him nothing.* In truth, Agathe could not imagine why the decoration had been given to Joseph. But Philippe, become a count, Philippe with sufficient strength of mind to shun the gaming table, Philippe, a guest at Madame's entertainments, Philippe, the brilliant colonel who rode by at reviews and in processions, dressed in a magnificent costume and decorated with two red ribbons, realized Agathe's maternal dreams. On the occasion of a certain public ceremonial, Philippe had banished from her mind the last remembrance of the odious spectacle of his destitute appearance on the Quai de l'Ecole, by passing her at the same spot, riding before the Dauphin, with plumes in his *schapska,* and a fur cape glistening with gold! Agathe, who had become a sort of devoted Gray Sister to the artist, had no feeling of motherhood save for the audacious aide-de-camp of His Royal Highness, Monseigneur le Dauphin! She was proud of Philippe and she would soon be leading a life of ease, thanks to him; she forgot that the lottery office by which she lived came to her from Joseph. One day Agathe found her poor artist so worried by the sum total of his color-dealer's account that, while cursing art, she insisted upon paying his debts. The poor woman, who kept the house with the profits of her lottery office, was very careful never to ask Joseph for a sou. So she had no money; but she relied upon Philippe's kind heart and his purse. She waited, expecting a visit from her son from day to day, for three years; she fancied him bringing her an enormous sum, and enjoyed in anticipation the pleasure she would have in giving it to Joseph, whose opinion of Philippe was as unchangeable as Desroches'.

Without Joseph's knowledge, then, she wrote the following letter to Philippe:

"To Monsieur le Comte de Brambourg:

"My Dear Philippe,

"You have not given your mother the least little token of your existence in five years! That is not right. You ought to remember the past a little, were it only for your good brother's sake. To-day Joseph is in need, while you are swimming in wealth; he works, while you are flying from fête to fête. You have the whole of my brother's fortune. In fact, according to young Borniche, you have two hundred thousand francs a year. Come and see Joseph! While you are here, put twenty thousand-franc notes in the skull: you owe it to us, Philippe; nevertheless, your brother will consider himself your debtor, to say nothing of the pleasure you will give your mother.

"Agathe Bridau, née Rouget."

Two days later, the servant brought to the studio, where poor Agathe and Joseph had just finished breakfast, the following terrible letter:

" MY DEAR MOTHER,

"One does not marry Mademoiselle Amélie de Soulanges by offering her empty nutshells, when one has, beneath the name of Comte de Brambourg, that of

"Your son,

"PHILIPPE BRIDAU."

As she fell back, almost fainting, upon the divan in the studio, Agathe dropped the letter. The slight noise that it made in falling, and Agathe's low but agonized exclamation, attracted the notice of Joseph, who was entirely oblivious of his mother at that moment, for he was working furiously at a sketch; he looked around the side of his easel to see what was going on. At the sight of his mother lying back upon the divan, the painter dropped palette and brushes, and ran to raise what seemed to be a corpse. He took her in his arms, carried her to the bed in her own room and sent the servant to summon his friend Bianchon. As soon as Joseph was able to question his mother, she confessed that she had written to Philippe and had received a reply from him. The artist picked up the letter, whose concise brutality had broken the poor mother's sensitive heart, overturning the stately edifice erected by her maternal preference. Joseph, when he returned to his mother's bedside, had the good sense to hold his peace. He did not mention his brother during the three weeks that the poor woman's death-agony—which can hardly be called an illness—lasted. Bianchon, who came every day and ministered to the invalid with the devotion of a true friend, told Joseph the truth the first day.

"At your mother's age," he said, "and under present circumstances, it is useless to think of anything except making her death as pleasant as possible."

Agathe, too, was so conscious of the fact that God had called her, that she requested, on the very next day, the religious ministrations of Abbé Loraux, who had been her confessor for twenty-two years. When she was alone with him and had poured out all her sorrow into his heart, she repeated what she had said to her godmother; words which were constantly on her lips.

"In what can I have offended God? Do I not love him with all my soul? Have I not walked in the path of salvation? What sin have I committed? And, if I am guilty of some sin of which I know nothing, have I time to correct it?"

"No," said the old man in a gentle voice. "Alas! your life seems to be pure and your soul seems to be without stain; but God's eye, poor sorrowing creature, is more penetrating than that of His ministers! My own are opened a little too late, for you yourself have deceived me."

When she heard those words from lips that had hitherto had none but sweet and soothing words for her, Agathe sat up in bed, her eyes filled with fear and anxiety.

"Tell me! tell me!" she cried.

"Be comforted," the old priest rejoined. "From

the way in which you are being punished, we may
look forward to your forgiveness.   God's hand falls
heavily upon none but His elect upon earth.   Woe
to them whose sins are favored by chance; they
will be kneaded again in humanity until they in
their turn are severely punished for simple errors,
when they reach the maturity of celestial fruit.
Your life, my daughter, has been one long error.
You have fallen into the pit you have dug for yourself, for we are found wanting only in the direction in which we have weakened ourselves.   You
have given your heart to a monster in whom you
have seen your glory, and you have misprized that
one of your children who is your real glory!   You
have been so profoundly unjust that you have not
noticed this striking contrast; you owe your existence to Joseph, whereas your other son has constantly robbed you.   The poor son, who loves you
without the recompense of equal affection from you,
brings you your daily bread; while the rich son,
who has never given you a kind thought and who
despises you, longs for your death."

"Oh! as to that!—" she began.

"It is true," continued the priest; "your humble
condition is a drawback to his proud hopes.—Mother,
this is your crime!   Woman, your suffering and
your anguish announce to you that you will enjoy
the peace of the Lord.   Your son Joseph is so noble-
hearted that his affection has never been lessened
by the injustice of your maternal preference; so
love him dearly! give him your whole heart in

these last days; pray for him; I go hence to pray for you."

Unsealed by such powerful hands, the mother's eyes embraced her whole life in a retrospective glance. Enlightened by this gleam, she perceived her involuntary wrong-doing and burst into tears. The old priest was so deeply moved by the spectacle of the repentance of one who had sinned solely through ignorance, that he left the room in order not to manifest his pity. Joseph returned to his mother's room about two hours after the confessor's departure. He had been to one of his friends to borrow the necessary money to pay his most pressing debts, and he stole in on tiptoe, believing Agathe to be asleep. Thus he reached his armchair and sat down, unseen by the invalid.

A sob, broken by the words: "Will he forgive me?" brought Joseph to his feet, with the perspiration streaming down his face, for he fancied his mother was in the delirium that precedes death.

"What's the matter, mother?" he said, terrified at the sight of her eyes, reddened with weeping, and at her expression of deep distress.

"Oh! Joseph, will you forgive me, my child?" she cried.

"Forgive you for what?" said the artist.

"I have not loved you as you deserve to be loved—"

"What nonsense!" he exclaimed. "You haven't loved me?—Haven't we lived together seven years?

Haven't you been my housekeeper seven years? Don't I see you every day? Don't I hear your voice? Aren't you the sweet and indulgent companion of my miserable life? You don't understand painting, eh?—That's of no consequence! Why I was saying only yesterday to Grassou: 'The one thing that consoles me in my struggles is that I have a dear, good mother; she's just what an artist's wife should be; she takes care of everything, she looks out for my material wants without making the slightest trouble—' "

"No, Joseph, no; you have always loved me! and I have not given you love for love! Ah! how I would like to live!—Give me your hand—"

Agathe took her son's hand, kissed it and held it against her heart, and gazed at him for a long time, her azure eyes beaming with the tenderness she had hitherto kept in reserve for Philippe. The painter, who was a connoisseur in expression, was so impressed by this change, he saw so surely that his mother's heart was opening to him at last, that he took her in his arms and held her close to his heart, exclaiming like a madman:

"O mother! mother!"

"Ah! I feel that I am forgiven!" she said. "God must ratify a son's forgiveness of his mother!"

"You must be calm and not worry; it's all right now: I feel that you love me enough at this moment to make up for all the past," cried Joseph, laying his mother's head once more upon the pillow.

During the saintly creature's two weeks' struggle between life and death, her looks, her gestures and the outpouring of her heart upon Joseph were so instinct with love that it seemed as if there were a whole life in each one. She thought of nothing but her son, she counted herself as nothing; and, strengthened by his love, she was no longer conscious of her suffering. She made such artless, innocent remarks as children make. D'Arthez, Michel Chrestien, Fulgence Ridal, Pierre Grassou and Bianchon often came to sit with Joseph and talked in undertones in the invalid's chamber.

"Oh! how I would like to know what color is!" she cried one evening, overhearing a discussion concerning a picture.

Joseph for his part was sublime in his treatment of his mother; he hardly left her room, he cherished her in his heart and responded in kind to her affectionate effusions. To the friends of the great painter, it was one of the spectacles that are never forgotten. Those men, all of whom equally possessed genuine talents and grand characters, were to Joseph and his mother what they were sure to be: angels who prayed and wept with him, not by repeating prayers and shedding tears, but by making themselves one with him in thought and action. With the instinct of an artist as great in the matter of sentiment as of talent, Joseph divined from his mother's expression the existence of a desire deeply-rooted in her heart, and he said one day to D'Arthez:

"She loved that villain Philippe too dearly, not to long to see him again before she dies."

Joseph begged Bixiou, who was now fairly launched in the Bohemian society which Philippe sometimes frequented, to induce the detestable upstart to play, if only for pity's sake, the comedy of pretended affection, so that the poor mother's heart might be wrapped in a shroud embroidered with illusions. In his capacity of cynical observer and sneering misanthrope, Bixiou desired no better amusement than to execute such a commission.

When he had described Agathe's condition to the Comte de Brambourg, who received him in a bedroom hung with yellow silk damask, the colonel began to laugh.

"Ha! ha! what the devil do you suppose I'd go there for?" he cried. "The only service the good woman can do me is to die as soon as possible, for she would cut a sad figure at my marriage to Mademoiselle de Soulanges. The less family I have, the better my position will be. You can understand that I would like to bury the name of Bridau under all the gravestones of Père-la-Chaise!—My brother annoys me beyond measure by parading my real name in the broad daylight! You are too shrewd not to understand my position! Look you! if you become a deputy, why you have the gift of gab, and you will be feared like Chauvelin, you can force them to make you Comte Bixiou, Director of Fine Arts: imagine that you've reached that point,

how would you like it, if your grandmother Descoings were still alive, to have the good woman, who
looked like a Saint-Léon, standing at your side?
would you take her to the Tuileries on your arm?
would you present her to the noble family you were
trying to enter? *Sacrebleu!* you'd long to see her
six feet underground, sealed up in a lead chemise.
Come, breakfast with me, and let's talk about
something else. I am a parvenu, my dear man, I
know. I don't choose to allow my swaddling-clothes
to be seen!—My son will be more fortunate than I;
he'll be a great nobleman. The rascal will long for
me to die; I expect that, for otherwise he wouldn't
be my son."

He rang; the valet de chambre answered the
summons.

"My friend breakfasts with me; serve us a delicious little breakfast."

"But your aristocratic friends wouldn't see you
in your mother's room," rejoined Bixiou. "What
would it cost you to make a pretence of caring a
little for the poor woman for an hour or two?"

"Bah!" said Philippe, with a wink, "you come
in their interest. I'm an old camel and I know
something about genuflections. My mother wants
to milk me for Joseph's benefit, on the strength of
her last illness!—Thanks."

When Bixiou described this scene to Joseph, the
poor painter felt a cold chill strike his heart.

"Does Philippe know that I am sick?" said
Agathe in a distressed tone on the evening of the

same day that Bixiou rendered an account of his mission.

Joseph left the room, stifled by his tears. Abbé Loraux, who was at his penitent's bedside, took her hand and pressed it.

"Alas! my child, you never had but one son!" he replied.

As a result of this reply, which she understood, Agathe fell into a convulsion, which marked the beginning of the death-agony. She died twenty hours later.

In the delirium which preceded her death, these words escaped her:

"Whom does Philippe resemble?"

*

Joseph alone attended his mother's body to the grave. Philippe had gone, on service, to Orléans, driven from Paris by the following letter, which Joseph wrote to him immediately after their mother breathed her last:

"MONSTER,

"My poor mother has died of the shock your letter caused her; put on mourning, but feign illness; I do not choose that her murderer shall stand by my side at her grave.

"JOSEPH B."

The painter, who no longer had the courage to paint, although perhaps his profound sorrow demanded the species of mechanical distraction afforded by work, was surrounded by his friends, who had an understanding that he was never to be left alone. Thus it happened that Bixiou, who loved Joseph as well as an inveterate scoffer can love anyone, was one of the party of friends assembled in the studio, a fortnight after the funeral, when the servant suddenly entered and handed Joseph this letter, brought, she said, by an old woman who was waiting in the porter's lodge for a reply:

"MONSIEUR,

"To whom I dare not give the name of brother; I must appeal to you, were it only because of the name I bear—"

29   (449)

Joseph turned the paper and glanced at the signature at the foot of the last page. The words *Comtesse Flore de Brambourg* made him shudder, for he foresaw some new horror of his brother's invention.

"The villain," he said, "would play the devil with the devil himself! And he is considered a man of honor! And he wears a string of gewgaws around his neck! And he cuts a wide swath at court instead of being stretched on the rack! And the rake is called 'Monsieur le Comte!'"

"And there are many others like him!" said Bixiou.

"After all, this Rabouilleuse deserves to take her turn at being *rabouillée*," said Joseph; "she's worse than the itch; she'd have let my head be cut off without so much as saying: 'He is innocent!'"

He threw the letter aside, but Bixiou quickly snatched it up and read aloud:

"Is it decent that Madame la Comtesse Bridau de Brambourg, whatever her sins, should be left to die in the hospital? If such is my destiny, if such is Monsieur le Comte's good pleasure and yours, let it be so; then do you, who are Doctor Bianchon's friend, induce him to use his influence to have me admitted to a hospital. The person who will bring you this letter, monsieur, has been eleven days in succession to the Hôtel de Brambourg on Rue de Clichy, but has failed to obtain the slightest assistance from my husband. My condition precludes me from sending for a solicitor in order to procure by process of law what I need, to die in peace. I know that I am beyond saving. And so, if you should prefer to have nothing to do with your unhappy sister-in-law, give me the necessary money to buy the means of putting an end to my sufferings; for I can see that Monsieur your brother desires my death and has always desired it. Although he told me that he knew three sure ways of getting rid of a woman, I had not the wit to provide against the method he used.

"In case you should care to honor me with any assistance and to judge for yourself of my condition, I live on Rue du Houssay, at the corner of Rue Chantereine, on the fifth floor. If I do not pay my arrears of rent to-morrow, I must go! And go where, monsieur?—May I sign myself your sister-in-law,

"COMTESSE FLORE DE BRAMBOURG?"

"What a ditch full of infamies!" said Joseph; "what is there behind all this?"

"Let us send for the woman first of all," said Bixiou; "she should be an entertaining preface to the story."

A moment later a woman appeared whom Bixiou described as a "walking bundle of rags." She was, in very truth, a mass of linen and old dresses one over another, garnished with mud on account of the season, the whole mounted upon a pair of stout legs and huge feet, scantily covered with patched stockings, and shoes which discharged water through their yawning seams. Above this heap of rags arose one of the faces Charlet has given to his street-sweepers, arrayed in a shocking silk handkerchief, frayed and worn at the folds.

"Your name?" said Joseph, while Bixiou sketched the woman as she leaned upon an umbrella of the year II. of the Republic.

"Madame Gruget, at your service. I've seen better days, my little man," she said to Bixiou, whose smile offended her. "If my poor girl hadn't had the hard luck to be too fond of someone, I should be something different from what you see me. She jumped into the water, saving your presence, did my poor Ida! Then I saw the folly of sticking to a combination of four figures; that, my dear monsieur, is why, at seventy-seven, I watch sick folks for ten sous a day and feed—"

"But not dress yourself!" said Bixiou. "My grandmother, dear old soul! dressed herself while she cherished her little pet of a three-figured combination."

"But, out of my ten sous a day, I have to pay for a furnished room."

"What has this lady you are nursing?"

"She has nothing, monsieur—in the way of money, I mean! for she has a disease to make the doctors shudder—She owes me for sixty days, that's why I keep on watching her. Her husband, who's a count,—and she's a countess—will pay my bill, I suppose, when she's dead; that's why I let her have all I had—but I haven't anything more: I've taken everything to the *mau pi-é-té!*—pawnshop— She owes me forty-seven francs twelve sous, besides my thirty francs for nursing; and when she wanted to kill herself with charcoal, I says to her: 'That's all wrong.'—Just the same, I told the concierge to watch her while I was out, because she's quite up to jumping out of the window."

"But what's the matter with her?" Joseph asked.

"Why, monsieur, the doctor came from the convent, but as to the disease," said Madame Gruget, assuming a bashful expression, "he said she must be carried to the hospital. It's a fatal case."

"Let us go there," said Bixiou.

"Stay," said Joseph, "here are ten francs.

Plunging his hand into the famous skull to take all his available cash, the painter went to Rue Mazarine, took a cab and drove to Bianchon's house, where he was fortunate enough to find him. Bixiou meanwhile hurried to Rue de Buci to find Desroches. The four friends met an hour later on Rue de Houssay.

"This Mephistopheles on horseback called Philippe Bridau," said Bixiou to his three companions as they climbed the stairs, "has steered a villainous course in order to get rid of his wife. Our friend Lousteau, you know, who is very glad to receive a thousand-franc note monthly from Philippe, kept Madame Bridau in the same set with Florine, Mariette, Tullia and La Val-Noble. When Philippe saw that his Rabouilleuse had become accustomed to handsome dresses and expensive pleasures, he ceased to give her money and left her to get it for herself—you know how. In this way Philippe forced his wife down a little lower, from three months to three months, for a year and a half; finally, with the assistance of a dandified young subaltern, he gave her a taste for liquor. As he rose, his wife fell, and the countess is now in the gutter. The girl, born and brought up in the country, has a tough constitution, and I don't know how Philippe went to work to rid himself of her. I am curious to study this little drama, for I have a little account to settle with our friend. Alas! my friends," said Bixiou, in a tone that left his companions in doubt as to whether he was joking or speaking seriously, "all you have to do to get rid of a man is to guide him into the path of vice. *She was too fond of dancing, that's what killed her!* says Hugo. There you are! My grandmother was fond of the lottery, and Philippe killed her by means of the lottery! Père Rouget loved obscene stories, and Lolotte killed him! Madame Bridau, poor woman, loved Philippe, and she died through his means!—Vice! Vice! my friends.—Do you know what Vice is? It's the pimp of death!"

"You will die with a joke on your lips, won't you?" said Desroches, with a smile, to Bixiou.

From the fourth floor the young men ascended one of the steep staircases which resemble ladders, and by which you climb to the attic rooms in some houses in Paris. Although Joseph, who had seen Flore when she was so lovely, anticipated some shocking contrast, he was totally unprepared for the hideous spectacle presented to his artistic eye. Beneath the sloping roof of a bare-walled attic, upon a folding bed whose wretched mattress was stuffed with husks perhaps, the young men espied a woman, as green as a body two days drowned, and as thin as a consumptive two hours before dying. The loathsome body had upon its hairless head a wretched cotton cap. There were red circles around the eyes and the lids were like the inner lining of an egg. And of that body, once so ravishingly beautiful, naught remained but a vile mass of bones. At the sight of the visitors, Flore drew across her breast a fragment of muslin, which must at one time have been a small window curtain, for the edges were rusted by the rod. The only furniture in sight consisted of two chairs, a wretched commode upon which was a candle stuck in a potato, a few plates scattered over the floor and an earthen stove at the corner of a fireless hearth. Bixiou noticed the rest of the paper purchased at the grocer's for the purpose of writing the letter, which the two women had doubtless evolved by their united efforts. The word disgusting, the positive degree of an adjective that has no superlative, is the only word we can use to express the feeling aroused by such a depth of misery.

When the dying woman caught sight of Joseph, two great tears rolled down her cheeks.

"She can still weep!" said Bixiou. "This is a decidedly interesting sight; tears issuing from a domino board. It explains the miracle of Moses."

"How she has dried up!" said Joseph.

"In the fire of repentance," said Flore. "And I can have no priest, I have nothing, not even a crucifix to see God's image!—Ah! monsieur," she cried, raising her arms, which resembled two pieces of carved wood, "I am very guilty, but God never punished anyone as I am punished!—Philippe killed Max, who urged me to do horrible things, and he is killing me too. God uses him as a scourge!—Look to yourselves, for we all have our Philippe."

"Leave me alone with her," said Bianchon, "so that I can find out whether she can be cured."

"If she should recover, Philippe Bridau would burst with rage," said Desroches; "so I propose to have a sworn report of his wife's condition; he has never proceeded against her as an adulteress and she is entitled to all a wife's rights; he will have the scandal of a lawsuit. First of all, we will have Madame la Comtesse taken to Doctor Dubois's hospital on Rue du Faubourg Saint-Denis, where she will be well taken care of. Then I shall proceed against him for restitution of conjugal rights."

"Bravo, Desroches!" cried Bixiou. "What a pleasure it is to do good that will do so much harm!"

Ten minutes later, Bianchon came down and said to them:

"I am going at once for Desplein; he can save the woman by an operation. Oh! he will see that she's well taken care of, for excessive indulgence in drink has developed a magnificent disease that was thought to have disappeared."

"Go to, you wag of a doctor! Is there nothing but disease in the world?" said Bixiou.

But Bianchon was already in the courtyard, he was in such haste to tell Desplein the great news.

Within two hours, Joseph's unhappy sister-in-law was taken to the respectable establishment conducted by Doctor Dubois, which was afterward purchased by the city of Paris.

Three weeks later, the *Gazette des Hôpitaux* contained an account of one of the most audacious operations recorded in modern surgery, on a patient designated by the initials F. B. The woman died, rather because of her enfeebled physical condition than as a result of the operation.

Colonel Comte de Brambourg at once called upon the Comte de Soulanges, in deep mourning, and informed him of the *sad loss* he had met with. It was whispered in society that the Comte de Soulanges was about to bestow his daughter upon a parvenu of great merit, who was to be made a lieutenant-general and colonel of a regiment in the Garde Royale.

De Marsay imparted the news to Rastignac, who mentioned it at a supper at the *Rocher de Cancale* at which Bixiou happened to be one of the guests.

"That shall not come off!" said the clever artist to himself.

Although, among the friends Philippe had slighted, there were some, like Giroudeau for instance, who could not revenge themselves, he had been so ill-advised as to offend Bixiou, who, thanks to his shrewd wit, was received everywhere, and who never forgave an injury. On a certain occasion at the *Rocher de Cancale*, when Bixiou requested an invitation to the Hôtel de Brambourg, Philippe had replied, in the hearing of divers serious-minded men, who were supping there :

"You shall come to my house when you're a minister !"

"Must I become a protestant in order to be admitted ?" Bixiou retorted, in a bantering tone.

But he said to himself :

"You may be a Goliath, but I have a sling and there's no lack of stones."

The next day the practical joker changed his dress at the house of an actor friend of his, and was metamorphosed, through the agency of the all-powerful costume, into a secular priest with green glasses; then he took a cab and was driven to the Hôtel de Soulanges. Bixiou, being treated as a joker by Philippe, determined to play a joke upon him. Being admitted by Monsieur de Soulanges, upon his representation that he wished to see him upon important business, Bixiou played the part of a venerable man burdened with momentous secrets. In an assumed voice, he told the story of the dead countess's disease, the ghastly secret having been confided to him by Bianchon, the story of Agathe's death, the story of goodman Rouget's death, of which the Comte de Brambourg had boasted, the story of La Descoings's death, the story of the forced loan from the cash-box of the newspaper, and the story of Philippe in his evil days.

"Don't give your daughter to him, Monsieur le Comte, until you have made inquiries; question his former friends, Bixiou, Captain Giroudeau, etc."

Three months later, Colonel Comte de Brambourg gave a supper-party at his house to Du Tillet, Nucingen, Rastignac, Maxime de Trailles and De Marsay. The host accepted very nonchalantly the half-consolatory remarks addressed to him by his guests touching his rupture with the Soulanges family.

"You can do better," said Maxime.

"How great a fortune must one have to marry a Mademoiselle de Grandlieu?" Philippe asked De Marsay.

"You!—they wouldn't give you the ugliest of the six for less than ten millions," replied De Marsay insolently.

"Bah!" said Rastignac, "with two hundred thousand francs a year, you can get Mademoiselle de Langeais, the marquis's daughter; she's thirty years old and ugly, and she hasn't one sou of dot; that ought to suit you."

"I shall have ten millions in two years," Philippe rejoined.

"It is now the sixteenth of January, 1829," cried Du Tillet, smiling. "I have been working ten years and I haven't got that amount!"

"We will advise one another, and you will see how well I understand financial matters," said Bridau.

"How much do you possess in all?" Nucingen inquired.

"By selling everything, except my country estate and my city house, which I cannot and will not risk, for they are part of my *majorat*, I can get together some three millions."

Nucingen and Du Tillet exchanged glances, and Du Tillet remarked:

"My dear count, we will work together, if you like."

De Marsay surprised the glance Du Tillet had bestowed upon Nucingen, a glance which said: "To us the millions!" In truth, these two lights of the higher financial circle, being at the very fountain-head of matters political, were able to play against Philippe on the Bourse, with absolute certainty of winning, when all the probabilities seemed to be in his favor, whereas in fact they were the other way. And that was what happened. In July, 1830, Du Tillet and Nucingen had helped the Comte de Brambourg to make fifteen hundred thousand francs, so that he had not the slightest suspicion of them, finding them always loyal and judicious advisers. Philippe, having attained his exalted position by favor of the Restoration, and being misled by his profound contempt for the *pékins* believed in the success of the ordinances of July and desired to play for a rise; while Nucingen and Du Tillet, who believed in a revolution, played against him for a fall. The two shrewd worthies chimed in with Colonel Comte de Brambourg's ideas and pretended to share his convictions; they inspired him with the hope of doubling his millions and took measures to win them from him. Philippe fought like a man to whom victory was worth four millions.

His devotion to the king's government was so marked that he was ordered to return to Saint-Cloud with the Duc de Maufrigneuse, to advise with His Majesty. This mark of favor saved Philippe; for he intended to lead a charge to sweep the boulevards on the twenty-eighth of July, and he would in all probability have received a bullet from his friend Giroudeau, who commanded a division of the assailants.

A month later, Colonel Bridau possessed nothing of his immense fortune save his city house, his country estate, his pictures and his furniture. He was guilty of the further folly of believing in the re-establishment of the elder branch, to which he was faithful until 1834. When he saw Giroudeau a colonel, a feeling of jealousy, easy to understand, led Philippe back into the service, where, unfortunately, he was given command, in 1835, of a regiment in Algeria, and there he remained three years at the post of greatest peril, hoping to obtain a general's epaulets. But a malevolent influence, that of General Giroudeau, kept him where he was. Having become thoroughly hardened, Philippe went beyond all bounds in severity of discipline, and was cordially detested, despite his personal bravery *à la* Murat. Early in the fatal year 1839, as he was leading an offensive movement upon the Arabs during a retreat before a superior force, he rode furiously against the enemy, followed by a single company, which fell into a swarm of Arabs. A bloody, horrible combat ensued, man

to man, and only a small number of the French
cavalry escaped. When those who were at a distance saw that their colonel was surrounded, they
deemed it not worth while to attempt to rescue
him. They heard the words: "Your colonel! help!
a colonel of the Empire!" followed by frightful
yells, but they rejoined the regiment. Philippe
met a horrible death, for when he fell, almost
hacked to pieces by yataghans, they cut off his
head.

Joseph, who was married about this time, through
the influence of the Comte de Sérizy, to the daughter of a millionaire ex-farmer, inherited the house
on Rue de Clichy and the estate of Brambourg,
which his brother had been unable to dispose of,
although he was exceedingly anxious to deprive
him of his rights as his heir. The painter derived
the greatest pleasure from the fine collection of
paintings. His father-in-law, a sort of rustic
Hochon, is still adding to his store of crowns every
day, and Joseph already possesses sixty thousand
francs a year. Although he paints magnificent pictures, and renders valuable services to artists, he is
not yet a member of the Institute. By virtue of
a clause in the constitution of the *majorat*, he is
now Comte de Brambourg, a fact that often makes
him roar with laughter, among his friends in his
studio.

"Good counts wear good coats,"—*Les bons comtes
ont les bons habits*—says his friend Léon de
Lora, who, despite his celebrity as a landscape

painter, has not abandoned his old habit of dis-
torting proverbs, and who has a way of saying
to Joseph, apropos of the modesty with which
he receives the favors of destiny:

"Bah! *thirst comes with eating!*"—*la pépie vient
en mangeant!*

Paris, November, 1842.

LIST OF ETCHINGS

VOLUME XXV